D1130673

THE THEME
IS FREEDOM

THE THEME
IS FREEDOM

by John Dos Passos

Essay Index Reprint Series

 BOOKS FOR LIBRARIES PRESS
FREEPORT, NEW YORK

PREFACE

While I was getting together this collection of various writings of a more or less political complexion out of tattered back numbers of surviving and defunct publications and out of the already brittle pages of some of my own out of print books I kept thinking of Peletiah Webster's remark in the preface of his collection of Political Essays. "I cannot say I had all the success with these publications which I wished."

Peletiah Webster, whose greatest accolade while he lived was to be described in a note by Madison as an "obscure but able citizen," followed a somewhat unsuccessful career as a merchant in Philadelphia during the seventies and eighties of the eighteenth century. He was a Yale man, a cousin of the Noah Webster of primer and dictionary fame, and like so many studious young men from Connecticut in those days, started life as a preacher. He couldn't make a go of preaching and tried to support himself by a series of mercantile ventures. In the course of them he managed to be captured with his ship and cargo by the British off Newport and later when Howe occupied Philadelphia to be imprisoned by them as a patriot. When the redcoats abandoned the American metropolis Webster found himself in trouble with the redhot patriots for having done business there during the British occupation. Perhaps the origin of most of his difficulties lay in the fact that he was a man who gave more thought to the public interest than he did

v

to his own affairs. He kept coming out with untimely notions about the nature and operation of money and about credit and taxation and about a suitable form of government for the United States. These notions he was imprudent enough to air in the newspapers.

It was a time of intemperate controversy among men of the pen. If a man broached an unfashionable notion you branded him as a scoundrel. Peletiah Webster's communications though mild and commonsensical in tone produced violent irritation among those who disagreed with him, especially in a gentleman who wrote under the name of Timoleon, so much so that Webster was constrained to cry out in one of his articles "It is of no consequence whether Timoleon or myself have the blackest heart, the foulest mouth, or the most spiteful pen. I yield to him the palm in every article of personal abuse, sly innuendo or gross scandal, I mean to confine myself to such particulars as the public has an interest in."

In the end it was discovered that the public had so much interest in some of Webster's "particulars" that a number of his suggestions—of course he wasn't the only man who made them—were embodied in the federal Constitution. In his preface to the collection of his essays he printed a couple of years after that document had been adopted he made the candid remark which gave me such pleasure when I read it. "I cannot say I had all the success with these publications which I wished. . . . They crossed the favorite plans proposed by influential men . . . opposed great and strong interests which bore them down. . . . The subjects were new and the public mind had not time to fix itself on the ground of experience. . . . In fine, most people at that time were wrought up in such a passionate attachment to the American Cause that they had not the patience to examine and consider coolly the means necessary to support it."

CONTENTS

THE THEME
IS FREEDOM

THE BACKWASH OF OUR FIRST CRUSADE

It's hard to overestimate the revulsion wrought by the first world war in the minds of a generation that had grown up in the years of comparative freedom and comparative peace that opened the century. It's hard to remember in the middle fifties today that in those years what little military service there was in America was voluntary, that taxes were infinitesimal, that if you could scrape up the price of a ticket you could travel anywhere in the world except through Russia and Turkey, without saying boo to a bureaucrat. If you wanted to take a job it was nobody's business but yours and the boss's. Of course, as the labor people were busily pointing out, if you worked in a sweat shop for a pittance and happened to starve to death in the process it was nobody's business either. When Woodrow Wilson led the country into the European war, however little we approved this reversal of American tradition, most of us just out of college were crazy to see what war was like. We experienced to the full the intoxication of the great conflagration, though those of us who served as enlisted men could hardly be expected to take kindly to soldiering, to the caste system which made officers a superior breed or to the stagnation and opportunism of military bureaucracy. Waste of time, waste of money, waste of lives,

1

waste of youth. We came home with the horrors. We had to blame somebody.

The reformers we admired, the Bull Moose people, the Progressives from Wisconsin, Eugene V. Debs and the old time Populists had tended to blame everything that went wrong on malefactors of great wealth. Capitalism was the bogey that was destroying civilization. Cut the businessman's profits we said. Production for use. We thrilled to the word cooperative. Industrial democracy was the refrain of our song. In Europe we had picked up some of the slogans of Marxists and syndicalists. We agreed with them that democratic self-government had sold out to capital. Capitalism was the sin that had caused the war; only the working class was free from crime.

Most of us had been brought up in easy circumstances. If we were enlisted men in the army we found ourselves suddenly instead of top dog, bottom dog. An enlightening experience, but we couldn't help some cries of pain. We came home with the feeling that bottom dog must be boss. We must restore selfgovernment at home. If the people had had their way none of these disasters would have happened.

Greenwich Village met us at the dock. American Bohemia was in revolt against Main Street, against the power of money, against Victorian morals. Freedom was the theme. Freedom from hard collars, from the decalogue, from parental admonitions. For Greenwich Village art and letters formed an exclusive cult. The businessman could never understand. It was part of the worldwide revolt of artists and would be artists and thinkers and would be thinkers against a society where most of the rewards went to people skillful in the manipulation of money. The would be artists and writers felt out of it. The revolt of Bohemia was the last eddy in the ebb of the romantic flood that had flowed in various great waves through the literature of nineteenth century Europe. When artists and writers found it hard to make themselves a niche in industrial society they repudiated the whole business. Greenwich Village was their refuge, the free commune of Montmartre on American soil. Les bourgeois à la lanterne.

Greenwich Village wanted freedom and so did the working class. Only the people who worked in factories wanted freedom from certain very definite things, especially from low pay and bad conditions of work. They wanted to be treated as first class citizens the way businessmen were. Greenwich Villagers, mostly the sons and daughters of professional people, clergymen and lawyers and doctors, felt a sudden kinship with the working class. Of all strata of society only the artists and writers and the people who worked with their hands were pure. Together they would overturn the businessman and become top dog themselves. From the alliance between the trade unions and Greenwich Village the American radical was born.

The war had left an aftermath of ruin. Dislocated populations were starving and sick. The apocalyptic vision of capitalism's collapse that had haunted the working people of Europe was coming true. Revolution was the cure. Only a complete new order could bring health and cleanness back into the world. It was ordained by the march of progress. Only the bankers and industrialists and the old feudal hierarchies stood in the way of the millennium. In Russia the soviets had seized power. To the artists and writers of Greenwich Village the soviets were New England town meeting on a larger scale. Selfgovernment come to life again. Through the soviets the people who did the work of the world would conduct their own affairs. War was ruining civilization. Everywhere the

3

plain people wanted peace. Only the bankers and businessmen had profited by the war. Merchants of death. Down with the bankers and businessmen. With the working class in power, peace would be assured.

The American businessman met the failure of Woodrow Wilson's war to end war in two ways. He subscribed liberally to funds raised for the relief of the starving and the dispossessed abroad. For the first time relief became a career. At home he tried to root up discontent by force. Slackers and pacifists were hounded by vigilantes. The IWW was stamped out by the courts. Foreign agitators were deported by the boatload. Where Greenwich Village saw white the businessman saw black. After the radicals were suppressed new era financing would heal all wounds. Everybody would make a million on the stock exchange. Henry Ford had discovered that the wage earner was a consumer. Publicity began to be the national industry of the twenties. Instead of the full dinner pail, two chickens in every pot became the slogan; two cars in every garage.

Still even for Greenwich Villagers jobs were plentiful. In spite of the great literature of consent presided over by Lorimer's Saturday Evening Post the country was showing a certain taste for the literature of dissent. The twenties proved a golden age for the young people of the typewriter and the pen.

Dutifully we tried to throw our weight behind the working man's struggle to organize trade unions. In the meetings of strikers we saw new organs of selfgovernment. The class war must be reported. The old Masses had gone under in the massive wartime suppression of dissenting opinions. To report the class war we launched the New Masses. I forget who put up the money. Money was easy in those days.

4

In June 1926 for a New Masses article I stole a headline from the daily press:

1. 300 Red Agitators Invade Passaic

The people who had come from New York roamed in a desultory group along the broad pavement. We were talking of outrages and the Bill of Rights. The people who had come from New York wore warm overcoats in the sweeping wind, bits of mufflers; and fluffiness of women's blouses fluttered silky in the cold April wind. The people who had come from New York filled up a row of taxicabs, shiny sedans of various makes, nicely upholstered. The shiny sedans started off in a procession toward the place where the meeting was going to be forbidden. Inside we talked in a desultory way of outrages and the Bill of Rights, we, descendants of the Pilgrim Fathers, the Bunker Hill Monument, Gettysburg, the Boston Teaparty. . . . Know all men by these presents. . . . On the corners groups of yellowish gray people standing still, square people standing still as chunks of stone, looking nowhere, saying nothing.

At the place where the meeting was going to be forbidden the people from New York got out of the shiny sedans of various makes. The sheriff was a fat man with a badge like a star off a Christmas tree, the little eyes of a suspicious landlady in a sallow face. The cops were waving their clubs about, limbering up their arms. The cops were redfaced, full of food, the cops felt fine. The special deputies had restless eyes, they were stocky young men crammed with sodapop and ideals, overgrown boyscouts; they were on the right side and they knew it. Still the shiny new doublebarreled riot guns made them nervous. They didn't know which shoulder to keep their guns on. The people who had come from New York stood first on one foot and then on the other.

"All right move 'em along," said the sheriff.

The cops advanced, the special deputies politely held open the doors of the sedans. The people who had come from New York climbed back into the shiny sedans of various makes and drove away, except for one man who was slow and got picked up. The procession of taxis started back the way it had come. The procession of taxis, shiny sedans of various makes, went back the way it had come, down empty streets protected by deputies with shiny new riot guns, past endless façades of deserted mills, past brick tenements with illpainted stoops, past groups of squat square women with yellow gray faces, groups of men and boys standing still, saying nothing, looking nowhere, square hands hanging at their sides, people square and still, chunks of yellow gray stone at the edge of a quarry, idle, waiting, on strike.

From sometime during this spring of 1926 or from the winter before a recollection keeps rising to the surface. The protest meeting is over and I'm standing on a set of steps looking into the faces of the people coming out of the hall. I'm frightened by the tense righteousness of the faces. Eyes like a row of rifles aimed by a firing squad. Chins thrust forward into the icy night. It's almost in marching step that they stride out into the street. It's the women I remember most, their eyes searching out evil through narrowed lids. There's something threatening about this unanimity of protest. They are so sure they are right.

I agree with their protest: I too was horrified by this outrage. I'm not one either to stand by and see injustice done. But do I agree enough? A chill goes down my spine. Do they frighten me because I'm really among the oppressors, because there is some little mustard seed of doubt in my mind about the value of their protest? Maybe I'm not sure enough that I'm on the right side. Evil is so various.

Whenever I remember the little scene I tend to turn it over in my mind. Why did my hackles rise at the sight of the faces of these good people coming out of the hall?

Was it a glimpse of the forming of a new class conformity that like all class conformities was bent on riding the rest of us?

Class conformity was not in my mind when I helped revive the old Masses. We wanted to raise a standard to which, in Washington's words, "the wise and good might repair." Most of us could hardly have been called Marxists. I hated classification the way the devil hates holy water. We radicals didn't all think alike. Damned if we would. Already an argument was on between the heretics like myself and the convinced militants of the gospel of Marx. It's amusing to remember that in those carefree days a Communist party-member and an anarcho-syndicalist and even some sad dog of a capitalist who believed in laissez faire could sit at the same table and drink beer together and lay their thoughts on the line. It wasn't that you respected the other fellow's opinions exactly, but you admitted his right to remain alive. Needless to say, this happy state didn't last very long. The right of a dissenter to remain alive has tended to go down the drain along with the other civil rights of the old order.

An echo of that argument from this same number:

2. The New Masses I'd Like

The comrade is responsible for these lines, for their existence if not for their disorder and scatterbrainedness. The other night he made off into the underbrush after calling me a bourgeois intellectual before I had a chance to argue with him. The salutary truth has rankled and finally come out in a rash of generalizations concerning professional writers, the labor movement in America, the *New Masses* and people in general. Admitting that generalizations are worthless, here they are.

First a restriction about proletarian literature. It seems to me that people are formed by their trades and occupations much more than by their opinions. The fact that a man is a shoesalesman or a butcher is in every respect more important than that he's a republican or a theosophist; so that when he stops earning an honest living and becomes a writer, agitator, poet, idealist, in his actions if not in his ideas he becomes a member of the great semiparasitic class that includes all the trades that deal with words from advertising and the Christian ministry to song writing. Whether his aims are KKK or Communist he takes on the mind and functional deformities of his trade. The wordslinging organism is substantially the same whether it sucks its blood from Park Avenue or from Flatbush.

And at this moment it seems to me that the wordslinging classes, radical and fundamentalist, are further away from any reality than they've ever been. Writers are insulated like everyone else by the enforced pigeonholing of specialized industry. As mechanical power grows in America general ideas tend to restrict themselves more and more to Karl Marx, the first chapter of Genesis and the hazy scientific mysticism of the Sunday supplements. I don't think it's any time for any group of spellbinders to lay down the law on any subject whatsoever. Particularly, I don't think there should be any more phrases, badges, opinions, banners, imported from Russia or anywhere else. Ever since Columbus, imported systems have been the curse of this continent. Why not develop our own brand?

What we need is a highly flexible receiving station that

will find out what's in the air in the country anyhow.

Under the gray slag of a print-pocked crust there are veins of lava to be tapped that writers at least know nothing about, among the shuffling people at strike meetings there are tentative flickers of thought that the agitators and organizers know nothing about, under the vests of fat men in limousines there are inquietudes that mean something. In these terribly crucial years when the pressure is rising and rising in the boiler of the great steamroller of American finance that's going to try to grind down even further the United States and the world, being clearsighted is a life and death matter. . . .

The House of Morgan was powerful in those days, but not that powerful. It was years before I learned that producing a bogy man was an emotional quirk that blocked clear thinking.

. . . If we ever could find out what was really going on we might be able to formulate a theory of what to do about it.

Why shouldn't the *New Masses* be setting out on a prospecting trip, drilling in unexpected places, following unsuspected veins, bringing home specimens as yet unclassified? I think that there's much more to be gained by rigorous exploration than by sitting on the side lines of the labor movement with a red rosette in your buttonhole and cheering for the home team.

The terrible danger to explorers is that they always find what they are looking for. The *American Mercury* explores very ably the American field only to find the face of Mr. Mencken mirrored in every prairie pool. I want an expedition that will find what it's out looking for.

I hope that it is not for nothing that the *New Masses* has taken that dangerous word *New* into its name. The tendency

9

of the masses has always been to be more disciplined in thought than in action. I'd like to see that state of things reversed for once. I'd like to see a magazine full of introspection and doubt that would be like a piece of litmus paper to test things by. . . .

. . . But the comrade says that scepticism is merely the flower of decay, the green mold on the intellect of the rotten bourgeoisie. He may be right. Anyway I don't think it is scepticism to say that November, 1917, is in the past. It shows an almost imbecile faith in the word New and the word Masses.

The *New Masses* must at all costs avoid the great future that lies behind it.

New York, June, 1926

The Marxists who are so skillful in the detection and the isolation of heresies used to inveigh against one particular heresy that pleased me particularly. They called it American exceptionalism. During these years of mounting protest against the way things were going in America that label was my refuge. It enabled me to join in the protests of the various breeds of Marxists who were being more and more effectively regimented by the Communist Party without giving up my own particular point of view. I could join my voice to theirs in the outcry against the wave of repression which culminated in the Sacco-Vanzetti case, whereby the great industrial manufacturers were able to use the machinery of the courts and the police power to harass every effort to organize working people into trade unions, without giving up the automatic responses of the plain American patriotism I'd been raised in. If we were going to bring about a revolution in America it must be an American revolution.

The year 1927 turned out to be one of protest meetings. It was a year of battle for the lives of Sacco and Vanzetti.

Here I saw white where other good men saw black. I still think we were right, though it was a strange experience a couple of years ago to read a set of interviews by a reporter for the New Bedford paper with the surviving jurors that sat on the case. They were still convinced of Sacco's and Vanzetti's guilt.

Any man, I suppose, is capable of any crime, but having talked to Sacco and Vanzetti themselves it's impossible for me to believe they could have committed that particular crime. Oh Pilate, Pilate how sharp was your question.

". . . To this end was I born, and for this cause came I into the world, that I should bear witness unto the truth." . . . Pilate saith unto him, "What is the truth?"

It was in trying to help the Sacco-Vanzetti Defense Committee that I first came into personal touch with men of the anarchist faith. I found them to be simple and truthful. They were fanatics of course but there was humanity in their fanaticism. I never found among them that Marxist stirring up of envy, hatred and malice that corrodes the character of men and women. The anarchists had extravagant ideas but most of them seemed to me generous, selfsacrificing, warmhearted, really good people.

3. The Sacco-Vanzetti Case

The evening of May 5, 1920, Nicola Sacco, an Italian, working as edger in a shoe factory, and Bartolomeo Vanzetti, also an Italian, a fishpeddler, were arrested in a streetcar in Brockton, Massachusetts. The two men were known as radicals and were active in Italian working class organizations.

A couple of weeks before, the afternoon of April 15, a peculiarly impudent and brutal crime had been committed in South Braintree, a nearby town, the climax of a long series of holdups and burglaries. Bandits after shooting down a paymaster and his guard in the center of the town had escaped in a Buick touring car with over $15,000 in cash. It was generally rumored that the bandits were Italians. The police had made a great fuss but found no clue to the identity of the murderers. Public feeling was bitter and critical. A victim had to be found. To prove the murderers to have been reds would please everybody. After a stormy trial they were convicted of murder in the first degree. Sentence was stayed by a series of defense motions for a new trial.

The most important new evidence brought forward by these motions consisted of a series of affidavits to the effect that operatives of the Department of Justice were active in the trial, and that lacking evidence on which to deport Sacco and Vanzetti as radicals, they helped in the frameup by which they were convicted as murderers.

"They were bad actors anyway and got what was coming to them," one detective was quoted as saying.

The Hearing of the Seventh Motion

Another hearing of a motion for a new trial. Six have been denied so far. Sacco and Vanzetti have been six years in jail. This time there are no guards with riotguns, no state troopers riding round the courthouse. No excitement of any sort. Everyone has forgotten the great days of the Red Conspiracy, the passion to sustain law and order against the wave of radicalism, against foreigners, and the "moral rats gnawing at the foundations of the commonwealth" that Attorney General Palmer spoke of so eloquently. In this court there are no prisoners in a cage, no hysterical witnesses, no credulous jury under the sign of the screaming eagle. Quiet, dignity; almost like a class in lawschool. The case has been abstracted into a sort of mathematics. Only the lawyers for the defense and for the prosecution, Ranney from the Commonwealth's Attorney's office, Thompson and Ehrmann for the defense, two small tables of newspapermen, on the benches a few Italians, some professional liberals and radicals, plainclothesmen with rumpsteak faces occupying the end seats.

The court attendants make everybody get up. The judge comes in on the heels of a man in a blue uniform. Judge Thayer is a very small man with a little gray lined shingle face, nose glasses tilting out at the top across a sudden little hawknose. He walks with a firm bustling tread. The black gown that gives him the power of life and death (the gown of majesty of the blind goddess the law) sticks out a little behind. Another attendant walks after him. The judge climbs up to his high square desk. The judge speaks. His voice crackles dryly as old papers.

Affidavits, affidavits read alternately by counsel in the stillness of the yellowvarnished courtroom. Gradually as the reading goes on the courtroom shrinks. Tragic figures of men and women grow huge like shadows cast by a lantern on a wall; the courtroom becomes a tiny pinhole through which to see a world of huge trampling forces in conflict.

First it's the story of the life of Celestino Madeiros, a poor Portuguese boy brought up in New Bedford. He learned Americanism all right, he suffered from no encumbering ideas of social progress; the law of dawg eat dawg was morbidly vivid in his mind from the first. Hardly out of school he was up in court for "breaking and entering." No protests from him about the

13

war. He and his sister and another man dressed up in uniform and collected money for some vaguely phony patriotic society: The American Rescue League. By the spring of 1920 he was deep in the criminal world that is such an apt cartoon of the world of legitimate business. He was making good. He was in with the Morelli brothers of Providence, a gang of freight-car robbers, bootleggers, pimps, hijackers and miscellaneous thugs. The great wave of highway robbery that followed the war was at its height. For three years the leaders of society had been proclaiming the worthlessness of human life. Is it surprising that criminals should begin to take them at their word?

Scared to death, blind drunk, Madeiros, an overgrown boy of eighteen, was in the back seat of the Buick touring car that carried off the tragic holdup outside the Rice and Hutchins shoefactory at South Braintree. Probably on his share of the payroll he went south, once he got out of the Rhode Island jail where another episode of breaking and entering had landed him. He came back north with his money spent and worked as a bouncer at the Bluebird Inn, a "disorderly" roadhouse at Seekonk, Massachusetts and fell at last into the clutches of the Masschusetts law through a miserable failure to duplicate the daring South Braintree holdup at Wrentham, where he shot an aged bank cashier and ran without trying to get any loot. At his trial he sat so hunched and motionless that he seemed an imbecile. Not even when his mother threw an epileptic fit in the courtroom and was carried out rigid and foaming did he look up.

At the Dedham jail he was put in the cell next to Sacco. He could see Sacco going out to meet his wife and kids when they came to see him. The idea of an innocent man going to the chair worried him. For him everything had crashed. It had been on his own confession that he had been convicted of the Wrentham murder. He seems to have puzzled for a long time to find some way of clearing Sacco and Vanzetti without inculpating his old associates, even though he had fallen out with them long ago. He tried to tell Sacco about it in the jail bathroom, but Sacco, seeing Department of Justice spies everywhere—and with good reason—wouldn't listen to him. So at last he sent the warden a written confession, asking him to forward it to the *Boston American*.

Nothing happened. The warden kept his mouth shut. Eventually Madeiros sent a new confession to Sacco enclosed in a magazine, begging him to let his lawyer see it. *"I hereby confess to being in the South Braintree Shoe Company crime and Sacco and Vanzetti were not in said crime. —CELESTINO F. MADEIROS."*

Circumstances sometimes force men into situations so dramatic, thrust their puny frames so far into the burning bright searchlights of history that their shadows on men's minds become enormous symbols. Sacco and Vanzetti are all the imigrants who have built this nation's industries with their sweat and their blood and have gotten for it nothing but the smallest wage it is possible to give them and a helot's position under the bootheels of the Arrow Collar social order. They are all the wops, hunkies, bohunks, factory fodder that hunger drives into the American mills through the painful sieve of Ellis Island. They are the dreams of a saner social order of those who can't stand the law of dawg eat dawg. This tiny courtroom is a focus of the turmoil of an age of transition, the center of eyes all over the world. Sacco and Vanzetti throw enormous shadows on the courthouse walls.

William G. Thompson feels all this dimly when, the last affidavit read, he pauses to begin his argument. But mostly he feels that as a citizen it is his duty to protect the laws and

15

liberties of his state and as a man to try to save two innocent men from being murdered by a machine set going in a moment of hatred and panic. He is a broadshouldered man with steely white hair and a broad forehead and broad cheekbones. He doesn't mince words. There is intense feeling in his words. The case is no legal game of chess for him.

"I rest my case on these affidavits, on the other five propositions that I have argued, but if they all fail, and I cannot see how they can, I rest my case on that rock alone, on the sixth proposition in my brief—innocent or guilty, right or wrong, foolish or wise men—these men ought not now be sentenced to death for this crime so long as they have the right to say, 'The government of this great country put spies in my cell, planned to put spies in my wife's house, they put spies on my friends, took money that they were collecting to defend me, put it in their own pocket and joked about it and said they don't believe I am guilty but will help convict me, because they could not get enough evidence to deport me under the laws of Congress, and were willing as one of them continually said to adopt the method of killing me for murder as one way to get rid of me.'"

The Commonwealth's Attorney's handling of his side of the argument has been pretty perfunctory throughout, he has contented himself with trying to destroy the Court's opinion of Madeiros' veracity. A criminal is only to be believed when he speaks to his own detriment. He presents affidavits of the Morellis and their friends denying that they had ever heard of Madeiros, tries to imply that Letherman and Weyand (who gave other affidavits favorable to the defendants) were fired from the government employ and had no right to betray the secrets of their department. He knows that he does not need to make much effort. He is strong in the inertia of the courts.

The defense will have to exert six times the energy of the prosecution to overturn the dead weight of six other motions denied.

Thompson comes back at him with a phrase worthy of Patrick Henry.

. . . "And I will say to your honor that a government that has come to honor its own secrets more than the lives of its citizens has become a tyranny whether you call it a republic or a monarchy or anything else."

Then the dry, crackling, careful voice of Judge Thayer and the hearing is adjourned.

"Hear ye, hear ye, hear ye, all who have had business before the honorable the justice of the superior court of the southeastern district of Massachusetts will now disperse. The court is adjourned without day.

"God Save the Commonwealth of Massachusetts."

The court has refused to grant a new trial. The court has decided that Sacco and Vanzetti must die.

God Save the Commonwealth of Massachussetts.

The Bomb Scare

How is all this possible? Why were these men ever convicted in the first place? From the calm of the year of our Lord 1926 it's pretty hard to remember the delirious year of 1920.

On June 3, 1919 a bomb exploded outside the Washington house of Attorney General A. Mitchell Palmer. In the previous months various people had received bombs through the mail, one of them blowing off the two hands of the unfortunate housemaid who undid the package. No one, and least of all the federal detectives, ever seems to have discovered who committed these outrages or why they were committed. But their result was to put a scare into every public official in the country, and

17

particularly into Attorney General Palmer. No one knew where the lightning would strike next. The signing of peace had left the carefully stirred up hatred of the war years unsatisfied. It was easy for people who knew what they were doing to turn the terrors of government officials and the distrust of foreigners of the average man into a great crusade of hate against reds, radicals, dissenters of all sorts. The Department of Justice, backed by the press, frenziedly acclaimed by the man on the street, invented an imminent revolution. All the horrors of Russian Bolshevism were about to be enacted on our peaceful shores. That fall the roundup began. Every man had his ear to his neighbor's keyhole. This first crusade culminated in the sailing of the *Buford*, the "Soviet Ark" loaded with alien "anarchists" and in the preparation of the famous list of eighty thousand radicals who were to be gotten out of the way.

The raids were particularly violent in the industrial towns round Boston and culminated in the captives being driven through the streets of Boston chained together in fours. There were raids in Boston, Chelsea, Brockton, Bridgewater, Norwood, Worcester, Springfield, Chicopee Falls, Lowell, Fitchburg, Holyoke, Lawrence and Haverhill. Unfortunate people after being beaten up and put through the third degree were concentrated at Deer Island under the conditions that have become public through U.S. Circuit Judge Anderson's decision on the cases that came up before him.

Now it is this ring of industrial towns round Boston that furnish the background of the Sacco-Vanzetti case. There is no doubt that the Americanborn public in these towns on the whole sympathizes with the activities of the detectives. The region has been for many years one of the most intense industrial battlegrounds in the country. People slept safer in their beds at the thought of all these agitators, bombsters, garlic-smelling wops, and unwashed Russians being under lock and key at Deer Island.

Eastern Massachusetts has a threefold population living largely from manufacturing of textiles and shoes and other leather goods. With the decline of shipping and farming the old simonpure New England stock, Congregationalist in faith, Republican in politics, has been pretty well snowed under by the immigration first of Irish Catholics, congenital Democrats and readers of Hearst papers, now assimilated and respectable, and then of Italians, Poles, Slovaks, transplanted European peasants tenderly known to newspaper readers as the scum of the Mediterranean or the scum of Central Europe. There's no love lost between the first two classes, but they unite on the question of wops, guineas, dagoes. The January raids, the attitude of press and pulpit, howling about atrocities, civilization endangered, women nationalized in Communist Russia, put the average right-thinking citizen into such a state of mind that whenever he smelt garlic on a man's breath he walked past quickly for fear of being knifed. A roomful of people talking a foreign language was most certainly a conspiracy to overturn the government. Read over the articles in the *Boston Transcript* on the Soviet conspiracy at that time and you will see what kind of stuff was being ladled out even to the intelligent highbrow section of the entrenched classes.

It was into this atmosphere of rancor and suspicion, fear of holdups and social overturn, that burst the scare headlines of the South Braintree murders. Pent-up hatred found an outlet when the police in Brockton arrested Sacco and Vanzetti, wops who spoke broken English, anarchists who believed neither in the Pope nor in the Puritan God, slackers and agitators, charged with a peculiarly brutal and impudent crime. Since that moment these people have had a focus for their bitter hatred of the new, young, vigorous, unfamiliar forces that are relentlessly sweeping them on to the shelf. The people of Norfolk county and of all Massachusetts decided they wanted these men to die.

Meanwhile the red delirium over the rest of the country had slackened. Something had happened that had made many people pause and think.

About dawn on May 3 the body of Andrea Salsedo, an anarchist printer, was found smashed on the pavement of Park Row in New York. He had jumped or been thrown from the offices of the Department of Justice on the fourteenth floor of the Park Row building, where he and his friend Elia had been secretly imprisoned for eight weeks. Evidently they had tortured him during that time; Mr. Palmer's detectives were "investigating" anarchist activity. A note had been smuggled out somehow, and a few days before Vanzetti had been in New York as the delegate of an Italian group to try to get the two men out on bail. After Salsedo's death Elia was hurried over to Ellis Island and deported. He died in Italy. But from that time on the holy enthusiasm for red-baiting subsided. The tortured body found dead and bleeding in one of the most central and public spots in New York shocked men back into their senses.

When Sacco and Vanzetti were arrested in the trolley car in Brockton the night of May 5, Sacco had in his pocket the draft of a poster announcing a meeting of protest against what they considered the murder of their comrade. They were going about warning the other members of their group to hide all incriminating evidence in the way of "radical" books and papers so that, in the new raid that they had been tipped off to expect, they should not be arrested and meet the fate of Salsedo.

Don't forget that people had been arrested and beaten up for distributing the Declaration of Independence.

The Psychology of Frame-Ups

But why were these men held as murderers and highwaymen and not as anarchists and advocates of the working people?

It was a frameup.

That does not necessarily mean that any set of government and employing class detectives deliberately planned to fasten the crime of murder on Sacco and Vanzetti.

The frameup is often an unconscious mechanism. An unconscious mechanism is a kink in the mind that makes people do something without knowing that they are doing it. A frameup is the subrational act of a group.

Among a people that does not recognize or rather does not admit that it recognizes the force and danger of ideas it is impossible to prosecute the holder of unpopular ideas directly. Also there is a smoldering tradition of freedom that makes those who do it feel guilty. After all everyone learned the Declaration of Independence and *"Give me liberty or give me death"* in school, and however perfunctory the words have become they have left a faint infantile impression on the minds of most of us. Hence the characteristic American weapon of the frameup. If a cop wants to arrest a man he suspects of selling dope he plants a gun on him and arrests him under the Sullivan Law. If a man is organizing a strike in a dangerously lively way you try to frame him under the Mann Act or else you get hold of a woman to sue him for breach of promise. If a representative votes against war you have him arrested for breach of decency in an automobile on a Virginia roadside. If two Italians are spreading anarchist propaganda, you hold them for murder.

The frameup is a process that you can't help feeling, but

21

like most unconscious processes it's very hard to trace step by step. Half the agents in such a process don't really know what they are doing. Hence the moderately fairminded newspaper reader who never has had personal experience of a frameup in action is flabbergasted when you tell him that such and such a man who is being prosecuted for wifebeating is really being prosecuted because he knows the origin of certain bonds in a District Attorney's safe.

In this neatly swept courtroom in Dedham with everything so varnished and genteel it is hardly possible to think of such a thing as a frameup and yet, under these elms, in these white old-time houses of Dedham, in front of these pious Georgian doorways, the court has for the seventh time affirmed its will to send two innocent men to the electric chair.

The Outlaw Creed

What is this criminal garlic-smelling creed that the people of Massachusetts will not face openly?

For half a century anarchy has been the bogy of American schoolmasters, policemen, old maids and small town mayors. About the time of the assassination of McKinley a picture was formed in the public mind of the anarchist; redhanded, unwashed foreigner whom nobody could understand, sticks of dynamite in his pocket and a bomb in the paper parcel under his arm, redeyed housewrecker waiting only for the opportunity to bite the hand that fed him. Since the Russian Revolution the picture has merged a little with that of the sneaking, slinking, Communist Jew, enviously undermining Prosperity and Decency through secret organizations ruled from Moscow.

Gradually among liberals and intelligent people generally certain phases of anarchism have meanwhile been reluctantly admitted into respectable conversation under the phrase "philosophical anarchist," which means an anarchist who shaves daily, has good manners and is guaranteed not to act on his beliefs. Certain people of the best society, such as Kropotkin and Tolstoy, princes both, having through their diverse types of anarchy made themselves important figures in European thought and literature, it was impossible to exclude them longer from the pale of decency.

What is this outlaw creed?

When Christianity flourished in the Mediterranean basin, slave and emperor had the hope of the immediate coming of Christ's kingdom, the golden Jerusalem that would appear on earth to put an end to the tears and aches of the faithful. After the first millennium, the City of God, despaired of on earth, took its permanent place in the cloudy firmament with the Virgin Mary at the apex of the feudal pyramid. With the decay of feudalism and the coming of the kingdoms of this world the church became more and more the instrument of the governing orders. Undermined by the eighteenth century, overthrown by the French revolution, the church was restored by the great reaction as the strongest bulwark of privilege. But in the tough memories of peasants and fishermen—their sons worked in factories—there remained a faint trace of the vanished brightness of the City of God. All our city dwelling instinct and culture has been handed down to us from these countless urban generations, Cretans, Greeks, Phoenicians, Latins of the Mediterranean basin, Italians of the hilltowns. It is natural that the dwellers on those scraggy hills in sight of that always blue sea should have kept alight in their hearts the perfect city, where the strong did not oppress the weak, where every man lived by his own work at peace with his neighbors, the white commune where man could reach his full height free from the snarling

23

obsessions of priest and master.

It is this inner picture that is the core of feeling behind all anarchist theory and doctrine. Many Italians planted the perfect city of their imagination in America. When they came to this country, many of the more ardent spirits, when they found the reality did not match their imagining, reverted to the anarchist creed. There have been terrorists among them, as in every other oppressed and despised sect since the world began. Respectable people generally have contended that anarchism and terrorism were the same thing, a silly and usually malicious error much fostered by private detectives and police bomb-squads.

An anarchist workman who works for the organization of his fellow workmen is a man who costs the factory owners money; thereby he is a bombthrower and possible murderer in the minds of the majority of American employers.

In his charge to the jury in the Plymouth trial Judge Thayer definitely instructed them that the crime of highway robbery was consistent with Vanzetti's ideals as a radical.

Yet, under the conflict between employer and workman and the racial misunderstanding, in themselves material enough for the creation of a frameup, might there not be a deeper bitterness? The people of Massachusetts centuries ago suffered and hoped terribly for the City of God.

This little white courthouse town of Dedham, neat and exquisite under its elms, is the symbol of a withered hope, mortgaged at six per cent to the kingdoms of the world. It is natural that New Englanders, who feel in themselves a lingering of the passionate barbed desire of perfection of their ancestors, should hate with particular bitterness, anarchists, votaries of the Perfect Commune on earth. The irrational features of this case of attempted communal murder can only be explained by a bitterness so deep that it has been forgotten by the very people it moves most fervidly.

Fishpeddler

During the spring of 1920 Bartolomeo Vanzetti was peddling fish in the pleasant little Italian and Portuguese town of North Plymouth. He was planning to go into fishing himself in partnership with a man who owned some dories. Early mornings, pushing his cart up and down the long main street, ringing his bell, chatting with housewives in Piedmontese, Tuscan, pidgin English, he worried about the raids, the imprisonment, the lethargy of the working people. He was an anarchist, after the school of Galeani. Between the houses he could see the gleaming stretch of Plymouth Bay, the sandy islands beyond, the white dories at anchor. About three hundred years before, men from the west of England had first sailed into the gray shimmering bay that smelled of woods and wild grape, looking for something; liberty . . . freedom to worship God in their own manner . . . space to breathe. Thinking of these things, worrying as he pushed the little cart loaded with eels, haddock, cod, halibut, swordfish, Vanzetti spent his mornings making change, weighing out fish, joking with housewives. It was better than working at the great cordage works that own North Plymouth. Some years before he had tried to organize a strike there and been blacklisted. The officials and detectives at the Plymouth Cordage, the largest cordage in the world, thought of him as a red, a slacker and troublemaker.

Shoemaker

At the same time Nicola Sacco was living in Stoughton, working an edging machine at the Three K's Shoe Factory, where star workmen sometimes made as high as eighty or ninety dollars a week. He had a pretty wife and a little son named Dante. There was another baby coming. He lived in a bungalow belonging to his employer, Michael Kelly. The house adjoined Kelly's own house and the men were friends. Often Kelly advised him to lay off this anarchist stuff. There was no money in it. It was dangerous the way people felt nowadays. Sacco was a clever young fellow and could soon get to be a prosperous citizen, maybe own a factory of his own someday, live by other men's work.

But Sacco, working in his garden in the early morning before the whistles blew, hilling beans, picking off potatobugs, letting grains of corn slip by twos and threes through his fingers into the finely worked earth, worried about things. He loved the earth and people, he wanted them to walk straight over the free hills, not to stagger bowed under the ordained machinery of industry; he worried mornings working in his garden at the lethargy of the working people. It was not enough that he was happy and had fifteen hundred or more dollars in the bank for a trip home to Italy.

The Red Menace

Three years before Sacco and Vanzetti had both of them had their convictions put to the test. In 1917, against the expressed vote of the majority, Woodrow Wilson had allowed the United States to become involved in a war with Germany. When the law was passed for compulsory military service a registration day for citizens and aliens was announced. Most young men submitted whatever their convictions were. A few of those who were opposed to any war or to capitalist war had the nerve to protest. Sacco and Vanzetti and some friends ran away to Mexico. There, some thirty of them lived in a set of adobe houses. Those who could get jobs worked. It was share and share alike. Everything was held in common. There were in the community men of all trades and conditions: bakers, butchers, tailors, shoemakers, cooks, carpenters, waiters. It was a momentary realization of the hope of anarchism. But living was difficult in Mexico and they began to get letters from the States telling that it was possible to avoid the draft, telling of high wages. Little by little they filtered back across the border. Sacco and Vanzetti went back to Massachusetts.

There was an Italian club that met Sunday evenings in a hall in Maverick Square, East Boston, under the name of the Italian Naturalization Society. Workmen from the surrounding industrial towns met to play bowls and to discuss social problems. There were anarchists, syndicalists, socialists of various colors. The Russian revolution had fired them with new hopes. The persecution of their comrades in various parts of America had made them feel the need of mutual help. While far away across the world the hope of a new era flared into the sky, at home the great machine they slaved for seemed more adamant, more unshakeable than ever. To the war heroes who had remained at home any foreigner seemed a potential Bolshevik, a menace to the security of Old Glory and liberty bonds and the bonus. When Elia and Salsedo were arrested there was great alarm among the Italian radicals around Boston. Vanzetti went down to New York to try to hire a lawyer for the two men. There he heard many uneasy rumors. The possession of any literature that might be interpreted as subversive by ignorant and brutal agents of the Departments of Justice and Labor was dangerous. It was not that deportation was so much to be feared, but the beating up and third degree that preceded it.

It was on May 3, 1920 that Salsedo was found dead on

Park Row. A rumor went around that a new raid was going to be made in the suburbs of Boston. There was a scurry to hide pamphlets and newspapers. At the same time the Italians of Boston couldn't let this horrible affair go by without a meeting of protest. Handbills announcing a meeting in Brockton were printed. Vanzetti was to be one of the speakers.

On the evening of May 5, Sacco and Vanzetti with the handbills on them went by trolley from Stoughton to West Bridgewater. They thought they were being trailed and had put revolvers in their pockets out of some confused feeling of bravado. If the police pounced on them at least they would not let themselves be tortured to death like Salsedo. The idea was to hide the handbills somewhere until after the expected raid. When they found they couldn't use Boda's car they started back to Stoughton. They were arrested as the trolley entered Brockton. They thought they were being arrested as reds in connection with the projected meeting. When they were questioned at the police station their main care was not to implicate any of their friends. They kept remembering the dead body of Salsedo, smashed on the pavement of Park Row.

The Trap Springs

When Sacco and Vanzetti were first grilled by the chief of police of Brockton they were questioned as reds and lied all they could to save their friends. Particularly they would not tell where they had got their pistols. Out of this Judge Thayer and the prosecution evolved the theory of "the consciousness of guilt" that weighed so heavily with the jury. After they had been held two days they were identified, Sacco as the driver of the car in the South Braintree holdup and Vanzetti as the "foreign looking man" who had taken a potshot at a paytruck of the

L. Q. White company at Bridgewater early on the morning of Christmas Eve, 1919.

In spite of the fact that twenty people swore that they had seen Vanzetti in North Plymouth selling eels at that very time in the morning, he was promptly convicted and sentenced to fifteen years in the Charlestown penitentiary. The fact that so many people testified to having bought eels was considered very suspicious by the court that did not know that the eating of eels on the fast day before Christmas is an Italian custom of long standing. Later Vanzetti was associated with Sacco in the murder charge. On July 14, 1923, both men were found guilty of murder in the first degree on two counts by the Norfolk County jury, a hundred per cent American jury, consisting of two realestate men, two storekeepers, a mason, two machinists, a clothing salesman, a farmer, a millworker, a shoemaker and a lastmaker.

Bird in a Cage

The Dedham jail is a handsome structure, set among lawns, screened by trees that wave new green leaves against the robins-egg sky of June. In the warden's office you can see your face in the light brown varnish, you could eat eggs off the floor it is so clean. Inside, the main reception hall is airy, full of sunlight. The bars are cheerfully painted green, a fresh peagreen. Through the bars you can see the waving trees and the June clouds roaming the sky like cattle in an unfenced pasture. It's a preposterous complicated canary cage. Why aren't the birds singing in this green aviary? The warden politely shows me to a seat and as I wait I notice a smell, not green and airy this smell, a jaded heavy greasy smell of slum, like the smell of army slum, but heavier, more hopeless.

At last Sacco has come out of his cell and sits beside me.

The faces of men who have been a long time in jail have a peculiar frozen look under the eyes. The face of a man who has been a long time in jail never loses that tightness under the eyes. Sacco has been six years in the county jail, always waiting, waiting for trial, waiting for new evidence, waiting for motions to be argued, waiting for sentence, waiting, waiting, waiting.

Two men sitting side by side on a bench in a green bird cage. When he feels like it one of them will get up and walk out, walk into the sunny June day. The other will go back to his cell to wait.

He looks younger than I had expected. His face has a waxy transparence like the face of a man who's been sick in bed for a long time; when he laughs his cheeks flush a little. At length we manage both of us to laugh.

It's such a preposterous position for a man to be in, like a man who doesn't know the game trying to play blindfold chess. The real world has gone. We have no more grasp of our world of rain and streets and trolleycars and cucumbervines and girls and gardenposts. This is a world of phrases, *prosecution, defense, evidence, motion, irrelevant, incompetent* and *immaterial*. For six years this man has lived in the law, tied tighter and tighter in the sticky filaments of law-words like a fly in a spider web. And the wrong set of words means the Chair.

All the moves in the game are made for him, all he can do is sit helpless and wait, fastening his hopes on one set of phrases after another. In all these lawbooks, in all this terminology of clerks of the court and counsel for the defense, there is one move that will save him, out of a million that will mean death.

If only they make the right move, use the right words.

But by this time the nagging torment of hope has almost stopped, not even the thought of his wife and children out there in the world, unreachable, can torture him now. He is numb now, can laugh and look quizzically at the ponderous machine that has caught and mangled him. Now it hardly matters to him if they do manage to pull him out from between the cogs. And the wrong set of words means the Chair.

Nicola Sacco came to this country when he was eighteen years old. He was born in Puglia in the mountains in the heel of Italy. Since then up to the time of his arrest he has had pretty good luck. He made good money, he was happily married, he had many friends, latterly he had a garden to hoe and rake mornings and evenings and Sundays. He was unusually powerfully built, able to do two men's work. In prison he was able to stand thirtyone days of hunger strike before he broke down and had to be taken to the hospital.

In jail he has learned to speak and write English, has read many books, for the first time in his life has been thrown with nativeborn Americans. They worry him, these nativeborn Americans. They are so hard and brittle. They don't fit into the bright clear heartfelt philosophy of Latin anarchism. These are people who coolly want him to die in the electric chair. He can't understand them. When his head was cool he's never wanted anyone to die. Judge Thayer and the prosecution he thinks of as instruments of a machine.

The warden comes up to take down my name.

"I hope your wife's better," says Sacco.

"Pretty poorly," says the warden.

Sacco shakes his head. "Maybe she'll get better soon, nice weather."

I have shaken his hand, my feet have carried me to the door. The warden looks into my face with a curious smile. "Leaving us?" he asks.

Outside in the neat streets the new green leaves are swaying in the sunlight, birds sing, klaxons grunt, a trolleycar screeches round a corner. Overhead the white June clouds wander in the unfenced sky.

Bartolomeo Vanzetti

Going to the Charlestown Penitentiary is more like going to Barnum and Bailey's. There's a great scurry of guards, groups of people waiting outside; inside a brass band is playing *Home Sweet Home*. When at length you get let into the Big Show, you find a great many things happening at once. There are rows of benches where pairs of people sit talking. Each pair is made up of a free man and a convict. In three directions there are gray bar and tiers of cells. The band inside plays bangingly: *Should auld acquaintance be forgot*.

A short broadshouldered man is sitting quiet through all the uproar, smiling a little under his big drooping mustache. He has a domed, pale forehead and black eyes surrounded by many little wrinkles. The serene modeling of his cheekbones and hollow cheeks makes you forget the prison look under his eyes. This is Vanzetti.

Bartolomeo Vanzetti was born in Villa Faletto, in a remote mountain valley in the Piedmont. At the age of thirteen his father apprenticed him to a pastrycook who worked him fifteen hours a day. After six years of grueling work in bakeries and restaurant kitchens he went back home to be nursed through pleurisy by his mother. Soon afterward his mother died and in despair he set out for America. When, after the usual kicking around by the Ellis Island officials, he was dumped on the pavement of Battery Park, he had very little money, knew not a

32

word of the language and found that he had arrived in a time of general unemployment. He washed dishes at Mouquin's for five dollars a week and at last left for the country for fear that he was getting consumption. At length he got work in a brick kiln near Springfield. There he was thrown with Tuscans, first learned the Tuscan dialect and read Dante and the Italian classics. After that he worked for two years in the stone pits at Meriden, Connecticut. Then he went back to New York and worked for a while as a pastrycook again, and at last settled in Plymouth where he worked in various factories and at odd jobs, ditchdigging, clamdigging, icecutting, snowshoveling and a few months before his arrest, for the sake of being his own boss, bought a pushcart and peddled fish.

All this time he read a great deal nights sitting under the gasjet when everyone else was in bed, thought a great deal as he swung a pick or made caramels or stoked brick kilns, of the workmen he rubbed shoulders with, of their position in the world and his, of their hopes of happiness and of a less struggling less animallike existence. As a boy he had been an ardent Catholic. In Turin he fell in with a bunch of socialists under the influence of De Amicis. Once in America he read St. Augustine, Kropotkin, Gorki, Malatesta, Renan, and began to go under the label of anarchist-communist. His anarchism, though, is less a matter of labels than of feeling, of gentle philosophic brooding. He shares the hope that has grown up in Latin countries of the Mediterranean basin that somehow men's predatory instincts, incarnate in the capitalist system, can be canalized into other channels, leaving free communities of artisans and farmers and fishermen and cattlebreeders who would work for their livelihood with pleasure, because the work was itself enjoyable in the serene white light of a reasonable world.

33

And for seven years, three hundred and sixtyfive days a year, yesterday, today, tomorrow, Sacco and Vanzetti woke up on their prison pallets, ate prison food, had an hour of exercise and conversation a day, sat in their cells puzzling about this technicality and that technicality, pinning their hopes to their alibis, to the expert testimony about the character of the barrel of Sacco's gun, to Madeiros' confession and Weeks' corroboration, to action before the Supreme Court of the United States, and day by day the props were dashed from under their feet and they felt themselves being inexorably pushed toward the chair by the blind hatred of wellmeaning citizens, by the superhuman involved stealthy soulless mechanism of the law.

Boston, June, 1927

The protest against the denial of a new trial to Sacco and Vanzetti became world wide. Since every legal path seemed barred the governor was implored to grant a pardon or at least to commute the sentences. The governor passed the buck by appointing a commission of prominent laymen who were presumed to be above the battle to advise him on the matter. Both the president of Harvard University and the president of the Massachusetts Institute of Technology were members. The commission sent the governor in a report which justified every feature of Judge Thayer's conduct of the trial and showed a surprising ignorance of the political background of the case into the bargain. In those days college presidents were not yet liberals by definition. The two men were electrocuted in Charlestown Jail in August 1927.

Vanzetti left a statement: "If it had not been for these things, I might have lived out my life talking at street corners to scorning men. I might have died unknown, a failure. This

34

is our career and our triumph. Never in our full life can we hope to do such work for tolerance, for justice, for man's understanding of man as now we do by accident. Our words, our lives, our pains, nothing. The taking of our lives—the lives of a good shoemaker and a poor fish peddler, all. The last moment belongs to us. That agony is our triumph."

In Memoriam

This isn't a poem

This is two men in gray prison clothes.
One man sits looking at the sick flesh of his hands—
hands that haven't worked for seven years.
Do you know how long a year is?
Do you know how many hours there are in a day
when a day is twenty-three hours on a cot in a cell,
in a cell in a row of cells in a tier of rows of cells
all empty with the choked emptiness of dreams?

Do you know the dreams of men in jail?
Sacco sits looking at the sick flesh of his hands—
hands that haven't worked for seven years,

remembers hoeing beans at twilight in his garden
remembers the crisp rattle of the edger,
remembers the mold of his wife's back,
fuzziness of the heads of kids.
Dreams are memories that have grown sore and fes-
        tered,
dreams are an everlasting rack to men in jail.

Vanzetti writes every night from five to nine
fumbling clumsily wittily with the foreign words
building paper barricades of legal tags,
habeas corpus, writ of certiorari,
dead spells out of a forgotten language
taken from the mouths of automatons in black.

They are dead now,
the black automatons have won.
They are burned up utterly,
their flesh has passed into the air of Massachusetts,
their dreams have passed into the wind.

"They are dead now," the Governor's Secretary nudges
the Governor,
"They are dead now," the Superior Court judge nudges
the Supreme Court judge,
"They are dead now," the College President nudges the
College President.
A dry chuckling comes up from all the dead:
The white collar dead; the silkhatted dead; the frock-
coated dead:
they hop in and out of automobiles,
breathe deep in relief
as they walk up and down the Boston streets.

These two men were not afraid
to smell rottenness
in the air of Massachusetts
so they are dead now and burned
into the wind of Massachusetts.
Their breath has given the wind new speed.
Their fire has burned out of the wind
the stale smell of Boston.

Ten thousand towns have breathed them in
and stood up beside workbenches,
dropped tools,
flung plows out of the furrow
and shouted
into the fierce wind from Massachusetts.
In that shout's hoarse throat
in the rumble of millions of men marching in order
is the roar of one song in a thousand lingoes.

The warden strapped these men into the electric
    chair;
the executioner threw the switch
and set them free into the wind;
they are free of dreams now,
free of greasy prison denim;
their voices blow back in a thousand lingoes sing-
    ing one song
to burst the eardrums of Massachusetts.

Make a poem of that if you dare!
New York, October, 1927

II

FRONTIER OF A TOMORROW

Up to the last most of us who had worked on the case were confident that some way would be found to get Sacco and Vanzetti a new trial. We were astounded when we read the report of the college presidents. We could hardly believe our eyes when we read that Justice Holmes and Justice Brandeis had refused to issue a writ of habeas corpus. No jurisdiction, they claimed. The last props of our belief in impartial justice broke away from under us.

The case left an immense bitterness between those who believed the men were innocent and those who believed they were guilty. I remember receiving a letter from a man I'd liked and admired and been on friendly terms with in college formally breaking off relations. Since we hadn't seen each other for many years, and he lived on one side of the country and I on the other, it puzzled me that he should have taken the trouble. Undoubtedly he felt he was doing his duty as a citizen.

This violence of opposition lashed us radicals up into a fresh determination to make our views known. The execution of Sacco and Vanzetti coming on top of the general abrogation of civil liberties during the European war, made us feel that all the instruments of power had fallen into the hands of the enemy.

The communists had an answer: revolution according

39

to Marx. In this country they were then a small sect striving without too much success to form their own unions. Their strength was that they had a definite set of convictions they held to with religious fervor. Their movement offered men and women who subjected themselves to the discipline dedicated careers, the selfrighteous assurance that they were better than other men, and that sense of participation in history that takes the place of religion for the Marxist. Their weakness was that they had no way of appealing to the desire for personal independence and to the basic creed that there should be fair play for all, which, thank God, is just as strong among American working people as it is in the rest of the population. Outside of foreign language groups, still subject to the millennial illusions they had brought with them from Europe, they weren't making much headway in the labor movement.

Their great success lay, as it does today, in the skill with which they managed to direct the thinking of halfeducated and inexperienced young people among Americans of middle class origin. I remember noticing a stiffening of the party line at the New Masses, which by this time was completely in the hands of communist professionals. I still published pieces in its columns on the theory that it didn't matter where your work appeared, so long as it was published intact, but I'd ceased to get much nourishment from the discussions of the comrades. In the course of the Sacco-Vanzetti case I had been thrown a good deal with working class agitators of a different sort. I felt that from them maybe might come a doctrine which would be much nearer to the old aspirations for a truly selfgoverning republic.

Meanwhile what could a man do? You could write. You could publish. You were cut off from the highpaying magazines and the larger audience, to be sure; but looking back on that period of the late twenties it is surprising how many more outlets for dissident opinion there were then than there are now. The Nation and The New Republic were still liberal journals in the nineteenth century sense of the word. Albert J. Nock's Freeman stood for independence all around the clock. The problem that worried us eager beaver radicals at the time was how to reach a larger public. O'Neill and the Provincetown Players had opened up a path. Some of us became convinced that through the theater we could reach an audience larger than the sprinkling of brighteyed dogooders who read the weeklies.

We spent a lot of time in Europe in those years. In Europe the theater was in a state of eruption. In Europe the social revolution was even more intimately linked with the revolt of Bohemia than in America. The revolt of Bohemia was taking fantastic and highly entertaining forms.

We had a profound belief in the arts, anyway. This was the period in the twenties when the arts caught fire. All the artistic revolts of the nineteenth century had a last blooming. Now, looking back, those years seem years of afterglow. When we were living them they seemed the dawn of an immense, magnificent era.

The war had taught us Paris. We were hardly out of uniform before we were hearing the music of Stravinsky, looking at the paintings of Picasso and Juan Gris, standing in line for opening nights of Diaghilev's Ballet Russe. "Ulysses" had just been printed by Shakespeare and Company. Performances like "Noces" and "Sacre du Printemps" or Cocteau's "Mariés de la Tour Eiffel" were giving us a fresh notion of what might go on on the stage. We saw photographs of productions by Meyerhold and Piscator. In the motion pictures we were enormously stimulated by Eisenstein's "Cruiser Potemkin."

41

One of the first fruits of Eisenstein's influence was that it led us to make a new appraisal of old Griffith's "Birth of a Nation." Out of the clash of all these new methods of expression we hoped to find new ways of bringing our protest against the injustice and cruelty of the afterwar world home to the common wayfaring man. I was fresh from the great days of that modernism in Paris (which I already knew was past its prime) when I got a cable from a friend in New York telling me that a Medici-minded financier was putting up some money to start an experimental theater. Would I become one of the directors? Sure. I took passage back to New York. I got there in time to see the opening night (or was it the closing night?) of a play of my own written in what was then called the expressionist manner.

The theater was fun in a way. I enjoyed designing and painting scenery; it was surprising what talented people turned up and how hard they worked; but it wasn't too long before I discovered it wasn't my meat. The theater is a career for nocturnal types. You never get to bed when you work in the theater. If you happen to be a daytime worker too, you never get any sleep. Then there was the constant insidious underlying conflict with the hardshelled communists who were determined that any theater that had anything to do with working people should serve the party. It was horribly fatiguing. I began to feel a need for fresh air and sunlight.

I'd been in the Soviet Union, or at least in Georgia and Armenia, at the moment when the Red Army was taking them over, in the fall of 1921. Now I wanted to see what was happening in Moscow. It seemed more than one man could do to try to report this vast experiment. Maybe if I stuck to the theater I could get a notion through that of what was going on in people's lives. So in the late spring of 1928 I embarked for Copenhagen.

Brooklyn to Helsingfors

In Brooklyn, in a few patches of grass, in the fuzzy antlers of the ailanthustrees that sprout beside garbagecans in back yards, it was beginning to be spring.

There was something about the way the tugs hooted on the East River in the morning twilight, and the harbor wind had a new sniff to it; but the girl with the copper-riveted henna rinse in the cafeteria was just the same, her face wore the same sleepwalker's neverasmile when she rang up your change or talked to somebody named Deary into the telephone or threw back a kidding remark or a Nice day, Bum day, Rainy day as if it had burned her. It was always the same in the subway, the echoing passage stinking of elevatorshafts and urinals, the scattering people in overcoats on the platform, hurried eyes that looked at you but never into yours (when eyes meet on the I.R.T. the airbrakes go on, the train stops with a crash), jostling bodies packed together through the long tunnel under the river, and the whiff of grit and burned gas in your face as you climbed out onto Seventh Avenue; and always the halfwop loafers at the corner of Bleecker, waiting for what?

In Manhattan there are no seasons and for a long time there hadn't been any days, only nights in the little office with its perpetually clacking typewriter (when the typewriter stops in a New York office everybody's embarrassed; men start to quarrel or to make love to the stenographer or drop lighted cigarettes in the wastebasket); and the stuffy little theater, and the stage lit for rehearsals and the empty rows of seats stretch-

43

ing into the dark; and upstairs the smell of the gluepot over the gasburner and the brushes that are so hard to keep from dripping and the dusty painted flats; and effort, hurry, the rush to make a number of things understood that we are unable to make understood.

In Brooklyn it was beginning to be spring, but in Manhattan there were no more days, only jangled nights of empty streets gone sour. High time I took a trip: the Hudson tubes had a fresh powdery electrical ozone smell; Hoboken was all yesterdays melting forgotten into the gray vacant scentless cavern of the wharf.

There is no sleep so good as sleep in a ship's bunk.

Looking out of the window across Germany is not half so entertaining as looking out of the New York New Haven and Hartford between Providence and New York, but it is fine going on board the Finnish boat at Stettin. The boat is enameled and bright as a toy in a toyshop window, everybody's eyes are blue on top of shining freshsoaped faces; everybody talks languages I can't even pretend to understand, but is delighted to produce whenever necessary a few words of a neat copybook English. The midday meal is Valhalla brought down to earth (except alas for the mead); in the center of the diningsaloon there's a long table; down the center of the table lie two whole boiled salmon head to head, they are flanked by a good hundred dishes of smoked salmon, herrings smoked, pickled, salted and raw, haddock and whitefish in a number of forms, caviar, hot cheese dishes, salads, cole slaw, red cabbage, pickles, savories, spiced meat, smoked tongue, sugared ham. . . . No wonder the bourgeoisie of these parts rose on its ear to defend its fleshpots.

Helsingfors is all right except that the sea isn't salt here and the town looks like a cleaner Duluth and they have run entirely out of this year's supply of darkness. There is a big fuzzy park where two brass bands play cheerlessly through the livid night and stocky pinkfaced boys and girls walk round in fours and fives nudging and elbowing and stepping on each other's feet when they meet.

The Sundays waiting for a visa in Helsingfors are the longest anywhere. You take a little steamboat and steam through endless archipelagos of birchcovered islands like islands in the Great Lakes, then you come back and walk out of town and go swimming in the chilly unsalt sea, then you come back and walk around in the elegant empty clean as a pin railroad station; it's nine o'clock but it's a bright day; no place is open and there's nobody anywhere.

Through the windows of the big hotel opposite the station you can at least see waiters moving about. The cavernous dining room is a chilly pink with lugubrious hangings held over from the old regime. The waiter speaks a little English, denies that he knows any place where I can get a drink. I sit munching alone; then a voice from home comes drawling out from some table behind the portieres, emphasizing each pause with a rattle of phlegm: "The trouble with . . . European countries . . . is . . . now all these customs barriers. Well in the States . . . fortyeight of 'em . . . well sir there's nothing like that. A man in Connecticut can trade with a man in Louisiana with no difficulties whatsoever. There everything is done to promote trade friendship, here you do everything you can to interfere with it."

All of which is indubitably true.

Eating the canned pears that ended the meal I formed a project to talk to the invisible speaker and his soundless companion; maybe they'd know where a man could get a drink. The

45

voice honked and gurgled and then went on: "Now look at the great enormous city of New York . . . stretched over three states . . . fifteen millions of inhabitants if you count the entire metropolitan district. Now look at that great metropolis . . ."

I had.

The thing to do was to go to bed and lie there in the colorless evening light worrying about why the Russian visa hadn't come.

Two days later it came. In the clean and comfortable Finnish-style station I went to bed in a clean and comfortable Finnish-style third class sleeper. The train rambled out of the station and on through endless gray birchwoods in the pale gloaming. It was fine to lie half asleep looking out of the window joggling toward the actual existing to-be-seen-with-my-own-eyes so bloodily contested frontier between yesterday and tomorrow.

This was in the summer of 1928. Was I right or was I wrong? That frontier is closer to us now. Writing in the summer of 1955 we still cannot say that we have taken tomorrow away from the communists.

Rainy Days in Leningrad

The train ran into the station and stopped; an empty station without bustle, broad clean asphalt platforms, gray ironwork, a few porters and railroad officials standing around. Very quickly the American conducted tours were absorbed and disappeared bag and baggage. I waited on the empty platform for a man who was doing something about a trunk. This was where Lenin, back from hiding in the marshes, had landed and made his first speeches during the Russian October eleven years ago.

How could it be so quiet? I'd half expected to catch in the gray walls some faint reverberation of trampling footsteps, of machineguns stuttering, voices yelling: All Power to the Soviets. Could it have been only eleven years ago?

At length we got into a muchtoosmall cab driven by a huge bearded extortioner out of the chorus of "Boris Godunov," and start joggling slowly along the toowide streets under a low gray sky. In every direction stretch immense neoclassic façades, white columns, dull red, blue or yellow stucco walls, battered silent, majestic, and all like the Finland station, swept free, empty. How could it be so quiet when only eleven years ago . . . ?

We ducked out of the chilly rain under a porch held up by tired-looking stone women and through swinging doors into the vestibule of the museum. That vestibule of the Czar's old picture collection, full of people standing round waiting to check their coats and galoshes, was a tower of Babel. A party of Americans was being conducted up the stairs, a few German students in windjackets and shorts stood about, a horde of dark people from southeast Russia were speaking Tatar, there were pale blue-eyed soldiers from somewhere in the north. A young man standing next to me asked me something and I tried him on English thinking he was a Chinaman. He turned out to be a Kirghiz. My companion knew Russian.

We walked round together, and he was as pleased to be talking to two men from America as we were to be talking to a Kirghiz; none of us saw any of the pictures.

He was a metalworker, an unskilled laborer. He'd been in Leningrad a year just making enough to live. He and his brother had left the tent of their fathers on the Kirghiz steppes and their herd of shaggymaned ponies, because they wanted to find

47

out about the world and the revolution. His brother was a partymember and was studying at the university for eastern peoples. No, he himself wasn't a communist. Well, mostly because he had not seen enough yet, he had not made up his mind as to whether they were right or wrong. He didn't know. He was too young yet. He'd have to see the world and draw his own conclusions, Criticize? Yes the workers in his factory said about what they pleased . . . of course if someone made a habit of talking directly against the Party, the Gaypayoo might bring pressure to bear. He wasn't sure. As for him, it wouldn't convince him the Party was right if they locked him up, he thought they understood that. He had to see the world and find out for himself.

And his people, the nomad tribes of the great steppes of Central Asia, stockraisers still living in the age of Abraham, Isaac and Jacob? The ideas of the revolution were just beginning to reach them, through schools, through young men like himself who went to work in Russian cities. They talked about revolution in their tents at night, round their smoky fires. The old people still clung devoutly to Islam, but the young men were like him, they wanted to know what was right, what was good for the world. Perhaps five per cent of them were communists or comsomols. Many of the rest of them, like him, wanted to see for themselves.

We talked about books. He said he was reading Gorki and until he had read everything Gorki had ever written he wouldn't have time for any other books. It was only since the revolution that there had been books among the Kirghiz.

What about the position of women? At home it was very complicated, it was all a matter of money or cattle, getting a wife, neither party was free; but here among the Leningrad factory workers you could do pretty much as you pleased with your individual life, if a fellow and a girl liked each other well enough, they lived together, and then if they got very fond of each other, or if she was going to have a baby, they registered the marriage. The only place the police stepped in was if either party failed to chip in supporting the child.

But what about America? We must tell him everything about America, whether you could get work, how much pay you got, what the schools were like, whether life was good there, what kind of marriage we had, whether the workers had any power, how mighty was capitalism.

Yes he wanted to go to America, he must see as much as he could of the world, so that he could make up his mind.

Just as we were getting ready to turn down the stairs, in front of a Rembrandt I ran into a titled Frenchman and his wife I had met at Antibes, who were past grand masters in the most esoteric circles of modernart. Their eyes turned to mine with a connoisseur's glint of approval. "*Quelle rencontre!*" We were in the right spot at the right time. La Russie sovietique was the *dernier cri*. "*La Russie c'est formidahble,*" they chanted. I echoed: "*Formidahble.*"

We had just come out from the bare stone corridors of Smolny Institute, huge austerelyproportioned colonnaded building that stood serenely athwart the gray drizzly afternoon; we had seen the little room where Lenin lived and worked from the time the Bolsheviki seized power in the name of the peasants and workers until the government moved to Moscow, a bare room with a few chairs and a table and a little cot behind a partition: we walked down the road and out through the gate. Eleven years ago . . . and now Smolny was history, like the music of Bach, like Mount Vernon, like the pyramids.

We wanted to find a place to drink tea and asked two

49

youngsters who had also turned round to look back at Smolny.

The question of tea was lost for a long while in the questions about America they peppered us with. They were communists, students at the university at Odessa, in Leningrad on an excursion run by Narkompros. Smolny for them was the beginning of everything. They were too young to have much memory of the old Russia of the czar when Smolny had been a ladies' seminary for daughters of the nobility. To them the October days seemed as long ago as the fall of the Bastille. They had finished their two years in the Red Army and were studying to be teachers. It took a definite effort for them to imagine how things must be in the capitalist world outside. Our routine questions about freedom of opinion and the economic position of the peasants didn't interest them. It wasn't that they didn't care about these things, it was that their approach was from an entirely different side. For us, October, Smolny, Lenin were in the future; for them they were the basis of all habits, ideas, schemes of life. It was as hard for them to imagine a time when Marxism had not been a rule of conduct as it would be for an American high school kid to doubt the desirability of the open shop or the Monroe Doctrine.

Lord how things have changed. Marxism is still the rule of conduct beyond that frontier. The opportunistic trimmings of course change almost daily; but the basic creed has formed generation after generation. Meanwhile the Western world has shuffled up all its convictions. If you talk to an American high school boy in this year of 1955 he'll tell you that the open shop is the stratagem of designing businessmen. If he ever heard of the Monroe Doctrine he takes a dim view of it.

"Why," these two young Russians kept asking us, "why can't you understand what we are trying to do, why can't the workers in America understand that we are building socialism; why can't the workers in England realize that we are working for them as much as for ourselves?"

Today the shoe's on the other foot. We are asking them, plaintively, why they can't understand that by a peaceable rearrangement of our society, we've already accomplished some of the things their revolution set out to do. We try to understand you, we tell them, why won't you try to understand us?

All this time I was working hard to try to understand the language. The Russian language is no joke. There's a special kind of headache you get from the effort to remember the conjugation of the Russian verb. I went to every theater I could find, with a dictionary in my hand. My pockets were filled with endless scrawled lists of Russian words.

At the same time I tried to find out like every other American tourist before or since, how the Russians lived, what it would be like to live under socialism.

It is not easy to form in your head the sort of simplified diagram of a social system that's needed for even the most cursory understanding of it. The people you try to study have already become accustomed to their lives. They hardly notice the unnamed pressures that really matter. The human race can get accustomed to almost anything.

It was years before the experiences of that summer really sank into my consciousness.

Keep your mind a blank page I kept telling myself.

The man who was taking us round town that evening was the son of a rich man. He had joined the red guards and fought with them all through the October days. Later he had been a head of a division of the Red Army through the civil war. He had gotten into trouble somehow, been expelled from the communist party and spent a year in jail. People told me afterward that he wrote first rate poetry. He called himself, jokingly, a counter-revolutionary. He spoke English.

He showed us the great square where the monument to the October dead was and told us how it had been made on one of Lenin's Saturday Afternoons, when bunches of soldiers and factory workers would tackle some particularly unsightly corner of the city and dig it up into a park. He told us a little wistfully about the enthusiasms and comradeliness of those days. He showed us the streets where he had fought eleven years ago, the place where they'd held the barricade against a desperate attack from the cadets, squares where the red guards had camped for the night, houses they had taken shelter in. Maybe he almost wished things still were as they had been eleven, eight, six years ago, when it was still possible to kill and be killed for the revolution, and politics was as simple as the mechanism of the machinegun.

We came out on the bank of the Neva. It was about midnight. You could still see things dimly in a faint milky twilight. The stately palaces along the Neva, the spires of the Peter and Paul fortress, the wide bridges, the icy clear gray swift flowing river must have looked about the same as they looked to Pushkin a hundred years ago. We walked down the embankment until we came to a small park. A young man and a girl sat on a bench talking low. At the end of the park on a base of granite rock was a statue, a huge black mass rearing into the pale night, a man on a prancing horse. The man who had been showing us around pointed to it: "There's my favorite Russian in history," he said. "Peter the Great, who brought order out of chaos, the first bolshevik."

We take the train to a suburban station in a firwood. The framehouses scattered among trees and neglected gardens are like the houses in an American residential section of twenty-five years ago, except that the paint has worn off them. The critic my friend is taking me to see is a very charming man. His English is very good. He asks us to take tea and strawberries with him. (The Leningrad strawberries are the size of peaches and have as much taste as wild strawberries. Queen Victoria and Kaiser William considered them the best in the world. Dear Nicky used to ship them to his relatives in Germany and England every summer.) The critic is a man of humanity, refinement, real humor; he knows a great deal. Somehow he missed the red train that left one November. Other friends and associates of his, who also missed it, were able to catch it at stations farther down the line. He was left where he stood eleven years ago. He asks with that timid feverish interest all Russians seem to feel, about the world across the frontier. It's hard to explain how fast Europe is crumbling away, leaving a dreary madhouse instead of those pleasant parks where people talked about Verlaine as they let the foam settle on their beer, and those watering places where even the almost poor could live genially and idly. Life is hard for those who have lost the train; the authorities don't let them publish what they want, the Gaypayoo nags their relatives and children; they never know when they are going to be arrested or exiled. Still, he says, in the long run, it's better now for a writer than under the czar, at least you can

53

argue with these censors, they give you reasons, they listen to what you have to say. In the old days you might as well try to argue with a gorilla as with the czar's police.

Stalin changed all that. He skipped Peter the Great and went back to Ivan the Terrible. No arguing with Ivan's police.

The bus stopped at an inn for lunch before crossing the highest pass on the Georgian road. The stoutish gentleman with a beard was a technician, what kind he didn't say. He spoke some English and some French and too much German. He asked me to sit at the table with him and ordered my lunch for me. He looked at me severely through his noseglasses over the borsch. "Of course," he said, "you have invented the best industrial technique in the world . . . Taylor, Ford, Firestone. . . . There has never been anything like it in history." I bashfully assented that there never had. "But in your hands," he pointed at me with his spoon, "it can only lead to disaster . . . a period of horror for the human race such as has never been seen in history." I agreed that we were in for a period of horror, but that perhaps it was not entirely our fault. "It is the fault of the capitalist system and the plundermadness of the businessmen. . . . But you Americans are to blame. . . . You have no feudalism, you boast of being free, you should have gotten control of the system during the lifetime of Marx. . . . But we are learning your system. . . . It is like arithmetic, once it is invented anybody can learn it. What did your Shakespeare say? *The villainy you taught me I shall execute.*"

The Moscow Theater

There are traces of other Moscows still to be seen under this tremendous November Moscow of our day, humming over-

54

crowded city that is the key switchboard to which all the wires lead that hold together the forces that are building socialism over one sixth of the world. Of course there is the startling remnant of the Red Square and the very visible and operatic mediaeval shell of the Kremlin that brings to your mind the music of "Boris" and "Khovantchina," but beyond that, across the river stretches a less showy region of streets of eighteenth- and nineteenth-century merchants' houses, the Moscow of Ostrovsky's plays, across the Moscow River. These streets have a particularly desolate and forlorn appearance but there still lingers in them a faint flavor of the life of the counting houses in the days when the Russian businessmen, for all their bushy whiskers and their abacuses were getting rich fast and easily. I don't know why they should have attracted me (perhaps because the life in them had resembled so much American life) but I seemed to feel their imprint in walking round the city more than that of the ferocious furlined boyars who built the Kremlin. Not that the merchants were any less ferocious than the boyars or that I've ever personally felt very deeply for the heady excitement of buying cheap and selling dear to which their lives were dedicated; maybe it's that the hope of something for nothing is in the American blood. You can still see the last remnants of these businessmen in the old markets, where, trodden underfoot by the new order, always at the risk of being nabbed as speculators, they still managed to find a few odds and ends to haggle and chaffer over. Another place you see them is in the beer restaurants and in the café near the postoffice where the gypsies sing at night. They sit there in their leather jackets with their beady eyes and predatory faces, a crumpled cartoon of the bank presidents and realestate agents and bondsalesmen and speculators for whose benefit the game is always rigged at home. Here these people make up the down and out disinherited and criminal class. Penal institutions reform some of them, they say.

But the Moscow of now, the Moscow of today, the Moscow of the new order, how can you get hold of it?

I can't do anything about it.

I hear the tramp of it under my window every morning when the Red Army soldiers pass with their deep throaty singing, I see it in the kindergarten I sometimes go to see that's so far away at the end of a trolley line, I see it most among the youngsters who run the Sanitary Propaganda Theatre where Alexandra directs the plays, energy, enthusiasm, selfeffacement and that fervid curiosity and breadth of interest that is the magnificent earmark of the Russian mind. I see it in the communist friends I make who are all the time working, arguing, organizing, teaching, doing office chores and who, no matter how pale and haggard from overwork they are when they come home to those late afternoon Moscow dinners, are always ready to talk, explain, ask questions; but an onlooker in Moscow is about as out of place as he would be in the assembly line of a Ford plant. If you are an engineer or a mechanic or a schoolteacher you can do something but if you're a writer you're merely in the unenviable position of standing round and watching other people do the work.

Well you're a reporter, you tell yourself. You're gathering impressions.

What the hell good are impressions? About as valuable as picture postalcards or the little souvenir knickknacks people who'd been on trips used to bring home to set in rows on the glass shelves of the parlor cabinet.

Worthwhile writing is made of knowledge, feelings that have been trained into the muscles, sights, sounds, tastes, shudders that have been driven down into your bones by grim repetition, the modulations of the language you were raised to talk. It's silly to try to report impressions about Moscow; you can stay there and work or you can go home and work.

That's why the best thing to do if you're in Moscow is to go to the theater. Here's as much as you can digest at a sitting put into digestible form. Not knowing the language is hardly a barrier at all. You can look at the stage all the better for not following all the lines. You can look at the audience. You are part of the audience.

A New York theater is a too fancylooking building put up on a realestate speculation for the purpose of getting people to pay more than they can afford to come in and sit in the dark to see actors moving round on a stage (lit brightly or bluely according as the production aims for the box office or for "art"), saying lines they've learned off typewritten sheets without knowing what the play's about, making gestures taught them by a director with jumpy nerves. A lot of expert electricians and stagehands change the lights and move round the scenery. Everybody except the technical staff and the audience is there on speculation, hoping against hope to cash in on the various forms of exhibitionism involved, to see their names in electric lights, to make a million dollars. The author, the director, the actors, the boxoffice man, the manager, the promoter who introduced the manager to the angel that put up the original capital, stagestruck girls, culturefuddled old women, ticket speculators, officeboys, playdoctors, scenedesigners, all think that this time they've matched the buffalo and will wake up famous and rich, or just rich, which is more important.

In Moscow people go to the theater to feel part of the victorious march through history of the world proletariat.

Most of the New York critics who've been in Moscow

hasten home to report that the Russian theater isn't any good, but they are wrong. They were too flustered by the different living habits of the Russians to enjoy it. The show begins just about when the critic would ordinarily be eating dinner; if he didn't eat, he's hungry and if he did, it was probably in a hurry and he's getting a touch of indigestion. None of the audience is much dressed up; he wonders anxiously how often these dirty Russians bathe. The theater building looks raw and crude, probably an old theater stripped of its decorations, barny, painted in plain white or gray. The play begins without much formality; usually the house goes dark and the stage lights go on; bright nervous spotlights point out the action dogmatically, like the ferrule of a schoolteacher pointing out equations on a blackboard. Somebody's trying to translate for the New York critic; he can't understand Russian or the translator's English very well. He is worried for fear he's hearing propaganda and will be converted to communism without knowing it. The play lasts a long time, the intermissions are too long, the seats are hard; he misses the sense of luxury even the smallest movingpicture house gives him at home; he goes back to the hotel yawning and tired, afraid he may have picked up lice, and writes back to the folks at home that the Russian theater is much overrated and that it's all bolshevik propaganda anyway.

These gentlemen are completely wrong. All the liveliest tendencies in the European theater are developing in the Soviet Union. The audience is growing every day. Fresh new hordes of people, eager to take part through their proxies, the actors, in the tragic renovations of history they are living through, offer to playwrights and directors an opportunity for every kind of innovation. As in America, motion pictures are a strong competitor but here the stage with living actors doesn't seem to be giving any ground. The Russian theater is at the beginning of a period of enormous growth.

Certainly in the fall of 1928 the Moscow theater was a delight. You could see productions in every conceivable manner, from the rather precious stylization of the Kamerny and the Jewish theater to Stanislavski's classical productions of Chekhov still acted exactly as he directed them and the works of the then new school of socialist realism which soon was to become the established order. I can still hear the deep-throated choruses of Moussorgsky's "Khovantchina." There was a new staging of "Boris Godunov," refreshed by a painstaking reconstruction of the great amateur's own original score. Nobody who wants to understand Russian history should neglect "Boris." Both the music and the text are a mine of understanding. The most startling evening of all was Meyerhold's "Roar China." It's too bad that a sort of built-in Philistinism inhibits our political leaders from paying any attention to the arts. If some representative of our State Department could have seen and understood "Roar China," he would have seen there, painted huge in garish colors, the violent myth that has led the Chinese communists to victory.

Not that I have any reason to crow over those much abused gentlemen. Everything I thought and wrote that summer was based upon the notion, which Josef Stalin was immediately to prove false, that the violent phase of the Russian revolution was over, that the drive of communist fanaticism was slackening, that the magnificent energies of the Russian people would soon be set to work on making life worth living.

As it turned out, it was in Great Britain that parliamentary socialism had its day and in the United States that the people got a new deal.

Stalin's own taste had great influence on the arts. What he liked in the theater was the endless repetition of "Swan Lake." As early as the summer I was in Moscow all officialdom was in raptures over a ballet called "The Red Poppy" which seemed to me a tasteless and routine performance much closer to the exercises of the Rockettes than to the magnificent affirmations the exiled Russian dancers were putting on the stage under Diaghilev in France. The arts mean something after all; they are the litmus paper that gives you the mood of a society.

Another omen I should have paid more attention to was the new Moscow postoffice. I'd always claimed that you could measure the intellectual energy and the good and bad intentions of any ruling group by the buildings they put up. The early buildings of the bolsheviks, Lenin's tomb and the Lenin Institute, were simple, handsomely proportioned. A complete break with the czarist past, they seemed to point to a revolutionary style. But the just completed postoffice which I was shown with pride was a return to the inhuman tastelessness of the bureaucracy of the late czars. I don't know that Stalin had a hand in it, but I should have taken it as a premonition of his regime.

Terror

Englishmen who have lived too long in foreign countries get a crazy look in their eyes like the look in the eyes of Van Gogh's selfportraits. This man had asked me to come to see him. As soon as I came in he poured me out a glass of Kakhetian wine. It was good wine, a little like port; he apologized for the wine, said he had to take what he could get. His wife came in, a nervous, unhappylooking Russian woman. They both seemed nervous and uneasy. I sat looking at them, looking round the apartment. It was a small apartment crowded with furniture, oldfashioned heavy carefully polished mahogany furniture. The furniture was crowded in the room. It had evidently been made for much larger rooms. There was a great deal of Dresden china, and cutglass decanters on the sideboard. The things in the room looked huddled together like stuff saved from a fire. Everything was clean and polished but there was an air of hurry and dread about the way the things were arranged in the room. We sat there uneasily at the fine oval mahogany table while the wife fussed nervously about, coming in and out from the other room. It was evident that he wanted to tell me something and that the wife was trying to keep him from saying it.

All at once he started to talk: "I used to believe in them as you do," he said, "sometimes I still do, but most of the time it's a nightmare. I came here to work full of idealism because I believed in them, now I'd go away anywhere, but I can't make any money. They won't let her go out of the country. We don't dare make inquiries about leaving for fear they'll arrest her."

"It can't be as bad as that," I started to say.

He broke in and talked on and on. He hadn't believed in the terror either, but now he lived under it. She was a member of the old intelligentsia; there was nothing she could do to put herself right. They were doomed unless they could get out. After all let them stamp on the old nobles and the middleclass social revolutionaries if they got in their way, it was war, he could understand that; it was how they treated their own people . . . now it was the Trotskyites, the old revolutionaries who had created the Soviet Union, friends and co-workers with Lenin;

61

it was anybody who fell under the wheels.

Did I know about Kronstadt? It was learning the truth about Kronstadt that had turned it all into a bitter nightmare for him. The sailors who revolted at Kronstadt were the men who had made the October days, among them were members of the crew of the *Aurora*, they were real revolutionaries but they were misled by crazy anarchists and S.R.'s, very likely there were paid English agents there too. There was no doubt that the revolt was a great danger. In Petrograd they got the wind up terribly. Undoubtedly it had to be suppressed. The loyal troops recaptured the fortress after fierce fighting. The sailors capitulated on terms. The Tcheka agents had run like rabbits at the first sign of danger. They didn't dare come back until three days after the troops had recaptured the place. But then the prisoners were turned over to the Tcheka, the Tchekists had many of them been members of the old Okhrana, czarists, sadists, perverts of every hideous kind—"there's no cruelty like Russian cruelty, not even Chinese. They butchered even the miserable prostitutes in the brothels of Kronstadt. Some of the Tcheka agents had with them copies of *Le Jardin des Supplices* written by that filthy Frenchman to use as a textbook when their imagination failed. It's a nightmare, I tell you."

I got to my feet a little dizzily. It was terror I'd seen in the man's eyes, in the huddle of the oldfashioned furniture moved into this choked apartment, in the woman's nervous step. I felt sick. I cleared my throat. "But the Tcheka's gone. . . . They had most of them shot. The terror is over."

"You can say that. . . . You can come and go when you please. It'll never be over for us till we die or they get us, unless we can get out. We are doomed. You know they always come at night. No arrests are ever seen. No one who sees them ever dares tell anyone. Nothing is ever known."

It was a relief to get out into the casual street, to look into everyday faces, to see the streetcars crowded with people coming home from the theaters, to feel the soft brush of snowflakes in my face. But that night I couldn't sleep on account of the man's creaking voice and the crazy look in his eyes, and the terrified huddle of the old middleclass mahogany furniture in that choked room.

The Village

The country round Moscow looks like the rolling part of Wisconsin, only occasionally in a clearing you catch sight of a landlord's house, often with white Georgian columns like a southern plantation mansion, but usually on a bigger more princely scale. The mansions that weren't burned down by the peasants in the first flare of the revolution are now resthouses or schools or sanitariums. It was to one of these resthouses, the Writers', that I was being driven by an eightfoot grizzled *izvoshchik* when he asked me if I was a German. I said I was an American. "Americans are civilized but Germans are more civilized," he said. "Here in Russia what we need is more Germans. Now we have too much liberty. Every barefoot no-account in the village thinks he's as good as the next man. There is no discipline, too much liberty. With liberty everything goes to hell. Hindenburg, he's what we need. He's a great man. But the young men now they do nothing but talk about liberty. That will not make a great nation. To become a great nation Russia should have a great man to put every man in his place, a man like Hindenburg."

"Now Stalin, our Stalin is a man," the cabdriver added. To this day I can't imagine why I left that out.

63

In Russian when you want to say you're going to the country you say you're going to the village. The village where I went to visit the parents of a Russian acquaintance was not very far from Moscow. The village straggles for a long way over the rolling plain. The houses are set out in rows a hundred or more feet apart and far back from the road. The houses are built of logs, thatched with bark, with smallpaned doublewindows. Inside, a huge stove, built of earth and plaster fills up the center of the house. Sometimes there are no partitions, but often the house is cut up into a series of small rooms in which the strapping people in their padded winter clothes crowd incongruously big. In the enormous plain, under the enormous sky, packed with the big hulking redcheeked men and women, the houses and everything in them look small as dollhouses. Back of each house there are outbuildings, a pigsty, a yard enclosed by a rail fence, a woodpile, a strip of garden or the beginning of a narrow field that stretches away out of sight over the next hill. If you're a guest or a foreigner the samovar starts to steam and you have to sit in the stuffy front room full of the fragrance of the tea and the sweetsickly smell of the charcoal, drinking tea and eating bread and butter and raspberry jam interspersed with little glasses of plum brandy. People talk with that same soft-voiced innocence of manner and speech you find among farmers in outoftheway parts of the middle west. You feel that at last you're learning the truth.

It is a very simple truth. The village needs seed, clothing, agricultural implements, scientific knowledge about stockraising, poultryfarming and the care of children, a doctor and a school-teacher, books, radios, contact with civilization, that heady enthusiastic participation in the march of human history that is being substituted for the calendar of saints, the ikons and the onion domes and the deep bearded voices of the churchsingers.

The revolutionary bureaucracy needs grain, potatoes, cabbages, sunflower seeds, pork, support against reactionaries whose whole habit of life is buying cheap and selling dear, intelligent workers who will carry out the changing policies of the center, even helpful hardheaded criticism sometimes. We are Russia, we believe that the Communist Party will eventually benefit us, that the Communist Party is putting us in the forefront of history. But it is not easy for the bureaucracy and the peasants to learn to work together. It is not easy, but we will learn.

When my head was bursting with the stuffiness and the smell of the charcoal and the maddening prismatic puzzle of the Russian language I slipped out and walked away from the house over the hill. It was dark and the sleet had made a light crust on the snow. Overhead I could barely make out the low even lid of clouds. In a few steps the tiny string of lights of the village was lost in the snowy folds of the plain. The raw wind threw an occasional handful of sleet in my face. Everywhere the endless northern plain at the beginning of night, at the beginning of winter. No sense of locality; no ingrained quaintness of ancient local histories and customs. It might be Alberta or the Dakotas or Tasmania or Patagonia, any untrampled unfenced section of the earth's surface where men, tortured by the teasing stings of hope, can strain every apprehension of the mind, every muscle of the body to lay the foundations of a new order. It's a tremendous thing to walk alone, even a short distance, at night at the beginning of winter over the Russian plains.

Moscow, December, 1928

How hard it is to write truthfully. Reading over these lines I keep remembering things I forgot to put in. Why did I forget to put in about the enlarged photographs of Lenin as a baby I saw in the ikon corner in the peasants' houses in-

65

stead of the Christ Child? Why did I neglect people's hints about Stalin? There was a very pleasant actress whom I've called Alexandra who had worked with the Art Theatre I sometimes took evening walks with in Moscow. She came of the old revolutionary intelligentsia. I shall never forget the look of hate that would come into her face when we'd pass a large photograph of Stalin in a store window. She never spoke. She would just nudge me and look. As the years went on I understood what she meant. Of course in 1928 Stalin had not shown himself yet. He was working from behind the scenes. Trotsky was in exile but there were still people around the theater in Moscow whom their friends introduced half-laughingly as Trotskyites. The terror that English journalist was trying to tell me about still lurked in the shadows. It was not yet walking the streets.

Still, I remember falling into a real funk for fear they wouldn't let me leave the last few days I was in Moscow attending to the final passport formalities. Just like every other American I'd done my best to see the good, but the last impression I came away with was fear, fear of the brutal invisible intricate machinery of the police state. No fear was ever better founded.

Warsaw in those days was no paradise of civil liberties, but I still remember how well I slept in the sleazy bed in the faded hotel I put up at in Warsaw after piling out of the Moscow train. Warsaw was Europe. My last month in Moscow I'd been scared every night.

I wonder, too, thinking it over twenty-five years later, why I didn't note down some of the firstrate conversations I had with Russian theater people, like the Tairovs and with motion picture directors like Pudovkin and Eisenstein. Before I left Moscow a troop of the Japanese Kabuki arrived for a twoweeks run. I was amazed to discover that Eisenstein knew a certain amount of Japanese. Every Russian I met seemed to have spent weeks reading up on the Japanese theater. The shows were besieged. People invented dangerous stratagems to get themselves seats. Every bureaucratic string was pulled. They noted every move of the actors, they greedily sopped up every note of the music, every stylized gesture of the dancing. The way the revolving stage was used appealed to them particularly. By the time the Kabuki players left they had drunk the style to the dregs. Everything had been absorbed and filed away for future use.

In my mind I compared their intelligently directed enthusiasm with the complacent dogmatism of "artistic" people at home. The immense powers of absorption of the Russian mind left me baffled. I came away, as I always had whenever I found myself in competition with these great vague hungry dedicated people, with a frightened admiration for the amplitude of their interests, for their peculiar kind of efficiency, so differently organized from ours. When I wrote down my notes and impressions on my way home this was one of many things I couldn't cope with, of many things I hadn't absorbed enough yet to write about.

Then there were the inhibitions. I probably didn't write about the Tairovs and other friends I made in the Russian theater because I already felt that they were under a shadow. I was afraid something I might say would make their lives more difficult under the regime.

The other inhibition, of course, was the fear of writing something that would be seized on by anti-Soviet propaganda in the West. That was a period in which American capitalism seemed a much greater danger to the Russian experiment than the other way around. Today in 1955 the situation is reversed. The peculiar methods of bureaucratic tyranny which were developed by Stalin out of Lenin and Trotsky's military communism have become the dominant power in the world. In those days I was trying to be neutral, above the battle like Goethe.

It was puzzlement more than disillusionment I suffered from. I came away full of admiration for the energy and breadth of the Russian mind. I still felt that the Russians were nearer to finding a solution to the strange and horrible world industrial society had produced for mankind than we were in America. Even then I didn't pretend to like the solution. There must be a better way.

I tried to put that feeling into words: You don't have to make a decision yet I kept telling myself. As communist power grew that position proved untenable.

Passport Photo

Slipping unsurely with numb wet feet on the sleetslimed pavement the Americanski Peesatyel stumbles into the station and finds his way dazedly to his compartment in the train. In the trainshed it is like the Moscow winter afternoon outside, only darker and grayer. The dim electric bulbs make no light in the December murk, cold and heavy and gray as pigiron. Only the steam rising from the engine and our breaths make a little fragile stir of whiteness. The A. Peesatyel is dead tired, his nose stopped up with a cold, his stomach is full of cold herring and smoked fish, the vodka of many goodbyes has worked up into his head where it weighs and buzzes in an iron crown. All the day before, all night, all this day he'd slushed through the steelpitted snow of the streets, climbed gray stairs, tried to explain, to understand explanations, to say things in foreign languages, to ask how, to tell why; had stood face to face with great healthy young people in formless gray clothes; had been warmed and moved by the warmth and movement of their faces so alive in the eyes and lips, eyes strained to see beyond the frontier, beyond next week and next century, lips always forming questions; had left the questions halfanswered, halfunderstood and had shaken hands. This shaking hands and saying goodbye was like shaking hands with a surgeon you were friends with who had come to the door of the operating theater for a moment to strip off his rubber gloves and smoke a cigarette and try to explain something to you before it was time to go back to the lights and the blood and the glittering instruments of the theater where with desperate difficulty a baby was being born.

In the early morning there'd been a long drunkendrowsy trip in a taxicab to a suburb where you could hardly see the gray ramshackle houses against the long gray snowbanks disappearing under the gray sky, to visit an old peasant, a sharpfaced timeless man, who'd brought from some Volga villages a whole bagful of lacquered scraps of the middleages made up for sale into ashtrays and soupspoons and cigarette boxes, painted right today in the style of the Byzantine ikonpainters; and then back into the murk of Moscow, into the terrible jangling girderwork of the future again, and more unfinished talks, goodbyes, little glasses of vodka, goodbyes.

But all the old habits of thirty years of life are straining away toward the west and carpets and easychairs and the hot and cold bathwater running and the cheerful trivial accustomed world of shopwindows and women's hats and their ankles neat as trottinghorses' above the light hightapping heels, and the nonsensical lilt of advertisements and gimcracks and greenbacks. It's like waiting for the cage that's going to haul you up out of

69

a mine, like getting out of a cementfactory, like climbing the long greasy ladder out of the stokehold of a steamboat, like getting away from the rotary presses of a newspaper and stepping out onto the disorganized jingling street.

Groggily the A. Peesatyel drops his bags in his compartment (anyway made the train) and steps out on the platform to smoke one more of too many last cigarettes, and stands stamping his numb feet in the gray iron cold of the trainshed under the spiraling beckoning vaguelyseen steam. The woman who was the theaterdirector, the nice genial woman with the fine dark eyes, has come down to say goodbye; the company came with her, all the fifteenyearolds and eighteenyearolds I'd seen rehearsing the plays for the Sanitary Propaganda Theatre, the play about avoiding syphilis, the play about cleaning your teeth, the play about the world that will stand up so bright and shining when the dark murky scaffolding of today's struggle is torn away. "They want to say goodbye," she says as I am shaking the hard untrembly hands (they are all factoryworkers in the daytime and actors at night), under the probing of so many blue eyes curious and friendly, wanting to be told, to be with, to understand, to cross all these faraway frontiers. "They want to know," she says. "They like you very much, but they want to ask you one question. They want you to show your face. They want to know where you stand politically. Are you with us?"

The iron twilight dims, the steam swirls round us, we are muddled by the delicate crinkly steam of our breath, the iron crown tightens on the head, throbbing with too many men, too many women, too many youngsters seen, talked to, asked questions of, too many hands shaken, too many foreign languages badly understood.

"But let me see. . . . But maybe I can explain. . . . But in so short a time . . . there's no time."

The train is moving. I have to run and jump for it. They are gone in a whirl of steam, rubbed out by the irongray darkness. The train has pulled out of the station and is rumbling westward.

Warsaw, December, 1928

III

THE REVOLUTION OF 1932

The stockmarket collapse of 1929 and the partial breakdown of the free enterprise system of which it was a symptom provided the Marxists with their great I told you so. Things like that didn't happen in the Soviet Union. You didn't have to be a Marxist to blame all this misery on the slaphappy greed of the capitalists. Even from the perspective of today, after every effort to eliminate the bogyman from the picture, it still seems true that the American businessman had proved himself a conspicuous failure. For all his feeding at the government trough he had not been able to develop the responsible ruling class that Alexander Hamilton had looked forward to. Looking back on those years what most stands out is the businessman's panicky abdication.

The soft coal industry like many another was on its beam ends. The Communist Party at that time was trying to organize its own trade unions. With their flair for publicity, they induced a number of writers and journalists to serve as a committee to go to the Kentucky coalfields to see for themselves the violence that had met the efforts of communist-trained organizers to form a union. Theodore Dreiser, shy, opinionated, sensitive and aware as an old bull elephant, headed the committee. He looked like a senator, he acted like a senator and he got himself into a thoroughly senatorial

73

scrape. For all of that there was a sort of massive humaneness about him, a selfdedicated disregard of consequences, a sly sort of dignity that earned him the respect of friend and foe alike.

Depression in Harlan County

Breakfast in the station at Cincinnati. After that the train crosses the Ohio River and starts winding through the shallow valleys of the rolling section of central Kentucky. Change at Corbin onto a local for Pineville. The Louisville papers say Governor Sampson is sending a detachment of militia into Harlan County. As we get near Pineville the valleys deepen. Steep hills burnished with autumn cut out the sky on either side. There's the feeling of a train entering the war zone in the old days.

At the station is a group of miners and their wives come to welcome the writers' committee: they stand around a little shyly, dressed in clean ragged clothes. A little coaldust left in men's eyebrows and lashes adds to the pallor of scrubbed faces, makes you think at once what a miserable job it must be keeping clean if you work in coal.

At the Hotel Continental Dreiser is met by newspaper men, by the mayor and town clerk of Pineville, who offer their services "without taking sides." Everybody is very polite. A reporter says that Judge D. C. Jones is in the building. A tall man in his thirties, built like a halfback, strides into the lobby. There's something stiff and set about the eyes and the upper part of his face; the look of strain and bullying of a man who feels he's under criticism. When he comes up to us he draws himself up to his full six feet five or six.

"Well, they grow 'em big down here anyway," says Dreiser.

"Yes, sir, we grow tall down here in these mountains." They go on talking guardedly.

Somehow the judge comes around to the Harlan County jail, says it's a fine new jail, resents how it's been spoken of, says the food was so good Mrs. Wakefield gained three pounds in the month she spent there. He says the trouble is all over now, never was anything except a few outside agitators trying to make money out of the poor shiftless miners. Judge Jones says he's willing to answer any questions put to him about the situation in Harlan County. Mr. Dreiser and Judge Jones are photographed together on the steps of the hotel. Mrs. Grace of Wallins Creek, the wife of Jim Grace, a union organizer who was beaten up and run out of the county, comes up and asks Judge Jones why the sheriff's deputies raided her house and ransacked her things and her boarders' rooms. The interview comes abruptly to an end.

In the tradition of a congressional investigative committee, we settled down to take testimony. All the usual stories of violence legal and illegal against labor agitators, pushed a little further than usual in this case by the violent traditions of the Kentuckians. The miners' soup kitchens had been blown up. There had been gunbattles, mountain style between strikers and company men. As I remember we really tried to hear both sides. The party members who were trying to direct the course of the proceedings showed a scornful tolerance for our "liberalism."

Next day the committee and attendant newspapermen, accompanied by three officers of the state militia sent as "observers" by Governor Sampson, drive up the fine valley of the Cumberland River to Harlan. It is a smoky fall day, the woods flare with reds and yellows, hunting weather, mountain climbing weather; you feel what great country this must have seemed to the pioneers who first came over the gaps from Virginia. About halfway up we pass the swimming pool where the soup kitchen was shot up, where Jeff Baldwin's brother had been killed.

Harlan is a lively little town; stores and bank buildings attest to the slightly flimsy prosperity of the boom period; the handsome courthouse takes away a little from the gimcrack air of a Southern industrial town. That Friday was a big day. There was going to be a football game between the Pineville and Harlan high schools. In the afternoon a parade with a band and boy scouts, automobiles decorated with green and white streamers and pretty high-school girls, went through the streets taking the home team to the ball field.

Perhaps it was on account of the football game and perhaps on account of the newspapermen and militia officers, but the "gun thugs" we have been told about were nowhere to be seen. There was no particular feeling of terror in the air. Everybody seemed in good spirits, out for a day off, sniffing with pleasure the winy fall day.

In all the bustle only the group of white-faced miners and their wives, waiting in their shabby clean clothes to tell their stories in the lobby of the hotel, were still. They didn't seem to appreciate the football game or the fine afternoon. The townspeople wouldn't look at them as they ran in and out of the lobby. Finally, at the request of the management the whole business was moved upstairs to a large room in the front of the house. In a small bedroom next door a group of young men who looked strangely like company guards, kept watch on what went on.

Somebody said they had a dictaphone in there, though I can't imagine what they could have done with it, as the door was open all through the hearings and everybody who wanted to was invited to come in and ask questions.

In the afternoon, the coach of the Harlan High football team very politely invited the committee to go to the game, which was the big athletic event of the season for Harlan and Bell counties. (We refused a little toploftily; we were there on serious business.) Lester Cohen, Charlie Walker and I went around to the courthouse to try to get Judge Jones or Sheriff Blair to attend the hearing. Judge Jones was not to be found, Sheriff Blair was down in the basement counting ballots from the election, Mr. Ward of the Harlan County Coal Operators Association greeted us smoothly and said he would come over after the game; his boy was playing in the game and he felt he had to see it. As it turned out neither he nor Judge Jones were willing to talk to the committee. The statement of the point of view of the owners and the authorities came from Sheriff Blair, late that afternoon, and from the county prosecutor the next day.

Walking around the town we were spoken to on the street by a Dr. Nolan, who was chairman of the local American Legion post. He had been much impressed by Dreiser's remarks about a government of equity in his argument with the editor of the Pineville paper—(I think it was in the hotel lobby; Dreiser was magnificent)—and said he felt that the hearing should be carried on in the town hall. He helped us dig up the town clerk, but it turned out that the mayor had already gone to the game and had carried off the key in his pocket.

In the late afternoon the committee trooped over to the courthouse to talk to Sheriff Blair. He stood up against the wall for a long time answering questions and finally took the offensive himself by serving Bruce Crawford with a $50,000 slander suit. The next morning we drove up to Harlan again to talk to the county prosecutor. Harlan town didn't look so pleasant as the day before somehow. There were a good many toughlooking young men standing around with guns under their jackets. We got the impression that people's attitude had changed overnight. There was a war feeling in the air.

The attitude of the "better" people may be inferred from a talk I had with the county supervisor and two other members of the Kiwanis Club in the hotel lobby. They solemnly assured me that there was no strike and that there was no real misery among women and children in the county, that all the trouble had been caused by a few malcontents who were too lazy to work anyway. I suppose they believed what they were saying. When we urged them to sit in on the hearings for a while, they became uneasy and sheered off.

The Mr. Jones who kept breaking into the conversation in Mr. Brock's office, was an attorney who shared the office with him. A brother of his, an employee of the Black Mountain Coal Company, was killed in the Evarts battle, and he himself had taken part in raids on the houses of miners suspected of being connected with the N.M.U. He had a group of friends in the hall during the conversation, and for a minute it looked as if there might be trouble. He kept us from forgetting that this was a war.

The Free Speech Speakin's

Straight Creek is the section of Bell County that has been organized fairly solid under the National Miners Union. Owing, the miners say, to the fair-minded attitude of the sheriff, who has not allowed the mine guards to molest them, there has been no bloodshed, and a three weeks' strike ended the week before we were there with several small independent operators signing agreements with the union at thirty-eight cents a ton and allowing a union check weighman. (The boy who was check weighman told me that in the mine where he worked one cwt. weighed eighty pounds when he took over the scales.) They say that thirty-eight cents is not a living wage but that it's something to begin on. The committee had been invited to attend a meeting of the N.M.U. at the Glendon Baptist Church and walked around the miners' houses first.

Straight Creek is a narrow zigzag valley that runs up into the mountains from Pineville. The mines are small and often change hands. The houses are low shacks set up on stilts, scattered in disorderly rows up and down the valley floor. They are built of thin sheathing and mostly roofed with tarpaper. A good many have been papered with newspaper on the inside by their occupants in an effort to keep the wind out. The floors are full of cracks. I have seen similar houses in Florida shantytowns, but here in the mountains the winter is long and cold. It's hard to imagine how the miners and their wives and children can get any semblance of warmth out of the small coalburning grates. They have to pay for their coal too, though some of the operators allow the women and children to pick up what they can around the tipple. It wrings your heart the way the scantily furnished rooms have been tidied up for the visitors.

The visitors form a motley straggle through the little dooryards (there have been cows and pigs kept in some and you have to be careful where you step); a certain Mr. Grady, who I believe is the same gentleman who made such a fuss last year about losing his job as technician in Soviet Russia, had turned up and is putting everything down in a little notebook. When somebody asked him who he represented, he replied: "I have nothing to do with you people, I represent American citizenship." It would be interesting to know who is paying Mr.

Grady's carfare now that he has been fired by the Soviet government.

The A.P. man and the gentleman from the *Courier-Journal* have a harrowed look on their faces; they keep looking around behind things as if they felt the houses had been put up to hoax them. They refuse to believe that people can be so badly off as that. They crowd into the door of one shack to hear what Aunt Molly Jackson, the local midwife, has to say, but you can see them getting ready not to believe what she says, what their own eyes see.

While Dreiser asks his questions, one of the militia officers is standing on the back stoop looking out into the gathering dusk and remarking that as a military man he felt the absence of sanitation very keenly. Somebody explained that during the summer they'd had a cow for a while. The militia officer went on to wonder whether anything could be done to teach these people sanitation.

Afterward some of us drove up a heavily rutted road up one of the forks to a tumbledown shack where an old man lay dying. It was nearly dark. The little cabin was crushed under the steep black of the hill and the ramshackle structure of a mine tipple jutting up into the sky. The first step I took into the cabin the floor creaked so I put my hand against the wall to steady myself. The rotten boards gave. With several people crowding into it, the crazy cabin looked as if it would crumple up at any minute.

"Be keerful when you step in," a woman says and points out the weak boards in the floor. The kitchen has already caved in. The man was propped up in a chair in front of a flaring coal fire. His belly is so swollen from the infected wound he can't fasten his trousers. "A piece of coal fell on me when I was workin' under the tipple. You can see here it's all swelled up and stuff comes out like water. My sister paid the doctor. We don't pay him regular now but he hasn't quit comin'. He says he thinks I'll git well. I always paid my doctor bills before."

There is nothing in the tworoom house but a bed covered with rags where a little halfnaked girl sits shivering. The two women who are taking care of the wounded man are haggard. The man is very weak, his eyes glitter in the firelight. He is obviously going to die.

The hollow was completely black. To get to the Glendon Baptist Church, where the meeting was to be held, we had to cross a high-swinging bridge above the creek-bed. Young miners in their best clothes had been posted by the N.M.U. to guard the approaches to it. The low frame hall was packed with miners and their wives; all the faces were out of early American history. Stepping into the hall was going back a hundred years. These were the gaunt faces, the slow elaborations of talk and courtesy, of the frontiersmen who voted for Jefferson and Jackson, and whose turns of speech were formed on the oratory of Patrick Henry. I never felt the actuality of the American revolution so intensely as sitting in that church, listening to these mountaineers with their old time phrases, getting up on their feet and explaining why the time to fight for freedom had come again.

The chairman was a young preacher named Meek. He spoke of the crowd as a congregation and of the meeting as a service. The old slogans of religion seemed to serve him just as well for the new hopes of unionism. The comic relief was afforded by a fat woman who stood in the aisle with her arms akimbo during many of the speeches glaring at the speakers. She finally broke into something the chairman was saying to remind him he'd never paid her ten dollars he'd owed her for two years. She was the local agent of the Red Cross and the bookkeeper at the Carey mine.

Aunt Molly Jackson the mountain midwife sang her blues, and her younger brother, Jim Garland, made a funny speech about why the coal operators called the miners reds. He said folks might maybe call him a red because his people, father, grandfather and great grandfather had been so long in that country that if you went any further back you came to Cherokee Injun blood and that was red all right. Then he said maybe another reason you might call the miners red was that they'd gotten so thin and poor, from the small wages they got, that if you stood one of them up against the sun you'd see the red right through him.

The representative of the I.L.D. spoke right after asking for solidarity, and a young man from the *Daily Worker* reminded everybody that that night was the fourteenth anniversary of the Soviet Union and that this was probably the first time such an anniversary had been mentioned in the mountains of Kentucky.

One miner summed up the general feeling by saying, after he'd described how a march of a thousand men going out to strike under the U.M.W. of A. that spring had been broken up in spite of the fact that they came out with five American flags, "By God, if they won't let us march under the American flag, we'll march under the red flag."

The speaking at Wallins Creek next afternoon was in the gymnasium of the handsome high school on the hill above the town. The high school seemed to be the only visible sign left of the boom period of '20–21. It had been a surprise to us on arriving in the town to see a banner strung across the main street reading:

WELCOME, Writers' Committee, International Labor Defense, National Miners Union.

As the afternoon wore on a curious lonesomeness came over the hall. Miners and their wives, who had sat in their faded and threadbare Sunday clothes with a look of quiet and intentness on their pale lined faces, began to slip quietly out and start for home. An old miner had been speaking, striding up and down the platform and banging his fist on the table like a backwoods preacher. He'd stride up and down and then pause with his fist clenched over the table; then he'd stare into the crowd and let out a sentence. "Your laborleaders has led you into captivity; they git the money and you git the beans and bread," and bang would go his fist down on the table and he'd be off again. "I love my chillun a thousand times better than I love Herbert Hoover." Then bang would go his fist on the table. "The prettiest thing I'd like to see in Harlan County would be to see the laborin' man all stand together as one." Then bang would go his fist. "We don't aim to git rich, but we aim to make our livin' out of it; today the moneyed man in Harlan town is tryin' to press the workin' man down into an aggregation of poverty and sin . . . Dear companions there's things happened in this state and county you couldn't believe could happen in civilized Ameriky . . . We're on that lonesome road between starvation and heathenism." Then he sang an old time strike song about seventy cents a ton and sat down.

Aunt Molly Jackson sang her moaning blues again:

> This minin' town I live in
> is a sad an' lonely place,
> For pity and starvation
> is pictured on every face,
> Everybody hongry and ragged,

no slippers on their feet,
All goin' round from place to place
bummin' for a little food to eat.
Listen my friends and comrades
please take a friend's advice,
Don't put no more of your labor
till you get a livin' price.

Other women spoke about the flux and how the Red Cross wouldn't help the family if the man went on strike. That bright young man from the *Daily Worker* made a stirring speech about China and the international proletariat and the defense of the Soviet Union. Members of the Writers' Committee assured the strikers a little shakily that public opinion the whole country over was being aroused in favor of the striking miners of eastern Kentucky. A collection was taken up. But all the time this curious lonesomeness was coming over the hall.

There had been warnings that the gunthugs were coming from Black Mountain to break up the meeting, that Sheriff Blair and his deputies were coming over to arrest everybody present. People were listening to the speeches with one ear cocked for noises outside. Once somebody thought he heard a shot and a dozen men ran out to see what the trouble was. The clear fall afternoon light through the gymnasium windows was becoming stained with blue. Slowly and lonesomely the afternoon wore on. At last the speaking broke up.

On the hillside outside people were melting away into the violet dark. The lights were pumpkincolor in the little stores along the road in the creekbottom. The west flared hot with a huge afterglow of yellow and orange and crimson light against the sharp razoredge of the high dark hills that hemmed in the Cumberland River.

Walking down the hill we felt the scary lonesome feeling

of the front lines in a lull in the fighting. By the time we got back to the road the cars had all gone back to Pineville. We went up to a garage a little piece up the road. Dreiser was standing in the door of the garage looking out into the fading flare of the evening. Again that look of an old bull elephant at bay. The garageman said a taxi would be coming soon. We stood a long time in the door of the garage. I could feel the wonderful breathless hush I'd felt years ago on post in the Avocourt wood. This was war all right.

On the way to the meeting at Straight Creek I had walked down the road with a young miner of about twenty. The way the eyes looked out of his white lean mountaineer's face made me think of the desert Arabs I'd been with in Syria years before. The coaldust sticks in the lashes and eyebrows when a softcoal miner washes; it gives the same intent look to the eyes as the kohl the Bedawi decorate their faces with. These people too have the same direct affectionate manners. Their pure unmodernized English lilts in the air like Elizabethan lyrics. I'd asked this boy how he liked the Communist's speeches about the international workingclass, their struggles in Germany and China, miners' life in the Soviet Union. He said he liked them fine, there was a great deal of learning in them, every time he listened to them he learned something new. "Here in Bell County we lack learnin' and eddication. It's the greatest thing ever happened to the laborin' man in eastern Kentucky. Why if it warn't for the N.M.U. we'd be on our knees before the coal company beggin' for a glass of water right now."

Then he turned to me and said, "Are you in this business too?"

I said I was a writer, writers were people who stayed on the sidelines as long as they could. They were sympathizers.

85

He looked disappointed. "I thought maybe you was a lodgemember, in for a revolution too . . . because I'm in it . . . up to the neck."

Provincetown, January, 1932

Our little expedition wasn't without comic relief. With characteristic bravado Dreiser had brought along with him a handsome and welldressed young woman who certainly was not his wife. She had caught the eye of some of the sheriff's deputies in Pineville and they had amused themselves stacking toothpicks against the great man's door after the young woman had entered it rather late one night. The toothpicks were still there in the morning. The sheriff arrested Dreiser at breakfast for infringing some local morals ordinance.

Dreiser, playing so well the part of the pachyderm, seemed completely undisturbed. In court, so I was told later, he confounded everybody by announcing that nothing immoral could have taken place since he was an old man and impotent. I don't know whether he was telling the truth or lying. I don't even remember how the case came out. All I remember is the strange look he had of an old bull elephant at bay.

Some time after we had all left Harlan County a local grand jury indicted several of us under the Kentucky criminal syndicalism law. When I got back to New York the chairman of the Central Committee sent for me and asked me to go back and stand trial. I refused. They would have to come and fetch me. Of course they never did. Already I had the feeling that there was something a little too offhand about the way these human engineers were handling the Kentucky miners. There was something about the boss communist's sneering tone that made it a little too obvious that he enjoyed making monkeys of the warmhearted liberals.

The miners were even more pawns than we were. A whole series of small incidents in Kentucky had made me feel that the communists were treating the misery and revolt of the Harlan County miners with the same professional's sneer— their scornful attitude toward perfectly sincere I.W.W. and A.F. of L. men; the way they handled the cases of the miners in jail, denying help to men who wouldn't play their game.

I went to work to edit the testimony Dreiser's committee had collected. I still felt that the communists—by the violence of their protest and by their tireless dedication— were filling a useful function in ramming the plight of the wageworker into the public eye, but I was a little more wary in my dealings with them after that.

"Equity" was the word Dreiser used continually. He wanted equity. Like so many of his words it was a hard one to corner. I had trouble getting a sharp meaning out of it. It led him, strangely, into a communist camp in later years. I already had a suspicion that this equity meant taking away everything the rich had. We were an illeducated lot but I had already acquired enough political sophistication to know that wouldn't make the poor any richer. We had to learn our way as we went. American writers were babes in the woods in those days.

"Equity" called to my mind the statue of Justice you see in old courthouses with bandaged eyes and a pair of scales. Equity meant keeping those scales even. Things were already beginning to happen that proved to me, at least, that there were forces in the American republic, willing and able to even up those scales in so far as they applied to the working-man. He still had his vote. He learned to use it. It evidently didn't seem so to Dreiser or he wouldn't have let himself be used by those who were out, not to even up the scales, but to smash them.

Meanwhile my chief preoccupation was to try to find out what people were saying, what people were thinking.

Detroit, City of Leisure

The sun is hot on the fresh green of Grand Circus Park, but the wind that combs through the leaves of the trees and shrubs has a smack of the north woods in it. All round, the windows of the skyscrapers of the boom town stare out with dusty vacancy at the summer afternoon. Unemployed men lie out on the grass in a hundred helpless attitudes of sleep. Nearly all of them spread out newspapers before they lie down; got to keep that suit decent as long as possible. On the benches men sit talking unhurriedly, all the time in the world. Around the livelier benches groups stand, listening in; occasionally someone from the back pops off with a remark. Toward the eastern end it's more shady and the crowd is thicker; there are *Daily Workers* and *Labor Defenders* for sale; in an easy wellpitched voice (the traffic isn't so thick in the street behind him that he has to yell) a young man with a touch of an Italian accent is making a speech:

"If a lot of fellers go to walk through the woods, through real heavy woods, they'll all walk in single file, won't they? Well, suppose they walk an' walk an' the trail gets worse an' worse, all rocks an' brambles an' then deep swamps an' then no trail at all maybe; by an' by one feller yell out to the guys in front, 'Where the hell you boys leadin' us?' An' then they all begin to worry an' think maybe they've lost the road. Well, the American workin' class is just like that. Everybody say, 'Step along, Johnny, keep in line, pretty soon we have prosperity.' But the trail gets worse and worse. Pretty soon we got to ask, 'Where the hell are they leadin' us to anyway?' You bosses lead us into the swamp; our turn to lead the way now."

88

In a blind pig a newspaperman is talking. It's cool and dark in here at the small tables. The radio roars so loud it blows the foam off our beer. We get the radio turned off so we can hear the newspaperman telling what isn't in the papers. "Here's a story that keeps coming in that we don't dare touch. A bunch of men, sometimes forty of fifty of them, go into a chain grocery store, usually the store where they're accustomed to deal, and ask for credit. The clerk tells 'em the business is on a cash basis. Then they tell him to stand back, they don't want to hurt him, but they've got to have some groceries. They take what they need and go off quietly. In the case I'm thinking of, the clerk didn't phone the police, he phoned the general manager. The general manager told him he did right, the less anybody heard about stuff like that the better."

"You mean if others heard about it, they'd get the same idea?" The newspaperman nodded.

We drive out through miles of partly built-up subdivisions. Ten miles out we are still within the skeleton of streets and avenues. In a roomy suburban house exactly like the houses that have grown up rank on rank through the boom developments of every other American city, there's gathered a group of people with the standard clothes and faces of the whitecollar class. We sit around sipping California wine and gradually, unhurriedly, talking. What are we talking about in this early summer evening? About a moonlight steamboat ride being gotten up to raise money for unemployed relief, about Soviet Russia and about the style of revolution we shall have in America. Somebody brought up the Red Terror. "Well if you're using force, you're using force," said a sweetvoiced woman in a pale blue dress. "And when they're changing the social system, I guess they'll have to use force. Ford's service men are using force all right."

89

Some old radicals have organized a communal boarding-house in an old brick dwelling near the river that used to be Detroit's House of Mirrors. Upstairs the rooms are fitted up with cots, on the ground floor there's a social room where you can read or play pinochle or checkers, in the basement there's a thoroughly organized kitchen and lunchroom where you can get meals for five or ten cents, according to the state of your brokeness. I ate a darn good meal there. The kitchen was clean and the food fresh. The secret of their success is that they never buy any provisions. They keep track of stores and markets that can't sell their surplus and bum it. If a dealer gets in an extra large shipment of onions, say, they keep an eye on it, and if they don't seem to be selling, manage to bum a case or two off him that otherwise would spoil and have to be thrown out. These men understand that in a depression caused by overproduction of goods, no one need starve if he'll organize with his fellows and forget about money. One said he was living better now than he did when he worked.

There was nobody in the entry of the huge new office building, nobody in the elevator going upstairs. The lawyer sat and talked to us from behind his wide glasstopped desk, now and then glancing out the window at the sunny back lots, the street where crowds moved slowly, the ranks of automobile-tops like dominoes face down. "I don't know what it is," he was saying, "but something is happening. I used to be a union worker and a radical and all that when I was a kid, but it's something different now. None of the political parties catch it, nobody believes in the old parties and the socialists and communists don't fit in somehow. In the men out of work, in the crowd everywhere, I can feel something I can't explain, something that's going to burst out. It makes you want to give up everything you've been working and hustling and sweating for, this kind of life at a desk, and go back where you came from, where you belong, with the men on the street. It sounds goofy and I can't explain it. It has something to do with these men on the street, laying around in parks, what are they going to do when they get so they won't stand for it any longer? . . . The only trouble is I've got four families to support."

"Well, you can always look on, you can observe the show."

"I can't. I've been a man of action all my life. I'd be in this now if I only knew what was happening."

Back in Grand Circus Park men lie out asleep in the morning sun or else sit talking drowsily on the benches. A man's auctioning off *Daily Workers*, groups are arguing. In one group a middleaged roundfaced Negro with bright eyes is trying to convince a lanternfaced yellow boy with gold teeth. "Lemme reason with ye, lemme reason with ye," he keeps saying. They are arguing as to whether the workers could run the banks. The yellow boy keeps saying no, they don't know enough. He keeps trying to get away. The older man has hold of the lapel of his coat. "Look here, boy, lemme reason with ye, lemme reason with ye."

At last in desperation he kneels down on the pavement and draws two sides of a triangle with his finger in the dust. "Look here, boy, this here's one foot and this here's one foot, ain't it?"

"Mebbe," grumbles the yellow boy.

"Well, we'll just 'low that it is. Well, you don't know how long that third side is?" "No, nor you neither." "Well, that don't mean that nobody don't know. See what I mean? That don't mean that nobody don't know."

Detroit, July, 1932

Snapshots of Washington

Washington has a drowsy look in the early December sunlight. The Greco-Roman porticoes loom among the bare trees, as vaguely portentous as phrases about democracy in the mouth of a southern senator. The monument, a finger of light cut against a lavender sky, punctuates the ancient rhetoric of the Treasury and the White House. On the Hill, above its tall foundation baked with magnolia trees, the dome of the Capitol bulges smugly. At nine o'clock groups of sleepylooking cops in well brushed uniforms and shiny visored caps are straggling up the winding drives. At the corner of Pennsylvania Avenue and John Marshall Place a few hunger marchers stand round the trucks they came in. They look tired and frowzy from the long ride. Some of them are strolling up and down the avenue. The end of the avenue with its gimcrack stores, boardedup burlesque shows, Chinese restaurants and flophouses, still has a little of the jerkwater, outinthesticks look it must have had when Lincoln drove up it in a barouche through the deep mud or Jefferson rode to his inauguration on his own quiet nag.

Two elderly laboring men are looking out of a cigarstore door at a bunch of reds, young Jewish boys from New York or Chicago, with the white armbands of the hunger marchers. "Won't get nutten thataway," one of them says. "Who's payin' for it anyway, hirin' them trucks and gasoline? . . . Somebody's payin' for it," barks the clerk indignantly from behind the cash register. "Better'd spend it on grub or to buy 'emselves overcoats," says the older man. The man who spoke first shakes his head sadly. "Never won't get nutten thataway."

The Doughboy Thirteen Years Later

"Home, boys, it's home we want to be," we sang in all the demobilization camps. This was God's country. And we ran for the train with the flags waving and a new army outfit on and our discharge papers and the crisp bills of our last pay in our pockets. The world was safe for democracy and America was the land of opportunity.

They signed you up in the American Legion and jollied you into voting for Harding and the G.O.P. Beaucoup parades, beaucoup speeches, run the slackers and the pacifists and the knockers out of the country, lynch them wobblies, tell the reds to go back where they came from. The G.O.P. took care of the Civil War vets and the Spanish War vets, didn't it? Well, it'll take care of youse boys.

You went to work if you got a job; some kinds of jobs you made big money on, on others the bosses gypped you, but anyway you could eat, you could save up a little, get married, start payments on a home; boom times ahead.

When things slackened and you began to look a little Democratic around the gills, they handed you the bonus. The G.O.P. and the nation are behind youse boys. Well, we got some of it and we spent it and we didn't reckon on cyclic depression No. 8b. And now look at us.

A bunch of outofwork ex-service men in Portland, Oregon, figured they needed their bonus right now; 1945 would be too late, only buy wreaths for their tombstones. They figured out, too, that the bonus paid now would liven up business, particularly the retail business in small towns; might be just enough to tide them over until things picked up. Anyway, everybody else was getting a bonus; the moratorium was a bonus to European nations, the R.F.C. was handing out bonuses to railroads and banks, how about the men who'd made the world safe for democracy getting their bonus, too? God knows we're the guys who need it the worst. Every other interest has got lobbyists in Washington. It's up to us to go to Washington and be our own lobbyists. Park benches can't be any harder in Washington than they are back home.

So three hundred of them started east in old cars and trucks, hitchhiking, riding on frieght trains. (Maybe the words "direct action" still hovered on the air of the Pacific slope, left over from the days of the wobblies.) By the time they reached Council Bluffs they found that other groups all over the country were rebelling against their veterans' organizations and getting the same idea. It was an army. They organized it as such and nick-named it the Bonus Expeditionary Force.

Now they are camped on Anacostia Flats in the southeast corner of Washington. Nearly twenty thousand of them altogether. Everywhere you meet new ragged troops straggling in. A few have gone home discouraged, but very few. Anacostia Flats is the recruiting center; from there they are sent to new camps scattered around the outskirts of Washington. Anacostia Flats is the ghost of an army camp from the days of the big parade, with its bugle calls, its messlines, greasy K.P.'s, M.P.'s, headquarters, liaison officers, medical officer. Instead of the tents and the long tarpaper barracks of those days, the men are sleeping in little leantos built out of old newspapers, cardboard boxes, packing crates, bits of tin or tarpaper roofing, old shutters, every kind of cockeyed makeshift shelter from the rain scraped together out of the city dump.

The doughboys have changed, too in thse fifteen years. There's the same goulash of faces and dialects, foreigners' pidgin English, lingoes from the industrial towns and farming towns,

East, Northeast, Middle West, Southwest, South; but we were all youngsters then; now we are getting on into middle life, sunken eyes, hollow cheeks off breadlines, palelooking knotted hands of men who've worked hard with them, and then for a long time have not worked. In these men's faces, as in Pharaoh's dream, the lean years have eaten up the fat years already.

General Glassford has played the perfect host; his entertainment committee of motorcycle cops has furnished iodine and CC pills, helped lay out the camps, given advice on digging latrines (the men call them Hoover Villas), and recently set out some tents and bedding. One of the strangest sights Pennsylvania Avenue has ever seen was a long line of ex-servicemen, hunched under their bedticking full of straw, filing up a long iron stairway in the middle of a partly demolished fourstory garage that the police department had turned over to them. The cops and the ex-servicemen play baseball together in the afternoon; they are buddies together.

In the middle of the Anacostia camp is a big platform with a wooden object sticking up from one corner that looks like an oldfashioned gallows. Speaking goes on from this platform all morning and all afternoon. The day I saw it, there were a couple of members of the bonus army's congressional committee on the platform, a Negro in an overseas cap and a tall red Indian in buckskin and beads, wearing a tengallon hat. The audience, white men and Negroes, is packed in among the tents and shelters. A tall scrawny man with deeply sunken cheeks is talking. He's trying to talk about the bonus but he can't stick to it; before he knows it he's talking about the general economic condition of the country:

"Here's a plant that can turn out everything every man, woman and child in this country needs, from potatoes to washing machines, and it's broken down because it can't give the

95

fellow who does the work enough money to buy what he needs with. Give us the money and we'll buy their bread and their corn and beans and their electric iceboxes and their washing machines and their radios. We ain't holdin' out on 'em because we don't want those things. Can't get a job to make enough money to buy 'em, that's all."

Washington, D.C., June, 1932

Out of the Red with Roosevelt

They came out of the stadium with a stale taste in their mouths. Down West Madison Street, walking between lanes of cops and a scattering of bums, the crowds from the galleries found the proud suave voice of the National Broadcasting Company still filling their jaded ears from every loudspeaker, enumerating the technical agencies that had worked together to obtain the superb hookup through which they broadcast the proceedings of the Democratic Convention of 1932.

Well, they did their part: the two big white disks above the speaker's platform (the ears of the radio audience) delicately caught every intonation of the oratory, the draggedout "gre-eats" when the "great Senator from the great state of . . ." was introduced, the deep "stalwart" always prefixed to "Democrat" when a candidate was being nominated, the indignant rumble in the voice when the present administration was "branded" as having induced "an orgy of crime and saturnalia of corruption."

The page with the portable microphone in his buttonhole had invariably been on hand when a delegate was recognized from the floor. The managers for the N.B.C. had never closed an eye, stagemanaging, moving quietly and deftly around the platform, with the expression and gestures of oldfashioned photographers, coaxing the speakers into poses from which they could

96

be heard.

Telegrams had been read giving the minutetominute position of the nominee's plane speeding west. The radio voice of Wally Butterworth had whooped things up by describing the adverse flying conditions, the plane's arrival at the airport, the cheering throngs, the jolly ride from Buffalo, the governor's nice smile; but when Franklin D. Roosevelt (in person) walked to the front of the rostrum on his son's arm while the organ played *The Star-Spangled Banner* and an irrepressible young lady from Texas waved a bouquet of red, white and blue flowers over his head, to greet with a plain sensible and unassuming speech the crowd that had yelled itself hoarse for Al Smith three days before, that had gone delirious over the Wet Plank and applauded every phrase in the party platform, and sat with eager patience through the weeklong vaudeville show—nothing happened.

Courteous applause, but no feeling.

The crowd in the huge hall sat blank, blinking in the glare of the lights. Neither delegates nor the public seemed to be able to keep their minds on what the candidate, whom they had nominated after such long sessions and such frantic trading and bickering downtown in their hotel rooms, had to say. As he talked the faces in the galleries and boxes melted away, leaving red blocks of seats, even the delegates on the floor slunk out in twos and threes. After all, what is a man, a tiny bundle of nerves and muscles only six feet tall, compared to the giant muddling awesome blurs, a hundred times amplified on the radio and screen?

You came out of the stadium and walked down the street. It's West Madison Street, the home address of migratory workers and hobos and jobless men all over the middle west. Gradually the din of speeches fades out of your ears, you forget the cracks and gossip of the press gallery. Nobody on the street knows about the convention that's deciding who shall run their government, nor cares. The convention is the sirens of police motorcycles, a new set of scare headlines, a new sensation over the radio. There are sixday bicycle races and battles of the century and eucharistic congresses and bigleague games and political conventions; and a man has got a job, or else he hasn't got a job, he's got jack in his pocket, or else he's broke, he's got a business, or else he's a bum. Way off some place headline events happen. Even if they're right on West Madison Street, they're way off. Roosevelt or Hoover? It'll be the same cops.

You walk on down, across the great train yards and the river to the Loop, out onto Michigan Avenue where Chicago is raising every year a more imposing front of skyscrapers, into the clean wind off the lake. Shiny storefronts, doormen, smartly dressed girls, taxis, buses taking shoppers, clerks, business men home to the South Side and North Side. In Grant Park more jobless men lying under the bushes, beyond them sails in the harbor, a white steamboat putting out into the lake. Overhead pursuit planes fly in formation advertising the military show at Soldiers' Field.

To get their ominous buzz out of your ears, you go down a flight of steps, into the darkness feebly lit by ranks of dusty red electric lights of the roadway under Michigan Avenue. The fine smart marble and plateglass front of the city peels off as you walk down the steps. Down here the air, drenched with the exhaust from the grinding motors of trucks, is full of dust and grit and the roar of the heavy traffic that hauls the city's freight. When your eyes get used to the darkness, you discover that, like the world upstairs of storefronts and hotel lobbies and battles of the century and political conventions, this world too has its leisure class.

They lie in rows along the ledges above the roadway, huddled in grimed newspapers, gray sagfaced men in wornout clothes, discards, men who have nothing left but their stiff hungry grimy bodies, men who have lost the power to want.

Try to tell one of them that the gre-eat Franklin D. Roosevelt, governor of the gre-eat state of New York, has been nominated by the gre-eat Democratic party as its candidate for President, and you'll get what the galleries at the convention gave Mr. McAdoo when they discovered that he had the votes of Texas and California in his pocket and was about to shovel them into the Roosevelt band wagon, a prolonged and enthusiastic Boo.

Hoover or Roosevelt, it'll be the same cops.

Chicago, July, 1932

Herbert Hoover's Last Stand

So many people want to see Mr. Hoover that even Ninth Avenue is jammed, so crowded, indeed, that the cops can't get at the Communist demonstrators come to jeer, and their boos are lost in the shuffle of the enormous crowd. Ducking through the ranks of brave boys in blue who seem bent on not letting anybody, with or without a ticket, get into the hall, you can catch a glimpse of the placards of the unemployed council, peaceably massed under the El. After working through five lines of cops I find myself in a rush of people up a stairway and am catapulted into an aisle that comes to an abrupt end in a bunch of men and women mashed against a rail. Beyond their heads is the hall, a pink mist of faces and American flags and spotlights.

They are singing something about Hoover to the tune of *John Brown's Body*. The flags wave, the pink faces roar: ovation.

A small, dumplingshaped manikin has appeared on the manikin-packed platform in the middle of the hall. Through the glasses I can see as distinctly as in the newsreels, among the jowly faces of Republican magnates, the familiar jowls of Herbert Hoover. He's waving a hand in a short gesture, squinting from side to side into the glare.

At the other end of the hall a heckler is being ejected. That boo never had a chance. Everybody is quieting down. The Hoover manikin has been set out by itself in a pool of white light. From where we jam against the rail we look intently into its left ear. A dry phonograph voice comes from the loudspeakers that hang from the shadowy ceiling in the center of the hall. Through the glasses I can see the mouth barely moving. The expressionless face when he turns our way is like the face of a ventriloquist. We are listening to Herbert Hoover's great speech in Madison Square Garden in the last week of the losing campaign of 1932, the speech about the grass growing in the streets of a hundred cities.

Motorcycle cops charge by, opening a lane in the crowd. A black limousine follows. To me it looks empty, but the skinny man on the curb beside me says he saw Hoover sitting in it. "Sure he was in it, all hunched up wid a black robe thrown over him. Oder cars all went out de oder way." I'm carried across the street by the push of the crowd. Faintly from far away comes the sound of a boo that is echoed by the bubbling noise an old drunken Irishman is making in his throat as he lurches out of the way of a policeman's horse.

New York, October, 1932

As a reminder of the blindness of partisan prejudice its worth remembering that many of the measures we were soon to be applauding Roosevelt for actually originated during Hoover's administration. We were too busy booing the capitalist bogyman to look into the facts very carefully.

As the literal-minded young men of the F.B.I. have occasionally reminded me, I let my name be used in a list of literary people who said they were going to vote for Foster and Ford in that election. I actually did vote for them. I remember thinking how surprised some of my casual friends in Provincetown would have been if they had known it. It certainly wasn't that I wanted the communists to conduct the revolution in American government which I felt was needed. It was because I knew they had no chance of winning. It was the old theory of the protest vote. It's a perfectly good way of using the American political machinery. I seem to remember having voted for Debs after he was dead on the same principle. It was certainly on the same principle that I came to vote in later years for Mr. Dewey of New York.

If I'd known enough about the peculiar processes by which American exceptionalism weaves its own peculiar politics I might have guessed that the revolution I was wanting, some of it at least, was going to be carried through under the leadership of a sweet talking crippled man whose origins lay in Groton and Harvard and in the Hudson River aristocracy, instead of in Engels and Marx. Still in 1932, to a casual onlooker like myself Franklin D. Roosevelt seemed the unlikeliest man in the world to assume such a function.

The Radio Voice

Outside the tight frame house there's a northeast gale blowing. The slanting rain drums on the roof and sloshes down the windowpanes. The house is a tiny neat wooden box full of dryness, warmth and light, in the enormous driving drift of the night. It's full, too, of a lonely tangle of needs, worries, desires; how are we going to eat, get clothes to wear, get into bed with someone we love, raise our children, belong to something, have something belong to us? After supper people sit around in the parlor listening drowsily to disconnected voices, stale scraps of last year's jazz, unfinished litanies advertising unnamed products that dribble senselessly from the radio. A brash deferential organizing voice from N.B.C. breaks in. People wake up. People edge their chairs up to the radio . . . "In the Blue Room at the White House."

Then there is a man leaning across his desk, speaking clearly and cordially to you and me, painstakingly explaining how he's sitting at his desk there in Washington, leaning toward you and me across his desk, speaking clearly and cordially so that you and me shall completely understand that he sits at his desk there in Washington with his fingers on all the switchboards of the federal government, operating the intricate machinery of the departments, drafting codes and regulations and bills for the benefit of you and me worried about things, sitting close to the radio in small houses on rainy nights, for the benefit of us wageearners, us homeowners, us farmers, us mechanics, us miners, us mortgagees, us processors, us mortgageholders, us bankdepositors, us consumers, retail merchants, bankers, brokers, stockholders, bondholders, creditors, debtors, jobless and jobholders . . . *Not a sparrow falleth but* . . . He is leaning cordially toward you and me across his desk there in Washington telling in carefully chosen words how the machinations of chiselers are to be foiled for you and me, and how the myriad cylindered motor of recovery is being primed with billions for youandme, and youandme understand, we belong to billions,

billions belong to us, we are going to have good jobs, good pay, protected bankdeposits, a new dealing out of billions to youandme. We edge our chairs closer to the radio, we are flattered and pleased, we feel we are right there in the White House. When the cordial explaining voice stops we want to say "Thank you Frank," we want to ask about the grandchildren and that dog that had to be sent away for biting a foreign diplomat . . . "You have been listening to the President of the United States in the Blue Room."

Provincetown, November, 1933

It was somewhere during the years of the early New Deal that I rejoined the United States. I had seceded privately the night Sacco and Vanzetti were executed. It was not that I had joined the communists. The more I saw of the Party the more I felt that the kind of world they wanted had nothing in common with the kind of world I wanted. I wasn't joining anybody. I had seceded into my private conscience like Thoreau in Concord jail. A man needs to do that from time to time in his life.

That protest vote in 1932 was already a step back into the American way of doing things. It indicated a certain skepticism about the Marxist millennium. So far as I can remember I hadn't quite recovered from the plague on both your houses attitude toward the two conflicting systems. I remember an argument with a friend, who recently reminded me of it. When pushed to the wall I told him that the chances for individual freedom were about equal under capitalism and communism. This was before we thoroughly understood the monstrous excesses of Stalin's regime, and before the success of the moderate revolution that took place in the United States during Franklin Roosevelt's first administration.

IV

SPAIN: REHEARSAL FOR DEFEAT

It's almost thirty years since I first knew Spain. A few months after graduating from college at a most impressionable period of my life I lived a while in Madrid. The angry beauty of the countryside, the dignity of the people, the painting of Velásquez and Goya, the prose of Cervantes, the epic of the Cid and the salty verses of the Archpriest of Hita all hit me at once. Life still conducted according to the ritual of the seventeenth century gave to every day a quality of theater. As I learned the language I began to feel enormous sympathy for the people of this nation so various and so much themselves, so unaffected by the standardization of the life of our day.

In Spain it was a time of intellectual effervescence. All the currents of nineteenth-century liberalism seemed to converge in the brittle air of the Castilian plateau. The country was properous, though to an American the contrast between brutal wealth and brutal poverty was shocking indeed. There was saving grace in everything being so open and aboveboard. In the midst of the decay of the old pageantry a future was being prepared. Here all the liturgical phrases of the nine-teenth-century religion of progress, which had seemed hollow and platitudinous to a young man growing up in America in destestation of the Sunday supplements, rang true. The sort of Spaniards who were at home with reading and writing, journalists, lawyers, doctors, architects, felt an immense desire to further the good of mankind the way the men who launched our own American republic had furthered the good of mankind. Progress was their faith. The old monarchy was played out. A second republic was the coming attraction. The ancient dramas of starvation and riches were to be taken off the boards. These feudal aristocrats who had forgotten the duties of feudal lords, these peacock officers who strutted in such empty boredom through the lobbies of military clubs, these ecclesiastics who had forgotten that humility was a Christian virtue, all these thrones and principalities and powers would soon be turning in their wornout roles taught them in dark ages past. They were about to be enlightened. They would come back on the stage with the greatest good for the greatest number their order of the day. Every Spaniard would be reoutfitted as a citizen of the modern world. The beggars would learn useful trades, the prostitutes would become thrifty housewives, the bullfighters would take to raising fat steers for the market. Translated into Spanish the American creed of reform and progress rang freshly on the ears. It would be the republic of wellintentioned men.

Among the people who worked with their hands, textile operatives in Catalonia, miners in Asturias, daylaborers in Valencia, the doctrine of progress had taken a more virulent form. The millennium they aspired to was more immediate. The socialists believed a revolution could be performed by some miracle of the ballotbox which would put the people who did the work in charge of the mechanism of the state. Immediately all men would work for the public good and receive according to their needs the benefits of socialized industry. The more numerous syndicalists and anarchists saw no need for the machinery of the state to perform this miracle. One apocalyptic overturn would shake loose the rich from their hold on the instruments of production. Thereafter men would treat each other as brothers according to the principles of mutual aid. In their dissensions over the various paths to progress lay the germ of the contradictions which were later to destroy the republic of wellintentioned men. The villages of Spain were living in the seventeenth century, the towns and cities were in the full heyday of the nineteenth. At a time when the humane civilization of Europe was already deeply undermined by the horrors and hatreds of the European war, the Spaniards who were not experiencing that war, were still tuned to the hopeful fervors of the international comity that war was destroying. To have lived for a few months in that genial air out of a lost era was a most salutary experience.

The Republic of Honest Men

When Don Alfonso finished sorting out and burning papers in his office on the side of the palace toward the city, he walked round to the other side of the immense pilastered graystone building, through the tall state rooms ornate with overweening pomp of scrolling designs in stucco and gilt and bronze and crystal and damask and velvet, through the throne room with its lions and its black busts of antique Romans crowded under the huge ceiling where, for the first of the Bourbons in the gaudy days of the Sun King, the Venetian Tiepolo had painted, in that daze of blue empyrean light that was his speciality, the grandiloquently draped abstractions of Government and Power. He hurried between tasseled portieres, through the inlaid eighteenth-century doors, into the room where the Englishwoman his wife was having tea.

It was a narrower room with an open fireplace, that instead of looking out on the strident masculine city, looked out on the boxhedges of the royal gardens and on that magnificent stretch of rolling tawny country tufted with blue evergreen oaks that rises to the foothills of the Guadarramas, which Velásquez invented as a background for the sallow faces and jutting wolfjaws of the members of the house of Austria.

Don Alfonso, too, had the face for that background. Tourists smuggled on gala days into palace functions in the tooearly bright light of the Madrid morning had often cried out how like a Velásquez he looked, passing against the sweeping voluted draftsmanship of the figures on the tapestry, a step ahead of the mass of uniforms, decorations, colored ribbons, stars, chokers, sunbursts, stomachers of the grandees of Spain and of the ladies of the court; there were the dead bored eyes, the sallow skin, the humble haughty set of the mouth of Philip IV without his easy assurance and his poise, all dulled by the halfwit leer the painter saw on the face of helpless Carlos the Bewitched, who so feebly ended the great line of the house of Austria.

Alfonso brusquely told his wife that he'd packed his trunk and was off for the border. He could trust the navy. He was going to drive south. There was a battleship waiting in Cartagena. She could wind up her affairs and follow him to France when she was ready. He left and he lost no time about it.

It may have been the crowd crying, "Death to the king. Live the republic" as they ran from from under the hoofs of the horses and the flailing sabers of the Civil Guards; it may have been the uneasy recollection of Ramon Franco's airplanes within an inch of unloading their bombs over the palace; or the strikes, or the parades of university students, or the changed attitude of his friends the armyofficers, or the frown on the face of General Sanjurjo who commanded the Civil Guard, or a fit of pique because everybody was telling him what to do; or it may have been just that the fruit was ripe to fall from the tree. The last of the Bourbons left Madrid as stealthily as a defaulting bank cashier. Next morning the queen, who had learnt her profession in the stern vocational school of Victoria, left with more dignity by train, accompanied by her children, forty trunks and four carloads of furniture and knickknacks.

The crown of Spain was found poked into a green baize bag, in a wardrobe in the palace.

Meanwhile, in the streets and cafés of Madrid, the citizens were celebrating the Republic. You could shout *Viva la Republica* right into the mustaches and the mausers of the Civil Guard without being arrested. Trucks paraded the main thoroughfares crowded with armyofficers and sailors and workingmen in blue denim singing the Marseillaise together. In the Puerta del Sol an artillery officer appeared on the balcony of the Gubernación (the ministry that traditionally has charge of breaking the heads of dissenting citizens) and hoisted a new tricolor, red yellow and purple, to the flagpole. Spain was a republic. The Bourbons had gone back to France where they came from.

The grandees trod on each other's heels crowding across the border at Irún and Port Bou, not a few generals and politicos who'd made themselves unpopular under the old regime suddenly found that they needed to take the cure in French and German wateringplaces. Wealthy businessmen stayed at home with shutters closed and doors barred until they found out how a liberated Spain was going to behave. Even the dyedinthewool republicans were uneasy when they stepped out of doors that morning and found themselves in the middle of the glorious republic of honest men they'd so long talked about.

But the republic was very wellbehaved indeed. Property and persons were respected. Everybody was for law and order in the shape of the now republican Civil Guard led by the now republican General Sanjurjo. The only outrages were the chipping off of the royal arms wherever they could be reached on public buildings and the upsetting of the magnificent bronze statue of Philip III in the Plaza Mayor. A couple of grandees were hissed and a few nuns were hustled but everything passed off with the greatest good humor: Viven los hombres honrados.

On back streets and in the workingclass quarters there may have been a little singing of the Internationale but in the Puerta del Sol it was the Marseillaise and the Hymn of Riego that greeted Alcalá Zamora, the whitehaired and silvertongued head of the new government, when he addressed the people from the balcony draped with the new red yellow purple bunting. The liberal and socialist junta of Hombres honrados that had been in exile and in jail was hastily dusted off and presented as a ministry.

The generals had lost their nerve and failed. It was the turn of the intellectuals to spring to the defense of order, progress and the rights of private property.

The leading republicans were doctors, lawyers, college professors, literary men; the republic was rooted in the Ateneo.

The Madrid Atheneum was one of those agreeable organizations that grew out of the enthusiasm for the arts and sciences that boiled up among the rising middleclasses in the early nineteenth century. Some time in the eighties it was established in its present dark and musty building. Downstairs there were quiet parlors with deep carpets and cavernous armchairs that might belong to any club anywhere, and a lecturehall. Upstairs there was an excellent library. It might have been in Boston or London, except that the members talked more, smoked more and were permitted to drink coffee at their desks in the library and were rather more varied in their dress and feature than they would have been in an Anglo-Saxon country. For many years, in talk and lectures and debates among the *ateneistas* the opposition of the professional classes to the church, the army and the monarchy that formed a triple lid over their heads, had stewed and steamed. With the first republic under Pi y Margall that lid blew off only to be promptly clamped down again. This time it looked as if it had blown off for good.

It was no accident that Manuel Azaña, the dominant political leader of the liberal republicans, was president of the *Ateneo* before he was president of the council of ministers.

When the first republican *Cortes*, as the Spanish parliament was called, that was to write the constitution for a liberal Spain, was elected it followed logically that many of its members should be *ateneistas*. They moved their debates, their habits of thought and their academic aloofness to the roomier and more gaily decorated congresshall around the corner.

At the *Cortes* the coffee was better, the seats were more freshly upholstered, the attendants were more elderly and courtly, and the speakers were refreshed by large glasses of a soothing and nonalcoholic drink made from burnt sugar and water. It was the best café in Madrid and Madrid was above all the city of cafés.

Jobholders who go to their offices at ten and leave at one and then look in again from five to seven, have a great deal of time for talk, and people who have no jobs at all have more yet. Hence the magnificent, and civilized in the Athenian sense, institution of Madrid cafés.

The cafés were as important a source of the Second Republic as the *Ateneo*. They were always open, they were always cheerful. A man can sit brooding over a single cup of coffee from the time he gets up till it is time to walk home in the grayness of the early morning, or else he can talk with a group of friends or with a casual stranger. These groups are like informal clubs, tertulias, they call them. He's not on the make, there's nothing to be gained; jobs come from family pull, money comes from a salary or a stipend, or from the lottery or roulette; to have no money is no disgrace. Talk is a pure art. Its only limits are the patience of the listeners who, when they get tired, can always pay for their coffee or charge it with a friendly waiter and walk out. The only place of entertainment that can compare with a Spanish café in cheapness and democracy is an American movie palace. But at a movie we pay for forgetfulness, darkness, soft seats and the stupor induced by a narcosis of secondhand daydreams. In his café the madrileño pays for his mild stimulant and has free entrance to the agora of concepts and ideas where he can make his way on his own. As the Stock Exchange is the central nervous system of New York, the cafés are the brains and spinal column of Madrid.

The Cortes that made up the republican constitution was ever so much like a tertulia at one of the best cafés. There lay the republic's strength, but also its weakness. The life of a professor, of the holder of a sinecure in a government office, or of an entertaining talker in a café, offers little training in dealing with the grim coarse hardtoclassify and often deadly realities that are the daily business of government. The genial group of wellintentioned gentlemen who talked so well and so wittily, who arrived so late and sat so late polishing the phraseology of the constitution, helped create a Spain that they certainly did not intend.

They legalized the disappearance of Don Alfonso and his family, they gave Spain liberal divorcelaws and disestablished the Church, they abolished titles of nobility and confiscated (giving bonds in return) some of the estates of the grandees, but they also passed a Law of Public Order and a Law against Vagrancy that would have made old Fernando VII, the Bourbon who got most pleasure out of shooting down his subjects, stand aghast. They sanctioned casual arrests of batches of citizens, mass deportations of workingmen and shootings of the rebellious in a way that must have made that genial old lowlife, the benevolent dictator, Primo de Rivera, turn in his grave. Don Alfonso, in his cozy retreat in Fontainebleau must have had more than one bitter thought about the trickiness of history's lotteries, when he read about these events in the papers. He'd been put on the skids for carrying out the death penalty against two mutinous armyofficers, and here were the honest men of the Republic, in the name of progress and socialism, shooting down their fellowcitizens by the hundreds.

The disappearance of the Bourbons, in a thin whiff of smoke, like an old puffball when you step on it, was only an incident in the nationwide collapse of timeworn stage properties. Whenever the deputies to the first *Cortes* of the Second Republic stepped out of their comfortable and gaudily decorated clubhouse, they found themselves faced by a Spain older and newer than they knew. Nothing in their training had taught them how to cope with the murderous passions and the cold calculations of the century they lived in.

The last time I was in Spain, it's already some eighteen years ago, the civil war was at a stalemate.

Francisco Franco had started the classical military revolt against civilian rule that is one of the bad political habits of countries governed in the Spanish tradition. He was a brother of the liberal aviator Ramon Franco who had done so much, when planes were still a sort of a novelty, to scare Don Al-

113

fonso out of Madrid. The Francos were lively up and coming young men from the despised province of Galicia. They wanted careers. Ramon Franco died early. Francisco Franco became an able military commander and absorbed the line of talk of the newborn Nazis in Germany and of Mussolini's Fascists. He was backed by the upper echelons of the clergy, by the officers' clubs who saw slim pickings ahead of them under a republican regime and by some elements of the landowning aristocracy which had important social and financial links with ruling groups in England. It was a British plane that brought Franco home from exile in the Canary Islands. When the revolt began the republican leaders found that outside of a few loyal army officers and the powerless middle classes of the cities, the only elements they could rely on for support were the organizations of labor. The labor unions gave out rifles and shotguns. The workingmen marched out to meet Franco's trained troops.

The fighting was carried on with great ferocity on both sides. The Loyalists had to learn how to fight. Franco's most reliable troops turned out to be his battalions of Moorish mercenaries, who had scores dating back a thousand years to settle with Christian Spain. Franco swept everything before him till he reached Madrid.

The capital was stubbornly defended. When I reached the city the magnificent new buildings of the university which typified more than anything else the nineteenth-century humane spirit behind the Spanish republic constituted a no man's land. The republic of wellintentioned men was in its death throes.

Spain torn in pieces by the struggle between believers in all the divergent paths to progress found itself doubly invaded by the bloody Twentieth Century in the form of fascist fanaticism and technology on the one hand and of the more organized, more all-pervading fanaticism and technology of the Communist Party, on the other. The liberals were dying under their crossfire. Fascists and communists alike shot the best men first.

For those who were willing to see with their own eyes and to hear with their own ears the Spanish civil war was another salutary experience. There for the first time appeared the shape of the world we would have to live in.

The story of how I went to Spain is so typical of the blundering of wellintentioned American liberals trying to make themselves useful in the world that is worth telling. Ever since the fascist revolt started I had been working with various friends trying to find ways to induce the Roosevelt administration to allow the republican government, which after all was the legally constituted government of Spain, to buy arms in America. The Britishbacked policy of nonintervention blocked every effort, and our campaign was made very difficult by the fact that we were continually embroiled with the communists, who wanted to take the campaign over for their own purposes. Whether it was Franklin Roosevelt's fear of losing the Catholic vote, or the basic failure to understand the rest of the world that has been the curse of almost every American administration since Wilson's, no amount of argument could convince him that the best way of curbing fascism in Europe was to throw his weight behind the legal government of Spain. In the end it was decided that a documentary movie of the Spanish civil war would be a way to get the attention of the American public. Money was raised, a brilliant young Dutch director was produced to shoot the picture. A well-known American writer, who also knew and loved the Spanish people, was induced to join me in writing the script.

A few nights before I sailed for France, Carlo Tresca, then editing a libertarian Italian weekly in New York, took me out to dinner. Carlo Tresca combined the shrewdest kind of knowledge of men and their motives with profound information on the realities of politics he'd acquired in a lifetime of partisan warfare in the anarchist cause. "John," he told me "they goin' make a monkey outa you . . . a beeg monkey."

How could they? We were to have complete charge of the shooting of the picture.

Carlo laughed in my face. "How can you? When your director is a Communist Party member, when everywhere you go you will be supervised by Party members. Everybody you see will be chosen by the Party. Everything you do will be for the interests of the Communist Party. If the communists don't like a man in Spain right away they shoot him."

It didn't turn out quite that way but almost. As soon as I reached Spain I discovered that the brilliant young director was sure enough taking his orders from the Party. Already before leaving New York I'd been surprised at the number of familiar zealot faces I'd seen in the offices of the various organizations raising money to send munitions and men to help the republican troops defend Madrid. The same set of faces I'd seen in partysponsored organizations when I'd tried to work with the communists in the Sacco-Vanzetti case or in trying to help the striking miners in Harlan County, Kentucky. Professionals of the labor movement. Men and women who gloried in taking orders from the Central Committee. Rule or ruin had been their motto from the beginning. They had failed to take the Sacco-Vanzetti case away from the anarchists and liberals in Boston. In Harlan County they left the miners in the lurch. In Spain they were going to be successful all down the line, so successful that the republic was destroyed and the fascists won.

From the first day I landed in France the trip was an education in the power politics of Europe. The bureaucracy of France was divided between fascistminded officials who yearned secretly for Hitler and "liberals" who were willing to wink at the smuggling of arms and personnel into republican Spain. Not a few of them were willing to be paid for helping the good cause. As assistance from Hitler and Mussolini flowed in to the support of Franco, the Kremlin mobilized its resources in propaganda and its tight-knit organization in favor of the defenders of Madrid.

In that spring of 1937 Franco held about half the country. On the republican side the middleclass government of Catalonia in the east, the Catholic Basque nationalists and the radical Asturian miners in the west, and the labor organizations of the central plateau were still holding out. Franco was besieging Madrid but had not yet succeeded in cutting it off from the republican capital in Valencia.

Franco seems to have handled his allies more skillfully than the republican leaders did theirs. While he took what help he could get with a minimum of commitments, the republicans who were paying the Kremlin out of the Spanish gold reserve for every machinegun they got, let themselves be undermined from within by communist organization. The Kremlin saw to it that the munitions they sent were placed in the hands only of "reliable elements" which would obey orders. The munitions were procured through dummy corporations in France and central Europe mostly from the Skoda works in Czechoslovakia. They were shipped into Spain by bribing the French. The Russians set up a headquarters in a Madrid hotel to make sure that they should reach the proper hands. The result was that only the troops under Communist control went into the field with anything like adequate training and equipment.

The communists in Spain fought well against the fascists but they also fought against the syndicalists, the anarchists, the socialists who made up the bulk of organized labor and against the middleclass liberals of Catalonia and the Basque country. These were the elements from which the republic was born. Up to the arrival of an international communist general staff the Party in Spain had been infinitesimally small. The phrase "fifth column" had been Franco's invention. The communists used it to the full against any Spaniard who did not submit to their dictation. In the end their war against Spanish independence did as much as Franco's superior military skill to sap the republican will to resist.

Our poor little project to produce a documentary movie that would put the case of the Spanish people up to the American people immediately fell a victim to this great underground power. I'd hardly been in Valencia a day before I realized that we were licked before we started.

Introduction to Civil War

Getting off the train from Paris early in the morning at Perpignan, I stood on the platform blinking from the violent impact of the clear light of the Mediterranean coast; there were the planetrees with their sunmottled trunks, the light dust, the creamy rusty colors of the stucco houses, the violent brightness dazzling after the dim grays of northern Europe. It's a light that goes with the smell of figs and dust and rancid oliveoil. The man in the baggageroom was old and brown. I checked my rucksack that was bulging and heavy with cakes of chocolate and soap and sausage for the trip, and walked down the long empty early morning street toward the town.

The Café Continental turns out to be a fine place, a regular operatic smugglers' cave of a place. It's where the local buses stop. There's bustle and bundles and baskets and sacks of potatoes stacked out in front of the long scaling stucco façade hung with grapevines. Inside you find yourself in a narrow room with the bar and tables. When I ask about the trucks and show the letter to the barman, I'm introduced to a stout absentminded man dressed in dusty black with glasses askew on a broad face. Yes, the drivers are there. They are asleep. They are leaving at noon. The waiter shows me into a little back room where I can leave my bag when I bring it from the station. On the wall is a map of Spain with the fronts marked out with little flags. "Ours," he says, smiling, pointing to the Loyalist side. We look at each other smiling, we have a feeling of being among friends. When we go out into the front room, the waiter closes the door carefully behind us.

At noon the drivers are there, both French, one a light-haired man of thirty from the north, a husky laughing guy who'd been a sailor, the other a stocky Parisian in his forties who'd been an upholsterer and had taken up truckdriving because he'd lost two fingers in a furniture factory and couldn't upholster any more. We drank our apéro and then they took me to their hotel to eat lunch, a remarkably good lunch. We all ate a lot because we weren't so sure of what we'd get across the border. We said goodbye, a little lingeringly perhaps, to the bigbosomed Frenchwoman at the cashregister and walked across town to the garage where the trucks were, huge and shiny with new gray paint. We stopped for gas and were off down the white road that ran straight between an avenue of planetrees toward mountains that bulked gray under billowing piles of clouds: the Pyrenees.

At Cerbère, while the drivers dickered with the authorities, I sat a long time on a bench in front of a gray shingled beach in the light drizzle, smoking sour cigarettes, watching a little group of Spanish refugee children under the care of a gentle forlornlooking young man playing an endless slow dance and song game. The drizzle stopped, the green and slategray headlands that hemmed in the little harbor cleared. On the headland toward Spain the pointed vaults of a cemetery stood out sharp against the sky in the washed glassgray light. Between the fishing boats, painted blue and yellow and dull red and black, drawn up on the shingle, a couple of thin hounds were rooting for dead fish.

An airplane passed flying low far out toward Spain. A few old men came out of the café and looked apprehensively at the plane, shading their eyes with their hands although there was no sun. Loyalist? Fascist? The plane disappeared behind the headland and the cemetery. A train came hooting out of the tunnel. It came on to rain again. A sadfaced woman in black came down to the beach and shepherded the children off somewhere. I went into the bar where the old men were and drank a glass of flat sour beer and then went and sat in the truck and read.

When the drivers came back they said that the truck with the gasmasks would have to be left. The sailor, who had no visa on his passport, would have to stay with it. We said goodbye to him, and the upholsterer and I ground slowly in the truck with the field telephones through the pouring rain up the steep hill to the Spanish border. At the border post we had another long wait while the officer in charge phoned Cerbère and tried to pin on the officer there the responsibility for letting us through. At last negotiations broke down and it looked as if we'd be there all night until the upholsterer sagely suggested that the official draw up a paper, and have all the officials sign it. The paper stated that he was letting us through only in accordance with instructions and not upon his own responsibility. It seemed to relieve his mind. Everybody signed it and shook hands and we were off.

At the Spanish border post things were more cheerful. A group of healthylooking boys in militia uniforms of various shades of green and khaki raised their clenched fists to us in the Popular Front salute. We offered them cigarettes, everybody shook hands and wished us a pleasant journey and waved as we drove away. In Port Bou the buildings looked neat and paintedup after the soggy gray look of Cerbère, in spite of the fact that it was raining harder than ever. We had quite a search for the representative of the Valencia Ministry of War who was to give us an order for gasoline along the road, but when we found him he was energetic and cheerful. He was a small plump baldheaded man more or less of the business class. When we told him the other truck with the gasmasks had been stopped he smiled and said he'd get it through next day. I asked him how. "Combinations," he said. "At the border everything is combinations."

Sitges was pitchblack so we couldn't see what the town was like but the little bar and restaurant where we stopped was brightly lit. Two men and a heavyfaced woman behind the bar greeted the upholsterer as an old friend and set us up to a drink while the supper was being cooked. The place was crowded and lively. One man, who spoke French and had lived in France, had been wounded on the Aragon front and was back at work again, after convalescence. At the bar there was a greenfaced man busy getting himself drunk, who came over to us and made us try on a pair of metal eyeprotectors he used when he threw handgrenades. He too was from the Aragon front. The woman, a big sexy blackeyed meanlooking woman, was definitely the boss. The son had been a waiter in London and spoke English. I had a feeling that business was good. They were optimistic about the war. They felt that the fascists would soon be licked. The man who had been at the front was strong for the Valencia government and against Barcelona and all the local committees and tradeunions. "We must have a central command," he said.

We drove fast through the sunlight under the pale blue Levantine sky, bordered by white and lilactinted clouds piled above jagged hotcolored desert mountains, through the bright-green fields and the orangegroves and the white villages with baroque churches with bluetiled domes I'd seen from the sea four years before, scudding effortlessly down the coast on a schooner. What a yearning for a world at peace that recollection gave me. Some of the churches were closed, some had been turned into markets or storehouses; one was a café. In most of the squares recruits were drilling under the small trees.

In Castellón we said goodbye to our militiaman who, not content with having paid for our lodgings for the night, insisted on setting us up to some magnificent glasses of cold beer accompanied by two kinds of big roasted prawns. The drive was delightful. Too soon after leaving Castellón we found ourselves passing the alligator-backed hill from which the old walls of Saguntum cut into the sky, and tearing into the dusty pink and yellow suburbs and the glistening greener than ever huerta of

Valencia. Then the bridge, the mediaeval gates and the clatter and jangle of the town.

Valencia didn't look very different from other times I'd been there. There was still something about the look of it that grated on the eyes, a jumble of ancient mellowly ornate buildings, scarred with new construction elaborately hideous under the sharp searching sun. The streets were crowded with miscellaneouslooking people and peddlers and signs almost like at the time of the annual fair, the only difference was the sprinkling of assorted military uniforms and the rifles and pistolholsters and the tasseled militiamen's caps. Instead of bullfights the posters announced civil war.

We drew up in front of the Hotel International next to the station where the upholsterer had another friend who spoke French. Again it was the dead time of day when all the offices would be closed. Since there was no way of delivering the truck until later in the afternoon we decided we'd better settle down to eat. The hotel seemed to be a sort of headquarters for international brigades; in the swelter of heat and the clatter of dishes of the hotel diningroom, scattered among the local militiamen at the crowded tables among which sweating waiters scooted desperately, were Frenchmen, Belgians, Germans, Poles, Yugoslavs, Italians; a cross section of Europe in arms. After lunch the upholsterer and I separated. He was to deliver the truck and to go back to Paris by train.

Valencia still centers around the Plaza Castelar with its underground flowermarket and its yellow trolleycars and its Coney Island buildings now hung with bunting and republican flags and plastered with posters, but instead of the old afternoon quiet every inch of the city is packed with a rambling crowd in which young men enormously predominate. There's the feeling that the town's been turned inside out like an old coat and that all the linings show.

At an office of the censor of the foreign press its's cozy and a little embarrassing, like a club. You meet old friends, you read the mimeographed sheets telling you what the government wants you to know. You snap at rumors. Inside beyond a roomful of typewriters, the censor himself sits owllike in his big glasses at a little desk under a blue light.

The newspapermen are tendered a lunch by the minister for Foreign Affairs at the restaurant at the Grao, the big old restaurant on the beach where years ago . . . the rice comes in the same earthen dish but I swear in peacetime it used to taste better. Through the windows of the glassedin porch you can see a warship hulldown on the blue horizon. Nonintervention.

Alvarez del Vayo with his curious whistling diction makes an excellent speech, a heart to heart talk in two languages. There's no question about our feeling that he has right on his side. The wine is good. We eat the old famous paella with shrimps and little clams. But the food at official luncheons does not digest. It stays in a hard lump in your throat. You think of those who are being led. It all depends whether your heart is with the hounds or the hares. Official luncheons are hunt breakfasts.

We walk back to Valencia talking about the mysteries of the Mediterranean these days, the unannounced blockades, the unreported sinkings, the freighters with their names painted out that run without lights slipping through the blockade— that's what they call the Mexicans; some of them are Russian ships, but they can't all be Russian.

One of the Frenchmen tells of a contract through a Czecho-slovakian intermediary, between the Loyalist government and Krupp. Europe is a tangle that nobody has yet unraveled. There's rarely been a time when the wise guys knew so little.

Back in the town I meet an old friend who takes me to see the place where the paintings from the Prado are stored. Double cement vaults have been built under the already strong stone vaulting in a chapel of a high renaissance church. That's where the paintings are. A huge collection of tapestries from the royal palace in Madrid has just arrived. They are being unpacked before being put away by an old man and two young men. A couple of experts, museum directors in black suits, hover around. It's quiet under the frescoed dome. They unfold the tapestries for us on the clean marble steps of the chancel, the magnificent crucifixion that Charles V always took with him on his campaigns, a Marriage at Cana, some enormous apocalypses. We spell out the ornate symbolic figures, the horsemen of war, pestilence, famine and death. "It's like that now," the old man says. "These are the days we are living."

The young men look at the tapestries and at us and shrug their shoulders.

House of the Wise is what people call the converted hotel where the government has put up some college professors and literary people who have lost their homes and have nowhere else to go. Its real name has a Soviet sound: the House of Culture. It's dreary in the parlor there, dinner is a gloomy function there. It's like being in quarantine. We feel like old trunks in somebody's attic. There in every mouthful in every lowvoiced conversation in every gesture you feel the choking strands of the tangle that nobody dares unravel. There's a tightness about men's voices. Nobody is talking to say anything. Everybody is waiting for the next man to commit himself. It seems hours before the oranges come that signify the end of dinner.

It's a relief to get out on the pitchblack streets where there are unstrained voices, footsteps, giggling, the feeling of men and women walking through the dark with blood in their veins. We turn into a narrow street and walk toward a dim blue light. In the narrow stone street the smell of orangeblossoms from the groves outside the city is intolerably sweet. We duck into a narrow door and through a dank stone passage enter a little litup bar. There are militiamen, a couple of sailors, a sprinkling of civilians. It smells of coffee and brandy. As we settle at a small table a frogfaced soldier comes up and introduces himself. He's a Serb serving in the International Brigade. He wants to tell his story. We piece it out with a little English, a little French, a little Spanish. He's a political exile living in Brussels. He was living with a Belgian girl who had a little boy by a former divorced husband. It's not his child but he loves it as his own, such a smart little boy. He couldn't help it, he had to leave them to come to Spain to join the International Brigade to help save Madrid from the fascists. And now the former husband is trying to take the child away from the girl because they are reds. The court has granted the child to the husband. What can he do? He's heartbroken. It's all in a letter. He shows us the letter. What can he do? What can we do? We tell him he's a good guy and he goes away.

It's quiet at night in the Casa de los Sabios. Lying in bed it's hard not to think of what one has heard during the day of the lives caught in the tangle, the prisoners huddled in stuffy rooms waiting to be questioned, the woman with her children barely able to pay for the cheap airless apartment while she waits for her husband. It's nothing they have told her, he was just taken away for questioning, certain little matters to be cleared up, wartime, no need for alarm. But the days have gone by, months, no news. The standing in line at the policestation, the calling up of influential friends, the slowgrowing terror tearing the woman to pieces.

And the hostages penned in the tarpaper barrack eating the cold rice with a piece of stale meat in it, playing cards on gritty blankets in corners of the floor, and the sudden hush when the door opens and the officer steps in, behind him two soldiers with guns. He tries to keep his voice steady when he reads the names. Eyes stare out of pale faces. Feet shuffle on the dirty floor of the office. "I am obliged to inform you that you have been ordered to be shot . . . at once."

And the man stepping out to be courtmartialed by his own side. The conversational tone of the proceedings. A joke or a smile that lets the blood flow easy again, but the gradual freezing recognition of the hundred ways a man may be guilty, the remark you dropped in a café that somebody wrote down, the letter you wrote last year, the sentence you scribbled on a scratchpad, the fact that your cousin is in the ranks of the enemy, and the strange sound your own words make in your ears when they are quoted in the indictment. They shove a cigarette into your hand and you walk into the courtyard to face six men you have never seen before. They take aim. They wait for the order. They fire.

Valencia, April, 1937

One of the best things about my first stay in Madrid back in 1916 was the number of friends I made there. On the train to Toledo one Sunday morning I fell in with a young fellow who was a student at the university. Painting and architecture were my main interests at the time. We found

127

we had many common tastes. Painting and poetry were his. We went to see Greco's painting of the burial of the Count of Orgaz together and came away fast friends. After he graduated from college and married, he came to America to teach. He was a man of vigorous, skeptical and inquiring mind. Whenever we happened to be in the same city we saw a great deal of each other. He and his family were back in Spain on a summer vacation when Franco's revolt exploded. I knew that he had stayed on to see what he could do to help the republican cause.

When I left New York I expected to go to him first. I knew that with his knowledge and taste he would be the most useful man in Spain for the purposes of our documentary film. When I asked for him in Valencia faces took on a strange embarrassment. Behind the embarrassment was fear. No one would tell me where he could be found. When at last I found his wife she told me. He had been arrested by some secret section or other and was being held for trial.

I started on a new round of the officials. All right, if the man is being held for trial, what was he being accused of? I knew that he had a brother who was an army officer on Franco's side and that members of his father's family were royalists, but I also knew that there was no possible doubt of his devotion to the cause of the republic. How about arranging an interview with him so that I could help him with his defense? Again the runaround, the look of fear, fear for their own lives, in the faces of republican officials. In the end I learned the truth. He had been shot.

The higher-ups at Valencia tried to make me believe that he had been kidnaped and killed by anarchist "uncontrollables." It wasn't till I got to Madrid that I learned from the chief of the republican counterespionage service that my friend had been executed by a "special section." He added that in his opinion the execution had been a mistake and that it was too bad. Spaniards closer to the communists I talked to said the man had been shot as an example to other officials because he had been overheard indiscreetly discussing military plans in a café. The impression I came away with was that the Russians had him put out of the way because he knew too much about the negotiations between the War ministry and the Kremlin and was not, from their very special point of view, politically reliable.

Some of my associates in the documentary film project were disgusted with me for making all these inquiries. What's one man's life at a time like this? We mustn't let our personal feelings run away with us. But how in the world, I asked them, are you to tell what's going on except by personal experience? Sacco and Vanzetti were each just one man. Isn't justice one of the things we are trying to establish? If one honest Spanish patriot has been executed, it's likely that there are more. Our hope was to save the Spanish republic and all the heritage of civilization that went with it. If it has already been destroyed from within what are we fighting for?

I remembered Carlo Tresca's warning words, the communists were liquidating every man they couldn't dominate. While I worked as best I could on my part of the film—for all his Marxist discipline our brilliant Dutch director didn't know Spanish—I kept my eyes and ears open. By the time I left the country there was no doubt in my mind that the case of my friend was no exception. Carlo Tresca, as he always did, had his facts right. By their usual methods the communists were taking over control.

Everywhere I went people were calling, and with reason, for a central command. The central command was already there. I can't remember the name of the Madrid hotel the Russian staff officers occupied. It had an English name. There everything was efficient, at least on the surface. There was the impression of military polish you would get from the general staff of any of the major armies. There was the impression, too, of being with the conquerors in occupied territory. You felt their complete divorce from any feeling for the population that formed the raw material for their human engineering. A feeling so far from sympathy that it was mighty near hatred. The conquerors and the conquered. It was a surprise to find the receptionist a New York girl—one of those fanatical but humdrum faces I've been accustomed to see in communist-run organizations in America. Was this where the dogooders among the Greenwich Village radicals had been heading?

How to tell about it? You didn't want to help the enemy, to add to the immense propaganda against the Spanish republic fomented by so many different interests. At the same time you wanted to tell the truth. As Pontius Pilate so aptly put it, what was truth? There were things you suspected you couldn't yet be sure of.

Just describe what happens, I told myself. Through surface events give what hints you truthfully can of the great forces working underneath. How can I be sure my hunches aren't wrong?

What I was seeing, I know now, was the taking over of the dying liberal republic by an outpost of international communism. All I could write was what I saw on the surface.

The Fiesta at the Fifteenth Brigade

Driving across the rolling parklands of the old royal hunting preserve shaded with scattered clumps of liveoaks and huge corktrees the young lieutenant colonel who was taking me to the field headquarters in the foothills near the Escorial, told me about his life. Up to last July he had been a pianist and composer. He had lived a great deal in Paris. He'd felt that his days didn't tie up to anything. He wasn't a good enough pianist or a good enough composer. When the military revolt began he'd put himself under the orders of the Communist Party and been placed in charge of an arms depot. They found he had an organizing mind so first thing he knew he was in the field as an officer of the Fifth Regiment. Now he was in command of a brigade. He said he was happier than he had ever been in his life.

At a crossroads at the edge of the village, among the ugly summer villas of welltodo madrileños that deface the high boulderstrewn foothills of the Guadarramas, we got out of the car and stood at the edge of the road waiting in a little crowd of guests. There were officers of various nationalities in various uniforms and campaign clothes, newspaper men from Madrid, Loyalist staff officers, and the mayor and a group of leading citizens from the village, the schoolteacher, the doctor, the pharmacist. We stood around in the hot sun. Opposite us a couple of companies of internationals, Frenchmen mostly, were drawn up waiting. Somebody suggested that there'd be mighty good pickings for Franco's airmen if they chose this moment to attack this particular crossroads. A Russian newsphotographer was raking the group with his camera.

As we talked we saw staff cars drive up bringing General

131

Miaja (one of the few old line generals who sided with the republic) and a Russian staff officer who goes under the name of General Walter, and Colonel Rojo and various functionaries from the Ministry of War. The companies presented arms very snappily. The band played the Hymn of Riego. The mayor of the village made a small speech welcoming the heroic defenders of Madrid and the heroic foreigners who were giving their lives to drive the fascist traitors and the foreign invaders from the soil of Spain, and then everybody connected with the brass climbed into cars. The others walked.

"The fascists have supporters everywhere," said my friend the musician, "but their espionage service is lousy. They ought to be bombing us this minute."

We drove out a little way down a dusty road into the hills and parked in a row of cars. While the band played the Hymn of Riego again and then the Marseillaise we walked, through groups of countrypeople looking on, into a clearing among great boulders and stonepines where the brigade was formed in a hollow square round a truck hung with bunting arranged for the speakers. The band sounded brassy and merry, the keen wind rippled in the red purple and yellow flags and carried dust out from under the restless hoofs of the cavalry. Behind rose great boulders and pines and the bare blue folds of the foothills and the snowy wall of the sierra.

The speeches, some in French and some in Spanish, were translated sentence by sentence. A new phase had come in the history of the international brigades. They had played a heroic role independently. Now the time had come for them to add their experience and knowledge of the business of war to the fresh cadres of the new Spanish people's army. They had come as anti-fascists. They had helped save Madrid. Now they were to help build up a victorious army that would fight for democracy and liberty until the peninsula was cleared of the tyrant and invader. The old Fifteenth was dissolved, hurray for the new Fifteenth Brigade of the victorious army of the Center under General Miaja. Hurray for the Army of the Center. Hurray for General Miaja.

After the speechmaking the guests and the general and his staff moved back to the road, where a rough stand had been built, and reviewed the march past of the troops. First the internationals marched by with a firm step, their stained uniforms carefully brushed, worn cartridgebelts scrubbed, rifles cleaned, battered helmets cocked jauntily over leathery faces ribbed and lined by six months of war; in this brigade there were French and Belgians mostly with a sprinkling of German and Italian exiles; it was surprising how many of them were middleaged men; here and there the face of a new young boy stared out startlingly pale. Next came the brown and ruddy newlytrained Spanish youths in new uniforms, cavalry, artillery, trucks, ambulances. And in the tailend of the parade two old tobaccocolored countrymen on donkeys. The tiny feet of the little gray donkeys moved in a dainty trot over the white dust of the road.

When the last band and the last pennant and the last ambulance had passed we all got into our cars again and were driven to the handsome new stucco villa, decorated with arches of pine and firboughs for the occasion, that was the brigade's headquarters. The officers' mess had invited the guest to lunch.

At the head of the table sat Miaja with his indulgent paterfamilias air and the shavenheaded weatherbeaten Russian who went under the name of General Walter. Behind General Walter's chair stood his aidedecamp, a young man with popping black eyes and sleek black hair in an overtailored green uniform with a brand new mapcase over his shoulder. He was a very military young man. He tended to move in jerks like a jumping-jack. General Walter, after a little crack in pidgin andaluz, spoke in Russian, which his little bantamcock of an aidedecamp, who followed his every word with deferential devotion, translated into excellent schoolbook Spanish. Then three soldier-representatives from the old internationals came up and presented a gold watch to the tall grave Frenchman who had been their commander and who was leaving the brigade for the general staff.

The best speech was Lister's. Lister is the *gallego* stevedore and stonemason who has risen to be one of the most brilliant commanders in the young republican army. He's a man in his late twenties built like a welterweight with a mane of black hair above a very white face that looks like a prizefighter's until he speaks; he spoke of the difficulties they had to face and the need for learning from past mistakes and ended up calling for victory with cascading eloquence that carried everybody away.

After him one young man after another was called on. As they spoke it was hard not to feel mounting enthusiasm for these youthful commanders, most of them in their twenties, who less than a year ago had been carpenters, blacksmiths, musicians, doctors, some of them businessmen even, who had had to learn the profession of arms as they fought, and who were learning it out of the mistakes of amateur commanders and the terrible disorganizing slaughter suffered by the first civilian resistance. Writing several months after that fine April afternoon in the foothills of the sierra, I wonder how many of them are still alive.

In the middle of the speechmaking General Miaja and his staff left and with them the Russian followed by his little aide-decamp strutting two paces behind him. The table began to fill up with the rank and file, and speeches became more personal and humorous. Some very bad warm champagne appeared and with it a good deal of kidding back and forth.

Then I heard someone say, "Here they come." A tall pleasantfaced young man who had been a carpenter in Huelva until the fortunes of war had placed him in command of an army corps went out into the sunlight to meet them. He came back ushering two women into the shade of the awning. They wore broad straw hats on top of silk shawls drawn over their faces. He placed them in the chairs at the head of the table that the generals had left empty. They sat down panting and fanning. There followed them into the shade a little group of lean yellowfaced Andalusian men who had that look of undertaker gravity peculiar to singers of the *canto jondo*. When the women took off their hats and pushed back their shawls from their sleek black heads you could see that they were Pastora Imperio and Niña de las Peñas.

Pastora is one of the greatest Spanish dancers there has ever been and Niña de las Peñas is one of the very good singers. They were going to give a performance for the soldiers that evening.

Everybody clapped and an address of greeting was duly delivered. They sat at the end of the table smiling and bowing with that mixed expression of pain and pleasure that so becomes their carefully madeup pale tobaccocolored gypsy faces. Then with great grace Pastora got to her feet. "I can't make speeches, but when I see you young men and how you are fighting for our liberty and when I think of my Spain . . . my heart breaks."

Tears filled her eyes. She pressed her hand over her mouth and sat down.

People brought her wine and tried to get her to drink a little cognac but she sat there shaking her head with the tears running down her face. Niña de las Peñas wouldn't drink anything either. "A little water," she said in a choked voice.

Pastora reached for the earthen waterjug on the table with her small hand, still, after all these years as delicately molded as a child's at the end of the thick arm of a stout woman in late middle age, and poured out a glass. She asked for sugar. As she carefully stirred the lump around in the water with a spoon she began to smile. She took up the spoon and laid it on the table with a little precise tap and handed the glass to the singer, who took it almost laughing. "You see she's going to sing tonight," Pastora said with a black flash of her eyes round the table.

Madrid, April, 1937

There was a certain amount of discussion as to what the main theme of our documentary should be. Shots of the fighting would make up a good deal of it. Madrid itself was a great stony theater of tragedy. The front line was a short walk from our hotel. Franco's artillery shelled the city in a haphazard way every few hours. The people, particularly poor people, took stubborn pride in going about their business as if nothing happened. Whenever you walked out on the street you tended to come on little scenes of blood and agony which Goya had already etched in the cold light and black shadow of the Castilian plateau, a century and a quarter before.

It was at the censor's office in the skyscraper the International Tel and Tel had rashly built in the middle of the city, that I came to understand the full refinement of the agony the people of Madrid were going through. As communications center the Telefonica was the most shelled spot in Madrid. The shells were small and didn't do too much damage; still they were a hazard to life and limb. Everybody working there took the chance of being dead before night as a matter of course. As I got to know the man who handled the American desk of the censor's office and his wife I began to understand that the intense strain they both showed was not due to fear of the shelling, but to another fear, a fear that tortured every man or woman who was doing responsible work in the city. They were being watched. The secret sections were everywhere. No matter how gallantly a man risked his life for his country, no matter how well he did his job, he was likely to be suddenly arrested and hurried away and never heard of again. With their teamwork and their arms and their slogans the communists had brought with them their terror.

This was something you couldn't very well get into a documentary particularly when the communists had charge of it. Our Dutch director did agree with me that, instead of making the film purely a blood and guts picture we ought to find something being built for the future amid all the misery and the massacre. We wanted cooperative work, construction with the profit motive left out, to be the theme. We settled on an irrigation scheme being put through by a village collective.

Irrigation Project

Fuentedueña is a village of several hundred houses in the province of Madrid. It stands on a shelf above the Tagus at the point where the direct road to Valencia from Madrid dips down into the river's broad terraced valley. Above it on the hill still tower the crumbling brick and adobe walls of a castle of Moorish work where some feudal lord once sat and controlled the trail and the rivercrossing. Along the wide wellpaved macadam road there are a few wineshops and the barracks of the Civil Guard. The minute you step off the road you are back in the age of packmules and twowheeled carts. It's a poor village and it has the air of having always been a poor village; only a few of the houses on the oblong main square, with their wide doors that open into pleasant green courts, have the stone shields of hidalgos on their peeling stucco façades. The townhall is only a couple of offices, and on the wall the telephone that links the village to Madrid.

Since July, '36, the real center of the town has been on another street, in the house once occupied by the pharmacist, who seems to have been considered hostile, because he is there no more, in an office where the members of the socialist Casa del Pueblo meet. Their president is now mayor and their policies are dominant in the village. The only opposition is the syndicalist local which in Fuentedueña, so the socialists claim, is made up of small storekeepers and excommissionmerchants, and not working farmers at all. According to the mayor they all wear the swastika under their shirts. Their side of the story, needless to say, is somewhat different.

At the time of the military revolt in July the land of Fuentedueña was held by about ten families, some of them the descendants, I suppose, of the hidalgos who put their shields on the houses on the main square. Some of them were shot, others managed to get away. The Casa del Pueblo formed a collective out of their lands. Meanwhile other lands were taken over by the syndicalist local. Fuentedueña's main cash crop is wine; the stocks in the three or four bodegas constituted the town's capital. The Casa del Pueblo, having the majority of the working farmers, took over the municipal government and it was decided to farm the lands of the village in common. For the present it was decided that every workingman should be paid five pesetas for every day he worked and should have a right to a daily liter of wine and a certain amount of firewood. The mayor and the

138

secretary and treasurer and the muledrivers and the blacksmith, every man who worked was paid the same. The carpenters and masons and other skilled artisans who had been making seven pesetas a day consented, gladly they said, to take the same pay as the rest. Later, the master mason told me, they'd raise everybody's pay to seven pesetas or higher; after all wine was a valuable crop and with no parasites to feed there would be plenty for all. Women and boys were paid three fifty. The committees of the socialist and the syndicalist organizations decided every day where their members were to work.

The village produces much wine but little oil, so one of the first things the collective did was to arrange to barter their wine for oil with a village that produced more oil than it needed. Several people told me proudly that they'd improved the quality of their wine since they had taken the bodegas over from the businessmen who had been watering it and were ruining the reputation of their vintages. After wine the crops are wheat, and a few olives.

The irrigation project seemed to loom larger than the war in the minds of the mayor and his councilors. Down in the comparatively rich bottomland along the Tagus the collective had taken over a field that they were planning to irrigate for truck gardens. They had spent thirteen thousand pesetas of their capital in Madrid to buy pumping machinery and cement. A large gang of men was working over there every day to get the ditches dug and the pump installed that was going to put the river water on the land before the hot dry summer weather began. Others were planting seed potatoes. An old man and his son had charge of a seedbed where they were raising onions and lettuce and tomatoes and peppers and artichokes for planting out. Later they would sow melons, corn and cabbage. For the first time the village was going to raise its own green vegetables.

Up to now everything of that sort had had to be imported from the outside. Only a few of the rich landowners had had irrigated patches of fruits and vegetables for their own use.

This was the first real reform the collective had undertaken and everybody felt very good about it, so good that they almost forgot the hollow popping beyond the hills they could hear from the Jarama River front fifteen miles away, and the truckloads of soldiers and munitions going through the village up the road to Madrid and the fear they felt whenever they saw an airplane in the sky. Is it ours or is it theirs?

Outside of the irrigated bottomlands and the dryfarming uplands the collective owned mules, a few horses and cows, a flock of sheep and a flock of goats. Most of the burros were owned by individuals. People's private sheep and goats were taken out to pasture every day by the village shepherds under a communal arrangement as old as the oldest stone walls.

Occasional fishing in the river was more of an entertainment than part of the town economy. On our walks back and forth to the new pumping station the socialist mayor used to point out various men and boys sitting along the riverbank with fishingpoles. All syndicalists, he'd say maliciously. You'd never find a *socialista* going out fishing when there was still spring plowing to be done. "We've cleaned out the fascists and the priests," one of the men who was walking with us said grimly. "Now we must clean out the loafers."

"Yes," said the mayor. "One of these days we will have to shoot it out with the loafers."

I had hardly had a glimpse of Barcelona on the way down. On the way back I stopped off there for some days. Barcelona had always been the most European city in Spain. I found myself in the same big fine hotel we had enjoyed so

much a few years before in the huge square at the head of the
Ramblas. Not too much changed except that the waiters
wouldn't take tips. The Ramblas were full of people as usual,
but there were none of those Catalan dances with their very
local lilting music they call sardanas going on any more. The
time before we had found them in every corner of the city.
Madrid at least was putting a brave face on disaster. Barcelona
had a furtive gutted look, stores shuttered, people glancing
back over their shoulders as they walked. In every street there
was a smell of burning from the charred ruins of the churches.

The trouble with Barcelona was not lack of government,
but too many governments, each one enforced with the butt
of a rifle. The Commonwealth under a fairly able and wellintentioned group of middle class people was trying to set up
an autonomous national republic for all Catalonia. The syndicalist and socialist trade unions still had the arms they'd
used to quell the fascist rebellion. They had established their
own jurisdictions. A number of political parties had done the
same thing, each a law unto themselves. To cap it all gangs
from the lunatic and criminal fringe of the anarchist movement were cruising about the city at night in commandeered
cars robbing people they considered welltodo or employers
or merely people they didn't like the looks of. Half the time
after they had collected what loot they could they would
drag the men of the family out and shoot them against the
nearest wall for good measure.

Order had to be established; but while I was there the
Valencia government, instead of throwing its weight behind
the Commonwealth, which was perfectly capable of running
the basically well organized little country that always seems to
the traveler more like a part of Switzerland than part of
Spain, was moving to take over the police power in its own

right. *The Russian general staff was behind this move. The Russians had come to Spain fresh from the purges of Trotskyites at home. Wherever they went they had to find heresies to wipe out in blood. There weren't too many Trotskyites in Barcelona but the various groups of dissenting socialists would do as well. In war, or in peace for that matter, the Russians were unable to imagine a decentralized government. They were continually egging on the Valencia government to disarm the dissidents. In disarming the dissidents, or in refusing them arms and ammunition which was what it came down to, they eliminated half of the armed forces that were, skillfully or unskillfully, standing up against Franco's troops on the Aragon front.*

The Dissenters

The headquarters of the United Workingman's Marxist Party. It's late at night in a large bare office furnished with odds and ends of old furniture. At a big battered fakegothic desk out of somebody's library a man sits at the telephone. I sit in a mangy overstuffed chair. On the settee opposite me sits a man who used to be editor of a radical publishing house in Madrid. We talk in a desultory way about old times in Madrid, about the course of the war. They are telling me about the change that has come over the population of Barcelona since the great explosion of revolutionary feeling that followed the attempted military coup d'état and swept the fascists out of Catalonia in July of the past year. They said Barcelona was settling down, getting bourgeois again.

"You can even see it in people's dress," said the man at the telephone, laughing. "Now we're beginning to wear collars and ties again but even a couple of months ago everybody was wearing the most extraordinary costumes . . . you'd see people on the street wearing feathers."

The man at the telephone was wellbuilt and healthylooking; he had a ready child's laugh that showed a set of solid white teeth. From time to time as we were talking the telephone would ring and he would listen attentively with a serious face. Then he'd answer with a few words too rapid for me to catch and would hang up the receiver with a shrug of the shoulders and come smiling back into the conversation again.

When he saw that I was beginning to frame a question he said, "It's the villages. . . . They want to know what to do."

"About Valencia taking over the police services?"

He nodded. "Take a car and drive through the suburbs; you'll see that the villages are barricaded. . . ." Then he laughed. "But maybe you had better not."

"He'd be all right," said the other man. "They have great respect for foreign journalists."

"Is it an organized movement?"

"It's complicated . . . in Bellver our people want to know whether to move against the anarchists. In some other places they are with them . . . You know Spain."

It was time for me to push on. We shook hands. Both these men are dead now. I went out into the rainy night. Since then the P.O.U.M. leaders have been killed and their party suppressed. The papers have not told us what has happened in the villages. Perhaps these men already knew they were doomed. There was no air of victory about them.

The syndicalist paper had just been installed in a repaired building where there had once been a convent. The new rotary presses were not quite in order yet and the partitions were unfinished between the offices in the editorial department. They took me into a little room where they were transmitting news and comment over the radio to the syndicalist paper in the fishingtown of Gijon in Asturias on the north coast, clear on the other side of Franco's territory. A man was reading an editorial. As the rotund phrases (which perhaps fitted in well enough with the American scheme of things for me to accept) went lilting through the silence, I couldn't help thinking of the rainy night and the workingmen on guard with machineguns and rifles at sandbag posts on the roads into villages, and the hopes of new life and liberty and the political phrases, confused, contradictory pounding in their ears; and then the front, the towns crowded with troops and the advanced posts and trenches and the solitude between; and beyond, the old life, the titled officers in fancy uniforms, the bishops and priests, the pious ladies in black silk with their rosaries, the Arab Moors and the dark Berbers getting their revenge four hundred and fifty years late for the loss of their civilization, and the profiteers and wop businessmen and squareheaded German traveling salesmen; and beyond again the outposts and the Basque countrypeople praying to God in their hillside trenches and the Asturian miners with their sticks of dynamite in their belts and the longshoremen and fishermen of the coast towns waiting for hopeful news; and another little office like this where the editors crowded round the receiving set that except for blockaderunners was their only contact with the outside world. How can they win, I was thinking? How can the new world full of confusion and crosspurposes and illusions, dazzled by the mirage of idealistic phrases, win against the iron combination of men accustomed to run things who have only one idea binding them together, to hold on to what they've got?

There was a sudden rumble in the distance. The man who was reading stopped. Everybody craned their necks to listen.

There it was again. "No, it's not firing, it's thunder," everybody laughed with relief. They turned on the receiver again. The voice from Gijon came feebly in a stutter of static. They must repeat the editorial. Static. Black rain was lashing against the window. While the operator tinkered with the dials the distant voice from Gijon was lost in sharp clashes of static.

Barcelona, May, 1937

It was only later that I discovered that one of the Englishmen I met at the Barcelona hotel was George Orwell, a man for whom I have come to feel more respect with each passing year. 1984. The Animal Farm. He had been up at the front with the troops of the P.O.U.M., that illfated dissident socialist group which the Russians, accustomed to looking for the proscribed under every bed, insisted on labeling as Trotskyites. Orwell had been wounded. His face had a sick drawn look. I suppose he was already suffering from the tuberculosis that later killed him. He seemed inexpressibly weary. We didn't talk very long, but I can still remember the sense of assuagement, of relief from strain I felt at last to be talking to an honest man. The officials I'd talked to in the past weeks had been gulls most of them, or self-deceivers, or else had been trying to pull the wool over my eyes. The plain people had been heartbreaking. There's a certain majesty in innocence in the face of death. This man Orwell referred without overemphasis to things we both knew to be true. He passed over them lightly. He knew everything. Perhaps he was still a little afraid of how much he knew.

It was the difference I'd felt so often in the earlier war when I'd been a nameless ambulance driver instead of a goddam campfollower. The men at the front could allow themselves the ultimate luxury of telling the truth. It was worth

145

the dirt and the lice and the danger and racket of shellfire to escape the lying and the hypocrisy and the moral degradation of the people in the rear. Men who are about to die regain a certain quiet primal dignity. Orwell spoke with the simple honesty of a man about to die.

The Catalans of the Commonwealth had offered to drive me up to the French border in one of their cars. Just as I was getting ready to leave, an American socialist I'd known in New York slipped into my room. The man was haggard. He'd just come in from Valencia. Would I let him come along? Of course. What was the matter? I knew he had come over to fight for the Spanish republic. As he was more of an office-worker than a rifleman, like so many others he had been put to work at a desk job. In war you have to have a front, but you also have to have a rear. Desk work is part of the business. I'd seen him in some office or other in Valencia. What was the matter I asked him again. Questions, he guessed he'd asked too many questions. He'd slipped out of Valencia just in time. We arranged for him to come along with me in the Commonwealth limousine. It was too bad I'd already made plans to stop off on the way to visit a cooperative. (Anywhere in the world, still, I'll take any amount of trouble to visit a cooperative. I know they are unfashionable but I believe in them.) Anyway our poor passenger would be on pins and needles until we got to the border. If one of the special sections caught up with him it wouldn't be funny.

The Village Where They Hadn't Killed Anybody

San Pol is a very small fishingvillage on the Catalan coast. The secretary of the agricultural cooperative told me with considerable pride that here they hadn't killed anybody. He was a small, schoolteachery man in a dark business suit. He had a gentle, playful way of talking and intermingled his harsh Spanish with English and French words.

The town is made up of several short streets of pale blue and yellow and whitewashed houses climbing up the hills of an irregular steep little valley full of umbrella pines. The fishingboats are drawn up on the shingly beach in a row along the double track of the railway to France.

Behind the railway is a string of grotesque villas owned by Barcelona businessmen of moderate means. Most of the villas are closed. A couple have been expropriated by the municipality, one for a cooperative retail store, and another, which has just been very handsomely done over with a blue and white tile decoration, to house a municipal poolparlor and gymnasium, public baths and showers, a huge airy cooperative barbershop and, upstairs, a public library and readingroom. On the top of the hill behind the town a big estate has been turned into a municipal chickenfarm.

The morning I arrived the towncouncil had finally decided to take over the wholesale marketing of fish, buying the catch from the fishermen and selling it in Barcelona. The middleman who had handled the local fish on a commission basis was still in business; we saw him there, a big domineering pearshaped man with a brown sash holding up his baggy corduroys, superintending the salting of sardines in a barrel. "He's a fascist," the secretary of the cooperative said, "but we won't bother him. He won't be able to compete with us anyway because we'll pay the fishermen a higher price."

As we were walking back down the steep flowerlined street (yes, the flowers had been an idea of the socialist municipality, the secretary said, smiling) it came on to rain. We passed a stout man in black puffing with flushed face up the hill under a green umbrella. "He's the priest," said the secretary. "He doesn't bother anybody. He takes no part in politics." I said that in most towns I'd been in a priest wouldn't dare show his face. "Here we were never believers," said the secretary, "so we don't feel that hatred."

Paris, June, 1937

The cooperators at San Pol set us up to a magnificent lunch in a sunny loggia overlooking the sea. Out on the blue horizon we could see the smoke of the inevitable nonintervention warship blockading the coast. They were so used to the blockade that nobody even mentioned it. We had broad beans in olive oil, wonderful fresh sardines and speeches, cheerful cooperators' speeches. Everything on the table they told us except the wine and the coffee had been grown within the town limits. They did grow wine they admitted but it wasn't good enough for guests.

Our passenger wasn't enjoying his lunch very much; he didn't like to seem too much in a hurry. It was hard to tear ourselves away from these fine people. Finally we climbed into the Commonwealth's Hispano-Suiza again. Nobody stopped us on the way to the border. Nobody questioned our passenger's papers at the customs. In a sense crossing the border back into France was waking up out of a nightmare; it wasn't the kind of nightmare you can ever wake up from. The nightmare went along with us, back to Paris, back to the States. It's a nightmare you have to learn to live with all day and every day.

The Tserpa villager comes home from the glacier. He has seen the Abominable Snowmen. Let him try to describe them.

How to bring home to people in America that their own liberties depended to a certain extent on the liberties of Russians, Spaniards, Esthonians, Poles, Moroccans; that freedom in our world was indivisible? Trying to tell the truth is only part of it. You have to get people to listen.

For a while some of us still had hopes that the President might be brought to see that the war in Spain was merely a rehearsal for deadlier assaults to come on free institutions. To every man in power there comes a moment when he stops listening. That deaf and blind selfrighteousness overtakes him which the Greeks based their tragic drama on.

Franklin Roosevelt had already succumbed to the disease of power. He had stopped listening.

His own powers of persuasion were virtually hypnotic. I remember soon after coming back from Spain meeting in the bar of the Willard an American diplomat I liked and admired for various reasons. He had an appointment at the White House. He was going to tell the President there had to be a change in our policy toward the Spanish republic. If we let the Loyalists buy arms in America there was still a chance of checking the fascist advance in Europe. He was jumping up and down with determination. If the President disagreed he had his resignation in his pocket. I met the same gentleman a few days later at the same spot. No more talk of ending the blockade. No more talk of resignation. He and the President had agreed perfectly about everything. He had been talked around to "the larger view."

V

THE USE OF THE PAST

The collapse of the Spanish republic was a blow to the whole fabric of the civilization of Western Europe. The men of the republic were trying to revive in Spain the mellow freedoms of late nineteenth-century Europe. They made mistakes, but without the blockade by the nonintervention committee they might have established something like the semisocialized society the British Labour party stood for in England. The blockade forced them to buy their arms through the communists. With the arms came communist control, the disintegration of the revolutionary parties opposed to Franco, and defeat. On the other side Franco's victory encouraged Hitler to engage in new adventures to subvert the peace and freedom of Europe.

The communist victory in Spain—it was a sort of a victory because it was in the Spanish operation that the pattern laid down for infiltration, subversion and the seizure of power that was used to such victorious effect in Czechoslovakia and in China a few years later—would not have seemed so horrible if it had not come on the heels of the great purges and the mass deportations of country people in the Soviet Union itself. The dreadful paradox of the communism of the Nineteen Thirties was that it still managed to use the poor aspirations of the world's disinherited to justify power for its own sake attained through massacre and murder on a scale unimagined since the days of Attila and Genghis Khan and of Russia's own Czar Ivan.

Hitler in Germany, Mussolini in Italy, Stalin in Moscow, Franco in Spain. For an American there seemed little to chose between them. All we could learn from Europe was the horrible results of the mistakes made by the leaders of the selfgoverning countries. Could we learn in time?

It was only in America that the ground felt firm under a free man's feet. How firm was it?

Almost by accident it seemed Franklin Roosevelt's administration was accomplishing a moderate revolution. Our system of selfgovernment must have a strength we hadn't suspected in the days when we were burning up with protest over the persecution of the I.W.W., the Palmer raids, the Sacco-Vanzetti Case, the use of the police power against working people in labor disputes. Where did that strength come from?

My father had put in a good deal of thought and a good deal of money trying to get me an education, but I managed like some others of my generation to go through school and college without getting the faintest notion of what American history was about. At Harvard we were much too superior to be interested in politics. Now I found myself consumed with curiosity to know what the phraseology of democracy which I'd been bandying about with the noisiest of them, really meant in the terms of peoples' lives. To find out what all these great words mean now it would be a help to know what they meant to the people who first used them.

An Introduction to History

"I am sensible that there are defects in our federal government, yet they are so much lighter than those of monarchies, that I view them with much indulgence. I rely too, on the good sense of the people for remedy, whereas the evils of monarchical government are beyond remedy. If any of our countrymen wish for a King, give them Aesop's fable of the frogs who asked a King; if this does not cure them, send them to Europe. They will go back good republicans."

Jefferson to Dr. Ramsey, Paris, August 4, 1787

Every generation rewrites the past. In easy times history is more or less of an ornamental art, but in times of danger we are driven to the written record by a pressing need to find answers to the riddles of today. We need to know what kind of firm ground other men, belonging to generations before us, have found to stand on. In spite of changing conditions of life they were not very different from ourselves, their thoughts were the grandfathers of our thoughts, they managed to meet situations as difficult as those we have to face, to meet them sometimes lightheartedly, and in some measure to make their hopes prevail. We need to know how they did it.

In times of change and danger when there is a quicksand of fear under men's reasoning, a sense of continuity with generations gone before can stretch like a lifeline across the scary present and get us past that idiot delusion of the exceptional Now that blocks good thinking.

In spite of the ritual invocation of the names of the Founding Fathers round election time, Americans as a people notably lack a sense of history. We have taken the accomplishments in statebuilding of the seventeenth century colonists and of the thirteen states for granted as we took the rich forest loam and the coal and the iron and the oil and the buffalo. We have wasted and exploited our political heritage with the same childish lack of foresight that has wrecked our forests and eroded our farmlands and ruined the grazing on the great plains. Now that we are caught up short face to face with the crowded servitude from which our fathers fled to a new world, the question is how much is left; how much of their past achievement is still part of our lives? It is not a question of what we want; it is a question of what is. Our history, the successes and failures of the men who went before us, is only alive in so far as some seeds and shoots of it are still stirring and growing in us today.

In contrast to the agony of Europe, it begins to be apparent that our poor old provincial American order is standing up fairly well. Maybe the republic really is something more than a painted dropcurtain hiding the babyeating Moloch of monopoly capital. Maybe there is something more than campaign oratory and pokerplaying and pork and dummy bank accounts behind those Greco-Roman colonnades.

We can't get away from the fact that most everybody in the world today believes in his heart that life is more worth living for the average man in North America than anywhere else. Still we don't feel secure. In spite of the success of the New Deal revolution in keeping our society on an even keel, too many Americans still believe in their secret hearts that democracy is rotten. In spite of the ritual phrases and the campaign slogans out of our national folklore, like the frogs in Aesop's fable, many of us are croaking that we are sick of King Log and that we want to be ruled by King Stork. "When fascism comes to America," said Huey Long, one of the smartest aspirants for the position of King Stork that ever stuck his head out of our frog-pond, "it will come as antifascism."

How are these doubts to be answered? I myself believe that we are going to stick to our old King Log, that our peculiar institutions have a future, and that this country is getting to be a better place for men to live in instead of a worse; but unfortunately just putting the statement down on paper does not make it true. How are we to answer the angry young men of today? How are we going to reassure the great mob of secret subjects of King Stork? Are we sure that our King Log isn't as rotten as they say?

The answer is not in speeches or in popular songs, but in the nature of our political habits.

One reason why the communist cure in Russia has proved worse than the disease of an outrageously decrepit and brutal social order, is that the only political habits the bolsheviks had to work with were those of serfdom and subjection to a despot. In Germany the republic failed for much the same reason. German history has been politically the opposite of English history: it has been the history of the successive subjugation of the more western and selfgoverning aspects of Germany by the despotism of the Prussian drillmaster. None of the Russian or German Marxists had any idea of politics as an art. The Englishspeaking peoples are heirs to the largest heritage of the habits and traditions and skills of selfgovernment there has ever been in the world. Politics is our whole history. If we fail to cope with the problem of adjusting the industrial machine to human needs it won't be for lack of the political tradition.

By politics I mean simply the art of inducing people to behave in groups with a minimum of force and bloodshed. That was the purpose of the tribal traditions on which our common law is based; the patching up of private and public rows without

155

violence by the opinion of a jury or the counting of heads at a meeting.

Under the stresses of the last years we have seen nation after nation sink to its lowest common denominator. Naturally it's easy for us to see the mote in our brother's eye. The question we have to face is: What is the content of our own lowest common denominator?

If, in the bedrock habits of Americans, the selfgoverning tradition is dead or has been too much diluted by the demands of the industrial setup or the diverse habits of the stream of newcomers from Europe during the last century, no amount of speechifying of politicians or of breastbeating by men of letters will bring it back to life. We so easily take the word for the thing anyway, that even if what we consider our way of life were gone, we wouldn't quite know it. It's part of the way the human mind works that the verbal trappings of institutions linger on long after the institutions they referred to have faded away. We can study the past but about the present there are times when we can only state our hope and our faith.

What we can do is give that cantilever bridge into the future that we call hope a firm foundation in what has been. We can, without adding to the cloudy masses of unattached verbiage that make any present moment in political life so difficult to see clear in, at least point out that so far in our history the habits of selfgovernment have survived.

Often it's been nip and tuck. Our history has been a contest between the selfgoverning habits of the mass and various special groups that have sought to dominate it for their own purposes. So long as that contest continues the nation will remain a growing organism.

On the whole the struggle has been carried on thus far without destroying the fabric of society. In any cross section of our history you can find the political instinct running a binding thread through the welter of interests, inertias, impulses, greeds, fears, and heroisms that make up any event. Without overconfidence we can say that our people and the people of England have used the art of politics with more skill and have upheld the dignity of the citizen as a man better than the peoples of continental Europe, who at frequent intervals have gotten sick of King Log and called in King Stork and have been properly eaten up by him for their pains.

When we wake up in the night cold and sweating with nightmare fear for the future of our country we can settle back with the reassuring thought that the Englishspeaking peoples have these habits engrained in them. The reason so many angry young men were all for calling in King Stork in the form of the socalled dictatorship of the working class (we know now whose dictatorship it really is) was that they confused selfgovernment as a political method with a particular phase of the economic setup of production. It is fairly easy to demonstrate that uncontrolled government of monopolized industry by irresponsible men is headed for ruin, and that that ruin might carry a good deal of the social fabric down with it; but it doesn't follow that the selfgoverning republic, as a method of enabling people to live together in groups without conking each other on the head every minute, would necessarily go by the board too.

If all the monopolies folded up overnight, or if their bosses converged on Washington and seized the government, as they've occasionally been on the edge of doing in one way or another, the next morning we would still face the problem of politics. Would the men who held power want to make the rest of us do what they wanted with a minimum rather than a maximum expenditure of force? At the minimum end of the scale would still be selfgovernment and the need to argue, cajole, and bribe their fellowcitizens into doing what they wanted them to; at the maximum end would be the sort of military bureaucracy and personal despotism that has so often been the style of government of the world outside of the Anglo-Saxon family of nations.

In the last analysis, to be sure, the continuance of self-government will always depend on how much the people who exercise that liberty will be willing to sacrifice to retain it. A man in power will push his subjects around just as much as they'll let him. But even in a riot the members of the mob and the members of the police force will behave as they have been brought up to behave.

We must never forget that men don't make up much of their own behavior: they behave within limits laid down by their upbringing and group background. That is why individual men feel so helpless in the face of social changes. Modifications in the structure of any organization of men can't ever really take effect till the next generation. A revolution can keep people from behaving in the old way but it can't make them behave effectively in the new way. That is why a political system elastic enough to allow drastic changes inside of its fabric is one of the greatest boons any people can possess. Our occasionally selfgoverning republic has proved itself capable of bending without breaking under the terrific strains of the last ten years. The question is whether there is enough will to freedom in the country to make it keep on working. Social machinery, no matter how traditional, left to itself runs down; men have to work it.

Our history is full of answers to the question: How shall we make selfgovernment work? People like ourselves have been making it work with more or less success for centuries. And history is only dead when people think of the present in terms of the past instead of the other way round. The minute we get the idea that the records can be of use to us now, they become alive. They become the basis of a world view into which we can fit our present lives and our hopes for the future. We have never been told enough about the world view which the founders of the American republic held up to the men who followed them.

We need to look into that world view to see how it has changed with the years and whether enough of its brilliance is left to outshine the illusions which are at present leading millions to conquest and destruction in Europe. We consider their hopes lying and false, but there is no denying their enormous energizing force. Lenin and Trotsky, backed only by a few bookish enthusiasts and some starving and ragged partisans, managed to establish their system over one sixth of the globe against all the armies and the dead weight of the old order. There is something more than a magnificent chemical industry behind the immense explosive force of Hitler's Reich.

In our past we have the hope that kept Washington's army together the winter at Valley Forge. That was the world view of 1776. It still has meaning today.

Fascists and communists alike tell us that we have only the Almighty Dollar and the degradation and sluggishness that comes from too much property on top and too much poverty below. To answer them we don't need to fill ourselves up with the hope of another historical illusion like theirs, but we do need to know which realities of our life yesterday and our life today we can believe in and work for. We must never forget that we are heirs to one of the grandest and most nearly realized world views in all history.

If we can counter the deathdealing illusions of Europe with practical schemes for applying the selfgoverning habit more fully to our disorganized social structure, to the factories, unions,

159

employers' associations, chains of stores, armies that are imposed upon us by today's methods of production and destruction, then the creaking doubts will be quiet. Even if it means reversing the trend of our whole society in order to make it continually more selfgoverning instead of less so, the trend will have to be reversed.

If what we aim to do is to work toward increasing the happiness and dignity of every man, just because he is a man, that is what the founders of this country wanted too; in their lives and writings is a great storehouse of practical information on how to go about it. Our machinery has changed, but the men who run it have changed very little. That the republicans of the seventeenth and eighteenth centuries succeeded in starting something mighty in the world I don't think even the most despairing black advocate of tyranny can deny. If the first builders succeeded against great odds, why should we who have their foundations to build on, necessarily fail?

Provincetown, June, 1941

VI

MR. ROOSEVELT'S CRUSADE

The political act I have most regretted in my life was voting for Franklin D. Roosevelt for a third term. There seemed no alternative at the time. I certainly had misgivings. Now I know how wrong I was. If Roosevelt had retired from office at the end of his second term, as he should, it would have been as one of our greatest presidents. Now it's a case of what Shakespeare had Mark Antony say of Caesar:

"The evil that men do lives after them, the good
Is oft interred with their bones."

On his first reelection in 1936 I had voted for him with enthusiasm. It was the year of his greatest glamour. The New Deal in its early days had brought the country back to life. Even in the late twenties, when my political thinking came nearest to the Marxist theory of predestined revolution I had consoled myself with the heresy of "American exceptionalism." Here was a President who was a skillful enough political prestidigitator to prove that America was exceptional. The financial regulators of the economy had been shifted from Wall Street to Washington without anybody's firing a shot. To counterbalance the excessive weight of the great corporations Roosevelt had built up the great labor unions. However much one might quarrel with the details, a fairly dispassionate observer had to admit that the democratic process had been put to work with amazing skill to remedy the dislocation produced in society by the too rapid growth of the industrial machine. Under Franklin Roosevelt the poorest immigrant, the most neglected sharecropper in the eroded hills came to feel that he was a citizen again.

In a way it was as great a feat as Lincoln's; but like all great political achievements the New Deal brought along with it the defects of its qualities.

The federal government became a storehouse of power that dwarfed the fabled House of Morgan that had been the bogy of our youth. When you add to the coercive powers of government the power of the purse and a standing army, you have a situation that would have alarmed even the most authoritarian statesmen of our early history. The trouble with immense political power of course is that no man is good enough to wield it. It's the fear of the loss of power that lets the evil in. Consciously or unconsciously, Roosevelt could find no other way of consolidating the vast power—a hundredfold greater than that of any President before him—that the success of the New Deal measures brought him, than by leading the country into war. "War" Randolph Bourne wrote many years ago, "is the health of the state."

There may have been no way for us to keep out of the war in Europe but there was no excuse for the way we went into it, or for the insane lack of statesmanlike foresight with which the war was conducted from Washington. It was a minority opinion, I knew, but I had been among those who had felt uneasy about Franklin Roosevelt's foreign policy from the time of Franco's rebellion in Spain. It seemed to me that in the case of Spain as in the case of Czechoslovakia the administration in Washington could have brought more pressure to bear on the French and British politicians who were giving ground before every threat from the dictators. Looking back on the mistakes of those years we can see that they foreshadowed the much more disastrous mistakes that were to be made during the delirium of the conflict.

Pearl Harbor. No way of forgetting that December afternoon. Driving into New York from Long Island I went into a Second Avenue ginmill to make a phone call and heard disaster pouring out over the radio. As I walked back to the car I was thinking of Stephen Decatur's hackneyed toast. "My country right or wrong." What the ardent seadog had really said at that dinner in Norfolk, before he threw his wineglass over his shoulder into the mirror behind him, was "Our country! In her intercourse with other nations may she be always in the right and always successful, right or wrong." Much more to the point. I was heartily agreeing with him. If we are to continue to have a country, in times of acute emergency there is no other possible attitude.

Even before the election of 1940 there had been alarming premonitions of the war spirit. The prosecution of a local of a truckdrivers' union in Minneapolis for sedition under a disused Civil War statute seemed in strange contrast to the administration's benign tolerance of Stalin's own Communist Party in America. Evilminded critics suggested that it had something to do with the communists' control of the body of votes in New York City now known as the liberal block. Mr. Roosevelt needed those votes to carry New York State and he needed New York State to carry the nation. Putting those Minneapolis truckdrivers in jail looked like a symptom of a dangerous heightening of federal authority. Every administration that is grasping for more power has to send somebody to jail now and then to show who's boss.

There were other good reasons for rejecting a third term. Even the most hurried reading of American history leaves you with the impression that even a second term has been too much for most Presidents. In adjusting our government to our changing social order some traditions have to be scrapped: but the two-term tradition was a good one. A constitutional amendment has at least plugged that loophole for dictatorships.

Pearl Harbor set off the mightiest industrial effort in our history. The New Deal had given the American people new faith in themselves. There had been war booms before but this was a war boom that reached right down to the ditchdigger.

Being in no way a military expert I felt the thing for me to do was to report the social transformation that the war boom was bringing about. Thrown into direct contact with all kinds of people I found myself praising and blaming men for their skills, for their character, for themselves instead of for their position in the lineup of the Marxist class war. So vanished the last traces of the Greenwich Village radical who saw only certain limited classes of men as socially good.

What I saw in my comings and goings didn't fit any of the old preconceptions. In spite of such monstrous injustices and wartime hysterics as the herding of the loyal Japanese population of the Pacific Coast into concentration camps, in spite of the profiteering which is always one facet of war, the war effort on the whole seemed to be pushing the country closer than it had ever been toward our old Populist ideal of a classless society.

What is it going to do to us, I kept asking people. How is it going to shape our civilization?

Only a Handful of Men

In the palmgarden of the Mayflower Hotel music shrills above a din of tongues like the racket of an aviary at the zoo. The air smells of rolls and sizzling butter and cocktails and cigarette smoke. The mere fact of sitting there, packed under a little wicker table crowded by other tables, makes you feel like a very important personage. I have to shout at the man I'm lunching with to be heard above the racket.

"Who is it in Washington who corresponds to Doctor Schacht in Germany?" I am asking.

"The job of supply for the army is getting done all right. The army at least has men in this town who know how to get it done. Their job is seeing that we get places fastest with the mostest men and equipment, and they are doing it."

"But on the way the job is done depends the shape our society will have after it's over."

"You mean that as they do the job they ought to remember it takes wealth to create the money they are spending?"

"And that if the history of the United States has proved anything it has proved that liberty creates wealth . . . I mean," I cried above the din, "the turnover to war is reshaping the nation. What will it do to individual freedom?"

"They don't know about things like that in the army. They've got to get things done. What we have is some extremely efficient organizers on a short term basis. They know how to get the most money out of Congress and they know where to spend it."

"That means they can't help building up big business."

"Sure. . . . They are no more worried about where the money comes from or the future liberties of the average citizen than the hunters on the great plains were worried about where the buffalo came from. . . . They were brought up to think of this as the land of plenty."

In the Secretary of the Navy's anteroom an elderly man with a hammer under his arm is standing in front of the receptionist's desk holding out a large framed photograph, taken from the air, of the dark land of Kiska between the shining sea and the mist, and of transports and destroyers in formation steaming toward the island. Amphibious landing. The receptionist is telling him he can't hang it in Mr. Forrestal's office now, there is someone in there. If he'll lend her his hammer, she will hang it herself later. "I'd never get it back," he says, shaking his head. "I'll come back later." He stands the big photograph carefully up against the wall.

I was ushered into an office where James Forrestal sat with his back to a broad window open on the Potomac and the white buildings among green trees across the river and the broad morning sky above. Forrestal had a round light graying head. The bulge of his forehead and the flattening of the bridge of his nose and the small tight jaw gave him an almost comical look of determination. He had to overcome a trace of shyness to start talking. Immediately he forgot himself in what he was telling about. His smile became happy and confiding. You became more and more conscious of the man's immense quiet competence. There was a sort of poetry about the breadth of his outlook. He gave you the feeling of looking down from a great height on all the farflung theaters of war. He carried the whole war in his head.

When I mumbled something about his being pretty busy, he smiled and answered cheerfully, "Well, not so busy as last year. Then we were in a jam getting all this started. Now, the team is in the field. For better or for worse, the training program is launched. Then, we didn't have anything. We had to make everything up as we went along."

"What kind of a country are we going to have after the war?" I asked him suddenly.

The question didn't seem to faze him.

"A great country," he answered smiling with real warmth. "Two things have surprised me in the course of this work. One has been discovering the deep traditional selfless patriotism of the old line army men. . . . I always knew it was there, but I never knew how deep it went before. . . . And the other was the discovery that we have military brains in this country. We hadn't shown any particular sign of them since the Civil War. I suppose we didn't have any use for them. . . . That's why I don't feel too discouraged when people go around hanging crepe about how we'll never solve the postwar problems. Well, we found the brains for the army when we needed them. Maybe when it becomes absolutely necessary we'll find the brains for the postwar problems too."

About the only change war has brought to the procedure when you go to the President's press conference at the White House is that the secret service men have to find your name on a list at the gate before they let you walk across the drive to the entrance in the West Wing. If you are not a regular attendant, you are ushered into the long paneled room filled up by the great mahogany table Aguinaldo gave. The minutes pass. You sit on a red couch, one of a row of men you don't know. From the hallway outside comes a faint babble from the regular newspapermen in the hall. You go over your notes. You jot down appointments, you try to remember your expenses, that taxicab, the check at dinner. The minutes drag on.

All at once the newspapermen are pouring down the hall. A suave tall gentlemen in a cutaway has his arm across the door. As the crowd thins, he lets it drop. We come in at the tail end of the procession into the oval bluegray office. The brownish velvet curtains are new. The pictures of boats are the same, the flag and the eagle. Across the shoulders, past the ears of the newspapermen who got there ahead of you, you look down on the President of the United States seated at his desk.

On either side behind his chair stand secret service men. One of them is a burly middleaged man with a red beefy face, the other is a squarejawed expressionless young man who might be a floorwalker in a department store. Beyond you can see the green lawn sloping down the hill to the great enclosing trees. Lustrous in the crosslights behind the President's head stands a large globe of the world. It is against the blue Pacific Ocean that you see his head uptilted.

As always, he's handsomer when you see him face to face than he appears in his photographs. He hasn't changed so much since I saw him seven years ago in the early days of green-sickness and accomplishment of the New Deal. His hair is grayer. He still has the fine nose and forehead, the gray eyes blandly unabashed under the movable eyebrows. Looking down from this angle you don't notice the broad stump speaker's mouth, the heavy jowl.

Today he looks well rested. He's in high good humor. At breakfast they brought him the news of the capture of an island. The reporters shoot questions up over each other's shoulders. So long as it's on the foreign war it's fun. His manner is boyishly gay. He shoots the answers back with zest, blowing out

168

his cheeks the way he does when searching for a word, lifting his eyebrows to make the questioner feel he has all his attention, man to man, for a moment; cozily scratching an ear or the back of his head as he formulates one of his sparkling improvisations. The boys are being made to feel at home in the headmaster's study.

It's only when rationing, the coal strike, price control, come up that a frown appears on his forehead. He begins to talk about deep water. His manner becomes abrupt. A querulous note of vexation comes into his voice. He won't talk about these things. Congress will have to decide them, he says. His face takes on an air of fatigue, there's a sagging look under the eyes of having been up late at his desk, of sleepless nights.

"Thank you, Mr. President," a voice says. The President's gray face is hidden by the younger fresher unworried faces of the reporters turning to make for the door.

Harry Hopkins is sitting at a desk in a small office with a window behind him. He is a tall stooping man with a high forehead and nose glasses. For a flitting instant there's a recollection of Woodrow Wilson's long pale stubborn face. You can see that he has been ill. There's a waxy almost transparent look about his skin. At first he has a little difficulty finding his words as he talks. He stammers a little. There's no side about him. He doesn't talk like a man who's holding back half his mind. You feel that he trusts your respect for the seriousness and selflessness of his purpose, that he feels that if it is his purpose it must be a good one.

Harry Hopkins is patient about the interviewer's questions. He doesn't evade them or bristle at them. You feel that he doesn't hear them. Some time ago he made up his mind and closed its windows on the world. He starts talking about how the running of the war is necessarily in the hands of a few men. Only they know the facts. The President knows things nobody else knows. A great deal of his time, Harry Hopkins says, a great deal of his thinking, has to be on the level of the four leaders of the United Nations—Roosevelt, Churchill, Stalin, the Generalissimo. There are decisions that only these four men can make. Below that is the level of general staffs, of co-ordination of campaigns, the world-wide allocation of munitions, Lend Lease. The facts upon which these decisions are based are known only to a handful of men.

Several times he used the phrase "only a handful of men."

I mentioned Congress and strikes and food production. He frowned. A lot of that was politics. The press was always puffing up the importance of domestic problems. Problems made a great splash at first and gradually they were solved and people forgot them. In the White House they were bored with this way of looking at things. If the war were brought to a successful issue, all these troublesome things would fall into line. Did I realize how much work had to go into every separate decision as to what munitions were to go to what front, for an example, how much time had to be taken up on the level of the four leaders? Only a handful of men had the information on which to base an opinion. It was boring to come back to the petty misunderstandings of domestic problems. They should wait until victory. With the victory all these things would fall into line.

"How?" The small question was in my mind but I didn't ask it. It was time to go. He had talked pleasantly and patiently and he was a very busy man. I said goodbye.

As I walked out, past the limp guards, enjoying the civilian-in-uniform look these young men still had in spite of years of military training, and past the broadfaced secret service men in the little glass shelter, and out onto the hurrying noontime crowds and cars and taxicabs of the street that the flailing sunshine lashed like rain, I remembered my last glimpse of Harry Hopkins through the window. He was walking back with long unsteady strides across the secluded lawn to the central part of the White House where life went on on the level of the four leaders.

A stream of men, women, and children is flowing sluggishly down the platform toward the New York train. No seats in the coaches. Everything booked in the Pullmans. Just as I'm sliding into a place at a table in the diner, I see an official I know.

"Hello," he says, as he shakes hands. "You ought to have called me up sooner. I bet you've seen nothing but liberals." He grins. He has protruding brown eyes and a brown round face with a big jaw in it. We sit down side by side. "I used to think I was a liberal once. But they've turned out no good." He made a downward gesture with his hand. "I don't mean they don't mean well. They aren't tough enough to survive in the battle of Washington, they're too yellow to slug it out man to man, they're not efficient. My quarrel with a lot of these New Deal agencies is they don't deliver. I been in all of them. I'm working for the army now, thank God. . . ." He suddenly rubbed his hand across his forehead. "Here I am spilling my guts and I haven't even had a drink yet. Hey, waiter!"

We ordered some drinks and lunch. "Well, go on!" he shouted above the thumping of the train. "What have they told you? You spill something now."

"For sheer human suffering the foxholes of Bataan have

171

nothing on the foxholes of Washington."

" 'Don't cheer, men, the poor fellows are dying.' " He threw back his head and laughed uproariously.

"In all the conversations I've heard for and against this man and that man, nobody has ever mentioned whether he was doing a good job. Efficiency never seems to come up in Congress or in any of the powwows I've listened in on at all. It's all—is he right politically? Has he the right ideas?"

"The country does the job. Washington is no place for brighteyed idealists, even if their ideal is efficient work."

"Why not?"

"The stakes are too high. . . . Has there ever been a time since Cleopatra's barge when the stakes were so high? . . . . Ever read about the Roman Empire? Since the days of Caesar and Crassus and Pompey there's never been a time when so much direct power was within the grasp of a few men's hands."

"All the more need to work in the public interest."

"Interests in the plural is the thing in this town. Lately, I've had a good deal to do with the British. The difference between our boys and the Britishers is that the Britishers always put England first and the old firm second. With our boys, it's the other way around."

"Do you honestly think so?"

He nodded vigorously over his plate. "Look at your idealist. Look what happens to him. He comes down here in the public interest. That's what he thinks, anyway. If he has any brains he's probably had theories and spouted them around at some time in his life. The Dies committee gets on his trail. Right away he's a red. Maybe he's been a tulip fancier or gone in swimming without any clothes on. He's a crackpot. He's a nudist. The Kerr committee makes him miserable digging up

172

his past. He either runs to cover and stops trying to do anything
or else his boss puts him in cold storage. He's not a party man.
Say he's just out to save the American people some money. The
first time anybody needs to be fed to the wolves, out he goes on
his fanny. What comeback has he? A letter to the Nation. If
he's a real conspiratorial communist the Party protects him. He
sits pretty. If he's a crook he's got partners in crime. An unattached individual citizen has no more chance than a man trying
to fight a tank with a croquet mallet. We live in a world of machines. Some machines are made of steel; others are made up of
men."

"Isn't a good deal of the government machinery antiquated?"

"Antiquated! They've got an engine built for a sidewheeler,
one of those old excursion boats, and they're trying to fly an airplane with it. What do you expect?"

Provincetown, September, 1942

Meanwhile, in occasional visits to New York I would
hear about the other war, the secret war, the increasing war
for control of mankind by the Communist Party. From the
moment that Hitler had attacked Stalin, in spite of the communist sabotage of the war effort that had followed the
Hitler-Stalin pact, the administration had dropped its guard
entirely against the communists. The theory was that they
were another brand of New Dealer. Now that we were all
fighting Hitler's Germany they would continue to be our
loyal allies.

A few of us who had had experience with their mighty
organization thought differently. There was no way of getting
anybody to listen to our misgivings.

Carlo Tresca was the old-time Italian anarchist whose information I had found so accurate at the time of the Spanish Civil War. We had been friends for years and had been associated together in various enterprises to try to find homes for the thousands of anti-communist Spaniards who had been driven out of Spain by Franco's victory. The communists were taken care of by their own organizations and didn't need our help. From the moment that it became obvious that Italy would soon be knocked out of the war, Carlo would describe the moves the communists were making in Italian antifascist organizations in this country and in Europe to get control of the government that would take over in Italy after Mussolini's inevitable collapse. He was doing all he could to work against them. It was war without quarter for great stakes and he knew it. One day in January 1943 I had lunch with him in New York before taking the train out to the Cape. He talked about the pulling and hauling in Italian organizations in New York. Whomever Washington backed would rule the peninsula. The fight was getting hotter, he told me with glee.

Carlo Tresca was murdered that night on lower Fifth Avenue as he left the office of his newspaper, Il Martello.

A few days later a young man in the district attorney's office called me up and asked me to go to see him the next time I was in town. I hurried down to Foley Square full of hope that he would have some clue to the instigator of the crime. There was general agreement that the actual shooting had been done by a hired gunman. It turned out that he expected the same thing of me. I knew absolutely nothing. It was obvious that he didn't know much more. We sat looking at each other blankly. I don't know what he thought, but what I thought was that if we Americans didn't learn a little more about the world we lived in we weren't going to survive in it very long.

The Death of a Libertarian

Carlo Tresca was born in 1879 in Sulmona in the Abruzzi. Sulmona was an ancient stone town set in a bowlshaped, well-watered valley in the midst of the highest mountains of the range that forms the Italian peninsula's backbone. It was a town of cobbled streets and old churches and large irregular squares that filled up on market days with peasants and their carts and booths and jingling donkeys. Traditions reached far back into the Roman past. The main street was named after Ovid, who was born there. There was an aqueduct with pointed arches. Many of the thickwalled houses of squared stone had been built in the fourteen hundreds. The portals of the churches were ornamented with stone carving of the early Renaissance. In the first part of the nineteenth century Sulmona had been a prosperous center of many small industries. Hats were made there and violin strings and textiles. There were many tanneries. The surrounding country was rich in wine, olives, grains; sheep grazed on the grassy slopes, and in the oak woods in the mountains pigs were herded.

Carlo was the sixth child of a well-to-do family. They say that in later life he very much resembled his father, Don Filippo. His mother, Donna Filomena, came of a family of doctors, lawyers, and professional people much respected in the locality. Carlo grew up in a period when the town's prosperity was ebbing. Imported factorymade goods had put the handicraft industries out of business. Sulmona had become a railroad junction with roundhouses and repair shops and had a considerable population of railroad workers. Don Filippo's holdings of farming land had got tangled up in some unfortunate investments, and the family was coming down in the world.

Class lines were immensely rigid in the old Italian towns. The better people wore black broadcloth and starched collars and cuffs and scorned manual labor and everybody connected with it. Two of his elder brothers had managed to continue their studies in medicine and the law, but there was an effervescence about Carlo that kept him from fitting into the strict patterns of bourgeois life. He took to associating with the peasants and railroad workers. He was even seen eating and drinking with them in wineshops and taverns. He began to identify his life with their lives. He read Marx and Kropotkin. To his family he remained the favorite black sheep, somewhat indulgently nicknamed *il scapestrato*, the scatterbrain.

The social and economic organization of Italy was still semifeudal. The liberation of the country from the Bourbons had not brought the freedom the patriots of the early part of the century had dreamed of. All over Europe workingmen were boiling with the ideas of the Paris Commune. In Italy the Bourbons had gone, but the church remained, blocking the way to progress. A certain explosive and direct logic was inborn in the peoples of Latin speech, and they had never lost their early Christian faith in the millennium. Direct action would bring about the revolution which would set workingmen free to take over the good things of the world. Carlo became a socialist agitator and secretary of the new Railroad Workers' Union, and began to publish a paper called *Il Germi* (The Seeds), the seeds of revolution.

Impulsive, warmhearted, with a taste for food and wine and flowers and everything that was lively in men and women, with the special aptitude for leadership of a man born to be looked up to, and with the best type of cold shrewd Italian brains, he early became a danger to the established order. After a number of clashes with the authorities he had to run off to Switzerland to escape being clapped in jail. He was twentyfour years old.

Immigration to America was at the flood. It was natural that Carlo should be carried west with the great tide of his countrymen. He found himself in America still in Italy, but in an Italy set down in the middle of an unfamiliar exciting society. The immigrant was at the bottom of the heap, but he always had before him the hope of breaking through into prosperity by himself, instead of having to wait for the revolution. Meanwhile there was the struggle for labor organization, for better conditions on the job. Carlo Tresca, with his ready sympathy for anybody in trouble, with his passionate hatred of restraints on himself or anybody else, with his taste for danger, found himself a leader of his people in the class war. It was a time of bloody strikes, massmeetings, longfought engagements in the courts. Careless of money or security, he became a leader of guerrilla forces.

In fighting that war Carlo Tresca learned a great deal about the United States. He never really learned to speak English, but in a way he became an American. He even came to see some of the advantages of the illogical lawabiding, lawtwisting procedures of our peculiar type of political evolution. During the last ten years, in his last great fight against the fascists and communists, he became in the best sense of the word a conservative. His last campaigns were all aimed at protecting the Italian population he loved against a new influx of brutal European logic. The great European revolution had turned into a gang war on an immense scale.

Against the gang leaders trying to organize the Italians of America for the destruction of our form of government and of our existence as a nation, Carlo Tresca kept up a subtle and ruthless war. Like most good generals his defense was attack. One day last week he fell into an ambush and was killed. I think it can be truly said that he died in defense of America.

New York, January, 1943

Trotsky had been killed in Mexico. There had been disappearances of New York radicals on the outs with the Party. The man in the Kremlin had a long arm. Under the cover of the war effort the communists were entrenching themselves. The American liberals were too busy hating Hitler to see anything amiss. This was no time to argue with them.

In spite of all my telling myself it was my business to stay home, before long I found myself climbing into a war correspondent's uniform. I knew that the people who would really tell about the war were the young men and possibly the young women who were undergoing it, but the temptation just to take a look was too strong.

A war correspondent in World War II led a delightful life. He could go almost anywhere just by expressing the wish. The army and navy transport systems were his magic carpet. All the services were keen for public relations. I occasionally wondered what the enlisted men thought of me when I went around to see them fresh from the comforts of the officers' clubs. Poor devils, they were remarkably civil.

I found the young people in the services immensely appealing, but so much milder than the young men I'd known in the European war. I missed the high spirit, the feeling of crazy adventure, and yet the young men of this war had the whole world for their sphere. It didn't seem to interest them much. In the European war we sang all the time. Nobody

178

made up any songs any more.

The Pacific was a revelation.

Everybody had always told me that one of the worst things about American society was the crude way we discriminated against people of colors other than white. In Hawaii even under the dislocations of wartime I had a glimpse of a community where relations between the various races had taken a most unexpected turn. At the university there seemed to be no racial discrimination at all. Stratifications did exist, but not those that fitted in with the preconceptions of the New York radicals. The wealthy white offspring of the early missionaries seemed to be at the top. Then came the rare native Hawaiians, then the various riffraff of white newcomers from the continent, then the Chinese with their skill in amassing money. The Japanese made up the lower middle class. The Portuguese, my people, who were the latest comers were bottom dog. On the whole these islands seemed to be a museum of successful accommodation between different races and cultures. All anybody had ever told me about it before I got there was the wicked exploitation of labor by the sugar and pineapple kings. Our record in the few territories outside the United States where we have had to deal with mixed and various races deserves a better press than it has had. In some ways it is unique in modern history.

Another prejudice the Pacific cleared out of my mind was my enlisted man's prejudice against professional army officers. Forrestal had said during my short interview with him in Washington that the two things that had surprised and heartened him most had been the deep traditional selfless patriotism of the old line army and navy men, and the fact that Americans could produce military brains. I began to understand what he meant. I came home with a deep respect for many of the professionals of the army, navy and marine corps. The two great American inventions of the war, the floating base and the amphibious landing were the work of no mean intellects.

It's hard to describe the immense lift it gave you to feel that at last, in spite of the petty bickerings and the false moves so costly in lives that seem unavoidable in wartime, you were among fellowcitizens who were coping with new situations. It was only by coping with new situations, and coping with them fast, that we could preserve the essentials of our civilization in peace as well as in war. "We'll find the brains for the postwar problems too," Forrestal had said so jauntily. Maybe we would.

The Conquest of Supply

In the murk along the light-blue horizon ahead you can make out a faint crosshatching of crowded masts and superstructures of ships. As we draw nearer to the atoll, a few shadowy green streaks of islands rise to the surface. Signal flags flutter on our halyards and answering signals flicker and vanish on the foremasts of the cruisers and destroyers. Blinker lights keep up a continual conversation. Three fighter planes, rolling and tumbling in the sky overhead, fill our ears with the roar of their motors. As we slow down to approach the entrance to the anchorage, radar grids and gray masts and stacks and turrets bristling with guns rise out of the sea. We begin to make out a line of battleships and beyond them the great barns of aircraft carriers, planes with folded wings crowded close on their decks as bees swarming on a hive. There is a tangle of destroyers hull down far to the south behind ranks of long low tankers. In the broad lanes between whaleboats, bluntnosed landing craft of every size and description, tugs, destroyer escorts, patrol boats stagger in a churn of white water through choppy seas. Steaming into the Ulithi atoll is like steaming into a great port, New York or Liverpool, except that there's no land, only a few tiny drowned islets fringed with coconut palms along the reef.

At the entrance through the submarine net we cut down our speed. Our destroyers and cruisers go their way. The battleship with ponderous smooth dignity swings slowly into her anchorage in the line of battleships. As the chains rattle with the dropping of the anchor, a look of relaxation comes over the faces of officers and men busy with the shipping of accommodation ladders, the swinging-out of derricks and booms, the opening-up of hatches. The ship has made port.

We landed at a little pier of coconut logs filled with crushed coral. While we were waiting in front of a row of warehouses for a jeep to haul our bags up to the transient quarters, we watched a rusty landing craft coming in to the beach to unload. The beachmaster, a tall rangy man in sweatdrenched greens and a small visored cap like a baseball player's, was waving the landing craft in past the coral heads with the gestures of a traffic cop. At last it was in the right position and the ramp splashed heavily into the small waves on the beach. Several sunblackened men of the crew came wading ashore. They had that look of having been a long time away from home. They wore beards. Their hair was long and bleached out yellow. Several of them wore a single silver ring in one ear. They hauled on the cable to secure the landing craft in its position nose to the shore. Meanwhile a goodsized crane on a tractor was clanking down through the sand. The treads caught hold on the ramp. The crane tipped as it clambered clumsily aboard. It took some time to work the crane into the right position. The treads had to be blocked to steady it. Then a big sixwheel truck backed up the ramp and the unloading began.

The beachmaster turned to us. "That's what we do twenty-four hours a day," he said.

We asked what he was unloading. "Dynamite," he said, "and beer." He frowned. "I sure don't like the beer. Too much responsibility."

The quietmannered young Californian who was Public Relations Officer came around in the afternoon to see how we were faring.

"Who sees that all these ships don't run into each other?" I asked him.

"That's the port director. Suppose we drop in on him."

The port director was Lieutenant Commander J. A. Maloney. His office was in one of the headquarters huts, at the end nearest the harbor. He sat at his desk opposite an immense chart of the anchorages. He was a humorous roundfaced man with a flicker of blue in his eyes. He talked slowly and thoughtfully, as if it were somebody else's work he was talking about. He hadn't been home for two years. He asked me a little wistfully if New York still stood up on its hind legs. He had worked for the Shipping Board there. He'd had a little experience with the Port of New York, he said, but his real training for this job had been at Espiritu Santo. Eighteen months on Suicide Island. He'd moved up on October 8 and had operated off a destroyer tender. Two hours after they dropped anchor they were routing a convoy in.

It was pretty simple really, he went on, talking slowly with his eyes fixed on the chart. Of course the hours were long. No putting off till tomorrow in this work. He had thirty-two officers and a hundred men under him. They usually worked twelve to sixteen hours a day. A good many officers were sent to him for training. The main jobs were convoy routing. At a certain point in the Pacific convoys came under the management of this port. Before that they were routed from Pearl. For one thing they had to be diverted out of the way of Jap subs.

Then there was berthing and control of harbor activities.

And communications between ship and ship and ship and shore. Communications were a tough nut. This office alone handled seven or eight hundred messages a day.

The biggest headache was turnaround. There was a saying in supply that if you held up a Liberty ship for eight days it was the same as if you sank one. Floating warehouses were a help—barges and obsolete freighters put aside for that purpose—but that meant double handling of cargo. Well, perfect turnaround demanded a daily miracle, and miracles just didn't happen every day. He smiled wryly and got to his feet and walked slowly over to the chart.

"You see these circles." He pointed as he talked in his meditative tone. "They show the space a ship takes up swinging on her anchor chain. It's kind of fun working this stuff out. Each ship has to be placed as near as possible to the ammo or the fuel or the supply as the case may be. There's a terrible lot of lightering. We have to cut down the distance the lighters have to go as much as possible. And then while a ship's in here loading, she's using up her stores. Suppose she's in here a week. Each ship has to be topped off before she leaves."

Shaking his head, he walked slowly back to his chair. I could see him looking out of the corner of his eye at the yellow slips that had been piling up on his desk. He waved a bunch of the flimsy at me with a rueful smile. "Just while we were talking . . . it piles up."

"It's hard to believe," one correspondent said, looking around at the lights and the rows of bottles of the officers' clubs and the chairs and the glasses and the young men in laundered uniforms, "that we've only been on this island four months."

"Took us two months to clean house. . . ." One of the doctors spoke up in a reproachful tone, "You men land here and say it's dandy and then you're gone again next day. . . . You don't see the process. You can't imagine how much trash and litter there was on this island that's no bigger than a peanut, and the flies and the mosquitoes. A coconut palm makes as much litter as an Italian family on a picnic."

"Were you here when we had the typhoon?" somebody asked.

"We expected Japs, but what we got was a typhoon . . . most of our landing craft and small boats piled up on the reef."

"Does that mean," asked the correspondent, fishing in the damp breastpocket of his shirt for a notebook, "that we will have to move out of here before the typhoons start again next fall?"

"Might be."

"A typhoon sure would pick this place up and dump it into Greasy Creek," said the doctor bitterly.

"That's just what happens," said a skinny young man with a Dixie drawl who belonged to the seabees. "We just get a place fixed up nice when they tell us, 'Gentlemen, we've got a nice little pile of manure for you to clean up a thousand miles across the water. So shake the lead out of your tail and git goin'.' "

"Wasn't Ulithi part of the same change of strategy that landed us in Leyte instead of in Yap and Mindanao?" asked the correspondent.

"Uh huh," someone answered in matter-of-fact tones. "The

biggest base in the world five hundred miles inside enemy territory."

"I don't see why it isn't the biggest story in the war," said the correspondent.

"Try and tell it," somebody said.

At night, lying in an army cot listening to the crunch of the waves and the dry rustle of the palms I'd ruminate on what I had been seeing all day.

On these island bases where a sort of rudimentary civilization of airstrips and quonset huts and outdoor movies could be set up overnight, I was beginning to see the outlines of a new society under construction, a drastically simplified civilization of aluminium and plastics based on the airplane and the bulldozer. Weren't the agonies of our political systems due to lack of adaptation? The great backsliding of civilization that had happened in my lifetime, couldn't that come from the lack of adaptation of men's hopes and ideals to the industrial machine that molded their lives? Where you found men's energies fitting easily into the grooves of mechanized accomplishment, there even in spite of the dislocations of wartime, they got a certain happiness out of it.

When I was a young man and argued with businessmen about the wrongs of the workers, they used to come up with a pat question. Did you ever have to meet a payroll? I was beginning to understand what they meant. Before you could lay down the law about the physical and moral needs of any kind of people, you had to understand how they did their work.

No problems of selfgovernment in Ulithi, only the problems of government by an appointed elite.

Maybe the real strength of the communists, stripped of their nightmare ideologies of envy and hatred, lay in this:

185

their system offered authority, a whole society formed like an army in wartime. *It worked. It worked too well.*

What did we have in Ulithi that was different from that? Individual initiative, volunteers, the conviction that this was merely a temporary expedient. Stateside, as soon as we'd won the war we'd lead our private separate lives again. They taught that their system was a temporary expedient too. Only they postponed liberty into the great byandby. We were postponing it for a year or two.

When we got home we'd have to build liberty into the industrial scheme, or we'd be left with only the word. Your thoughts get a little mad sometimes on the atolls, in the dry rustling of the tradewind through the coconut palms, rock-happy the boys called it.

We found ourselves up at the bar beside the skinny seabee. "You come on down with me," he said, putting his arms around our shoulders, "to have a snack at our messhall and meet the Bougainville Bastards. Damned best outfit in the Pacific."

He piled us into his jeep and plunged into the cloudy night. Passing the pier, he stopped a moment so that we could look out at the dark bulk of the ships stretching out across the lagoon. Their masts and stacks and superstructures stood out against the moving fingers of searchlights. "Eighteen miles by eight," he said. "They have to signal by searchlight instead of by blinker, so many of the ships are hull down from one another." He threw the car into gear. "You folks are probably sick of sightseein' and want that snack."

The seabee camp was about a block further along the beach. He led the way up some steps into a messhall where, under a bright light over an immense gleaming refrigerator, a group of men sat at a table. At one end of the table was the half demolished carcass of a turkey, at the other a section of an immense pink ham, and in between a great white pile of army bread.

These men were older and varied more in feature and expression than the navy youngsters we'd just been talking to. Their faces were lined and creased by the experience of years, jobs, trades, skills learned, businesses started, techniques undertaken. They'd left families and broken off careers. There were short men and tall men, big bullchested longshoremen and slender longfaced machine operators. There were tough beefy men who had been around, smart quiet sinewy men who had knowhow. They were scarred with the scars of old accidents. Their necks were weathered and leathery. The sun and wind had tanned their hides. Some of them wore undershirts. Some of them were stripped to their shorts. They sat sweating round the table chewing on thick ham and turkey sandwiches and arguing with their mouths full as they chewed.

"Who wouldn't have a bitch," a brickcolored man was saying in a deep growling voice, "a goddam serious bitch? Here I thought all my life I was an engineer and they've got me smashin' crates like a nigger."

"You're drunk. We joined the navy to go where we'd do the most good, didn't we? Well, where's your bitch?"

A seriouslooking darkhaired man caught sight of us and got to his feet and said hoarsely in a loud stage whisper to the young man who had brought us, "Take 'em to see the lieutenant. He'll straighten 'em out. We don't want 'em to listen to this crap."

"At least we can let 'em have a snack. . . . I brought these gentlemen down to have a nice sociable snack."

"Make the boys a sandwich, can't you? I'll get some butter," whispered the darkhaired man, reaching for the refrigerator door.

"Make 'em a sandwich for crissake," shouted several voices.

Big mitts grabbed carving knives and started hacking off hunks of turkey. Butter was slathered on bread.

"Give 'em some stuffin' for crissake. Can't eat turkey without stuffin'."

"Here," the man who'd been bitching roared out of his barrel chest, "that ain't enough." He slashed off a pair of drumsticks and handed them to us. "I don't 'pologize," he growled, "but I won't let you boys go away hungry." He winked an enormous wink. "If you want chow, come to the seabees . . . If you want to know about the seabees, ask the marines. You know what they say." He got heavily to his feet and spouted with gestures:

"When we march into Tokyo with our cap at a jaunty tilt,
We'll walk in the roads that the seabees built."

"He's quotin' poetry, he must be awful drunk," hissed the darkhaired man.

With our mouths full and a sandwich in one hand and a drumstick in the other, we followed our friend down a path between the palm trunks to a lighted tent. A tall narrowfaced man was sitting at a table writing under the unshaded bulb.

"Lieutenant Newcomer," shouted our friend, "meet the press."

He got unhurriedly to his feet and opened the screen door for us. "Well," he said. "Well, well." His eyes narrowed as he looked us each in the face for a moment. Then he smiled a slow smile. "Come right on in," he said cordially. His drawl, the burr in his r's, his way of putting his words together, were pure Kansas.

While we chewed on our sandwiches, he listened to our

friend telling him he was the man to straighten us out about the seabees.

"Well, the first thing to remember about the seabees," he began, "is that Uncle Sam didn't have to pull any of us in by the scruff of the neck. We enlisted, and most of us not only didn't have to go, but could be makin' real big money now if we'd stayed home. . . . This bitchin' don't mean a thing. If the boys didn't get it up their nose sometimes an' kick the gong around a little, they'd get the Asiatic stare. . . . You watch what they do when there's work to be done."

And it was good tough work, he went on. Not a fourth of his outfit had done any stevedoring before they came out to the Pacific. Only two of them had had dock experience. They learned to run tractors. They learned to operate cranes and winches and they learned to supplement the heavy bull work with knowhow. . . . Getting a twenty-ton tank off a ship wasn't just a matter of heaving and hauling. It was a skilled operation and it took brains and experience. That was what reconciled most of them to the work. . . . Damn little rank in the seabees. Well, he couldn't help thinking sometimes that folks back home might wonder why he just stayed a lieutenant when other fellers got to be commanders and majors. Maybe the folks might think he wasn't doing such a good job. . . . But, hell, a man's only real satisfaction was in knowing himself he was doing a good job. Was that so or wasn't it? He came from plain people back in Kansas. His folks had been in every war since the Revolution. When they saw the old flag in danger, they just naturally had to go.

"Well, if you are goin' to serve, you serve, and way down that's what all the fellers work for me think" . . . . He put his long hand on my arm. "Don't imagine for a minute we do only stevedorin', we build roads, we build camps and wharves

189

and piers. We built every damn thing on this island. And if the Japs poke their noses into our business, we got some pretty good sharpshooters itchin' to get a shot at 'em. You ask Scrappy Kessing how long it took us to put up four hundred and fifty buildings for him. He'll take you to see the recreation building we put up for the men. He likes to show that . . ." He paused, and his voice slowed to a slow rural drawl. "But I'm gettin' off the track. What I started to say was: If you're goin' to serve, you might as well serve where it does the most good."

Everybody tells you about Commodore Kessing. Ashore and afloat he's affectionately known as Scrappy Kessing. He commands the anchorage and the miles of submerged reef and the few scraps of land scarcely above high-tide level that make up the atoll. He's not a man you find very often sitting at his desk. He's always plunging out to see how the work is going. His jeep with its single star is everywhere on tiny Azor Island. Or else he's storming around the bigger island where the airport is or buzzing in his Piper Cub from one thin strip of land to another along the fringes of the rough overpopulated waters of his domain. In the late afternoon you can see him playing a desperate game of softball on the sandy diamond between the recreation hall and the movie theater. Evenings after mess he's usually sitting in a big chair in his square hut on the windy corner of the island at the table in front of the refrigerator entertaining old friends from among the horde of admirals and captains riding at anchor on the lagoon. The talk is all navy, bluewater yarns, reminiscences that stretch back to Annapolis and to drowsy old days before World War One when warships were painted white with yellow stacks like yachts, through the period of spit and polish and diplomatic cruises and uniformed routine, through stifling leafy summer months in Washington, oldtime Army and Navy Club gossip, and stories of Guam and Manila and the China stations, to the day when the Jap bombers rumbling in a shuttle through the mountain gap on Oahu touched off the immense energies of the new navy and put every manjack of them on his mettle for life.

"Yes, he's in there," they say in the outer office when you go to call on him, indicating the open door to the inner office with a somewhat cautious gesture of the head, as if they were referring to a charge of dynamite or to a valuable but cantankerous bull. The commodore jumps up from his desk like a jumping-jack. He has a round head of closecropped grizzled hair set close to a pair of broad shoulders. There's a look of almost childish energy in the quick glance of his eye and the pugnacious set of his mouth. His attitude is that of a man ready to jump down your throat, but when he speaks the tone of his voice is unexpectedly considerate. While he is listening to what you have to say he is sizing you up.

Today the first thing he asks is, "Have you seen our new recreation building?"

"Yes indeed I have."

"Have you seen my seabees?"

"Yes indeed."

"A great bunch to work with. . . . You have to keep men active. That's my job. If you don't they start to run down. The hardest time in a base like this is when the rough work is over. Every officer has to play softball or something every afternoon. Hard work and plenty recreation . . . that's what keeps off the Asiatic stare."

"Let's go up in the wind and dry off a little," said the young man who was guiding me around. "I'll try to give you a notion of what a service fleet means."

We stood in the tepid breeze up in the bow looking out at the floating city about us. Anchored not far away was a big green vessel that looked like a Noah's Ark with a large sign alongside of the house that read Ritz Carleton.

"That's the barracks ship," he said, laughing. "Replacements. The old notion was that the fleet went back to a base for supply. Now the base comes out to the fleet. We operate thirty-eight different types of ships. The ship we are on is a floating office building, only one of them; it would take the Normandie to house all the feather merchants in the service squadron . . . feather merchants in the navy are the people who do the paperwork."

He spread out his arms to let the wind get at his armpits. "Well, I guess we're as cool and dry as we're going to get. . . . Suppose we go below and visit some of the leading feather merchants. . . . The first man I've got lined up is the Supply King of the Pacific."

Below decks the ship is a tangle of cramped dimly lit passages opening out into rooms crammed with tables and desks where men pale with perspiration stoop over stacks of papers under a whir of fans. On every bulkhead and partition hang charts and graphs that tell the story of the work being done.

The supply officer, Captain Novinski, is a man of about fifty with faintly crinkly light hair and an office pallor on his face. He has a serious unassuming way of speaking. He worked his way up in the navy from apprentice seaman. He first enlisted when he was fifteen, then he was a civilian again for a while, a bookkeeper for a meatpacking firm. "Always in the office game," he says deprecatingly. He'd been out here with Service Squadron 10 since October. He'd never worked so hard in his life. "We don't have hours on board here. If a message come at 3 A.M. we take immediate action. We don't even know what day of the week it is."

A fleet, he explained, required the same variety of services as a great city, and the further you had to bring the stuff, the more the problem grew, not in arithmetical but in geometrical proportion. Many thousands of items had to be on hand all the time. The storage problem was immense. "You can't substitute a fourpenny nail for a twentypenny nail."

A tall lieutenant commander with beads of sweat standing out on the white peak of his forehead above the brick-colored line of sunburn was hovering around the corner of the captain's desk. He was evidently in a hopping hurry about something. Time for us to move on.

The fuel officer, a young blond man from California named C. T. Munson, asked us up to his cabin. He handed us each a bottle of Coca-Cola and talked while he washed his face and changed into a dry shirt. He'd been in the oil business all his life. Had gone with Shell when he left college. The twenty officers he had under him were straight out of the oil business —about every American company was represented—but none of them had ever done anything like this. He spotted with his finger on a imaginary map the continuous train of evenly spaced tankers bringing out oil across the Pacific. It was a lot of oil, but to increase the flow on a given day meant planning three months ahead. What kept the oilmen up nights were the unpredictable factors. Suppose Admiral Halsey suddenly had to chase the Japanese fleet at full speed for five hundred miles; that meant he'd use two and a half times the oil that had been earmarked for that particular operation. And the wingwalkers, the aviators, they hardly knew from one day to the next how much high octane gas they were going to need. The solution was to keep floating tank farms—Dirty Gerties they called them, old cargo boats condemned for one reason or another and turned into tankers—as far forward as possible as a margin of safety. Sure, he'd been in the oil business, but the oil business had never been up against anything like this.

That evening, in the conversational period over coffee after dinner in the narrow salon under the pilothouse where the senior officers ate, I found myself sitting across the white cloth from Commodore Carter, who commands Service Squadron 10. He's a quiet grayhaired man with a round seagoing countenance and an unruffled rather scholarly manner. He's a man who has seen a great deal and thought privately about it and read a great deal and formed his own notions about what he's read. His father was a sailingship captain and his mother was a schoolteacher. He was born out in the Pacific, on the clipper ship *Storm King* outwardbound from Seattle to Honolulu. He rounded the Horn as a child. He had his schooling in the old shipbuilding town of Bath on the Kennebec. He's skeptical, he says with a smile, of the value of articles in magazines and particularly of articles by laymen on the problems of supply in the navy, but he can't help touching on the daily business of his life as we talk about other things.

He admits in that grudging downeast way that Nimitz has been heard to say that supply is his secret weapon. The fact that we've been able to establish floating bases halfway round the world has thrown the Japanese off balance and upset all their calculations. Obviously, without having invented a system of supply undreamed of in naval history we couldn't be threatening them in their home islands today. But it was equally obvious that the further we went west, the tougher the problem would become. The answer probably lay in increased speed in the service fleet and in continual tightening-up of efficiency all around. Nobody had believed we could do what we'd done up to now, and now perhaps it was hard to believe that we would be able to do what remained to be done.

"You think we can do it?"

He allowed himself a cautious scrap of a smile. "You've been around here all day, you answer that."

"I suppose the time will come when this whole floating base will move on west."

"It's conceivable," he said.

"How long would it take," I asked as I got up to say goodnight, "to move out of Ulithi?"

"Maybe twentyfive hours."

Tacloban, Leyte, February, 1945

This was the sort of thing Forrestal meant when, that day in Washington early in the war, he spoke of our having found military brains when we needed them. His was one of the great organizing minds behind the military victories. No man has ever been broken by overwork. It is frustration, disillusionment and despair that shatters a man's will to live. He had found the military brains. It was discovering he couldn't "find the brains for postwar problems too" that broke him. He was one of the few men in public office who saw the Abominable Snowmen. Long before the fighting stopped he understood that the peace would be a greater disaster for American aims than Pearl Harbor. As Secretary of Defense he beat his spirit to pieces against the massive incomprehension of the men he

195

had to deal with in the government until in the agony of a ruined mind, that night in the Bethesda Naval Hospital, he could find no way to go on living.

In the Philippines we found Americans, not professional soldiers at all, who out of that deep traditional patriotism Forrestal had talked about somehow found strength to remain alive. Some of them lived through the Japanese occupation. Some of them lived through it in style.

The Luzon campaign was bold and hasty. It could never have succeeded if the Japanese airforce hadn't been knocked out of the air. We were in Manila before we knew it. While the Japanese were still fighting like wildcats with their accurate little portable mortars in the streets of the burning city we correspondents were talking to the Americans interned in the buildings of the Spanish university of Santo Tomás.

Old Campaigners

We are sitting on a cot in one of the grim, highceilinged, gray dormitories in the main building at Santo Tomás.

"Guerrillas—I know a little about guerrillas," the man in the next cot says with a thin smile. He is a slender gray man with the shriveled caved-in look so many of the prisoners still have, even after two weeks of normal feeding. He starts talking in a low, quiet, expressionless voice. Sometimes he pauses to think up the right word.

His name is Charles J. Cushing. He's from Los Angeles. He came out to the Philippines in 1933, and married a Manila girl and had two children. When war broke out he was working at a gold mine in southern Luzon. He reported right away to USAFFE Headquarters. They set him to blowing oil supplies and dumps of explosives. During that time he enlisted in the 302d Engineer Regiment. They were sent to Bataan, where they got busy hauling sand and gravel and building dummy airfields and dummy guns to fool the Nips, and loading the bridges to blow up when the time came to retreat. The Japs were bombing day and night. At the end of January he was picked out along with a lumberman named McQuire, since they both spoke the dialects, to lead a party across the Jap lines.

Cushing has been staring down between his knees as he talked. He looked up. "My wife was in Manila. Maybe that's why I was willing to take a chance," he said.

They set out at night. They had to crawl by ones and twos past the sentry posts. What saved them was that these particular Jap troops weren't used to jungle fighting and made a lot of noise crashing through the dry bamboo as they walked their posts. The Americans could always tell where they were and wait for them to pass. It was a slow business. They had only rice and water to eat, and the hearts they cut out of swamp palm.

They managed to escape up into the Zambales Range that runs north along the west coast of Luzon. There they ran into a Negrito named Caballero. The Negritos, Cushing explained, were a pygmy black people you still found in odd corners of the Philippines. They shot with bows and arrows, and lived in the jungles and forests, and were very keensighted at night. There was a King Tom of the Negritos back up in there who liked Americans because they used to send him a little rice sometimes from Fort Stotzenberg. This little fellow Caballero knew all the trails, and led them up to Camp Sanchez on Penatuba Mountain. On the road they picked up an Igorot named Sergeant Smith. The Igorots and the Negritos got on all right.

"In fact," said Cushing, "I found all the pagan aborigines thoroughly reliable." His voice became deeper and firmer as he got into his story. "They are not all pagans by a long shot," he said, laughing; "a lot of them have American names because a colored American evangelist, named Bishop Brown, traveled back and forth in the mountains for years, baptizing them and giving them American names. He died a few years before the war. Sergeant Smith was one of Bishop Brown's boys. . . . Well, through this Sergeant Smith we managed to get a message back to Headquarters at Bataan, so that an officer was sent across the bay in a mosquito boat to us with a walkie-talkie set. We made big plans, assigned areas, laid out work, but the fall of Singapore and of Bataan took the heart out of us. Jap raids began to be troublesome. We were kept up for a while by the story of the six-hundred-mile convoy that never came. . . ."

While Cushing was talking, his wife had walked in and stood listening at the foot of the cot. She was a cool, oval-faced girl with a somewhat Spanish look about her. "Dear," he said, when he'd introduced her to us, "suppose you go ride herd on the children. They are running wild today."

When she had gone he started to speak again in a gruff whisper. He paused to swallow, then he continued in an expressionless tone, talking low, with his eyes fixed on the floor.

"It was on account of them I had to surrender. I walked into Taiug and handed my pistol to Colonel Mori. The garrison presented arms, the officer saluted, and I bowed in the Japanese style. Then they had me."

They made him write letters to other guerrillas telling them to surrender. They beat him for days and knocked out some of his teeth. They strapped him down and gave him the water cure . . .

that was the worst. They tie you down and pour water down your throat until every cavity is distended and then they jump on your stomach. The Filipino boy who cleaned up the mess told him afterward that the water spurted up fifteen feet. What was left of him they shut up in the execution chamber in Bilibid prison. There he got a little quinine for his malaria from a United States Army doctor.

His kidneys were injured so that he couldn't hold his water. He was just about dead. He was helpless in the hands of the Japs. They took him down to Cebu by plane, and made him write a letter to his third brother, Jimmy, who had been raising guerrillas in the Visayan Islands, begging him to surrender. He fooled them by writing "Dear James," instead of "Dear Jimmy." He'd never called him James in his life. Jimmy held out to this day and had just turned up in Tacloban. They took Charles Cushing back to the old Spanish dungeons of Fort Santiago down in the old town in Manila. "They kept me in with a lot of Filipinos that they beat up every morning," he said, "you get used to that stuff after a while. Then last summer they put us all back in Santo Tomás, and here we are. Of all the men that went out with me, I don't know of any other that is alive today."

His wife had come back leading a sallowfaced little boy by his hand. She sat down quietly at the end of the cot. The little boy stood beside her, looking with dark inquiring eyes from one face to the other. "This is Charley," said Cushing. He put his gray hand on the little boy's shoulder.

"Girl all right?" he asked. His wife nodded. "Well, here we are," he said again. They looked at each other and exchanged a tired private smile.

He was looking thoughtfully down at his little son's round brown head.

199

"At first we were getting away with it all right. Here and there we'd give a kind of a big brother talk. But we didn't have anything to back up our propaganda with. The morale of the Filipinos held up as long as they had Americans with them. They'd give us anything they had. They'd even kill their fighting cocks for us to eat. You know how much a Filipino thinks of his fighting cock. I remember all the people standing around in one village started crying when they saw that the rice we had was moldy. Somebody would always turn up to carry our packs. When my boys didn't have any shirts to wear, all I had to do was go into a barrio without any shirt on. People would give me their best. The same thing with shoes. . . . There were even racketeers going around collecting money, pretending it was for Americans. The trouble with us was we didn't have anything to back our propaganda with. Well they didn't get Jimmy. You better go down to Leyte and talk to Jimmy."

Down in the wellswept offices set out in the broad wooden headquarters building among the steaming palm groves at Tolosa on Leyte, a few days later, I asked about Jimmy Cushing.

"He's a Colonel Cushing now," the young officers told me. "He's a wonderful fellow. He stayed on in Cebu right along in spite of the fact that there isn't much cover on the island. Part of the time he had to travel around disguised as a Spanish priest with a long black beard and colored glasses. They've killed more Japs over there than on any other island. Planes fly over there twice a week. There's a hut at the airfield where the Ladies' Aid serves you coffee and doughnuts when the plane comes in. He was over here a couple of days ago. Would you like to go over and call on him? We might be able to fix it up."

While we were talking, a straightbacked young man in new suntans walked into the office. This was Captain Lorenzo Teves who had just hopped over from the island of Negros. He had neatly parted black hair and very white teeth he kept showing as he smilingly explained that this was the first time he'd met Americans since the war began.

Captain Teves had been in the Reserve Officers' Training Corps of Silliman University, the missionary college the Presbyterian Board of Foreign Missions has run for years over on Negros. He was in college preparing to study law when the USAFFE surrenders came in May, 1942. Right away, the Japs began a reign of terror, slapping people right and left and confiscating American and Philippine currency. Small units began to band together to fight them. The colonel who had commanded the training corps at Silliman was the only battalion commander who refused to surrender and who didn't order his officers and men to surrender. On August 3 he struck at Buenavista. His men ambushed seventeen Japs on a truck.

"We heard about it," said Captain Teves with a quiet smile, "in the concentration camp. We cadets were concentrated in the elementary school at Baclolod. Right away nine of us decided to escape. It was the night of September 10. It was raining hard and the rivers were flooded. An enlisted man watched the sentry while we went to the toilet. When the sentry went away, we jumped the barbed wire and ran for our lives through the banana groves."

He was sitting bolt upright on the edge of his chair, talking in a low voice. He pronounced his English correctly and precisely. "After we had run off, the Japanese threw a cordon of troops around the town. They didn't catch any of us." He gave a low abrupt laugh. "Some of us were arrested by the guerrillas. We had to prove ourselves. . . . How happy we were when in June of '43 the first shipment of supplies came in by submarine from General MacArthur. We determined to stay in the mountains forever if need be. Many officers married and had children for immortality's sake. My boy was born in a hut at three thousand feet."

He sat straight on the edge of his chair looking thoughtfully out of the window at the gray curving boles of the coconut palms. Around us typewriters chirruped. From the highway, cut through the immense plantation of palms, came the grind of trucks and jeeps and weapons-carriers. "Our most important work," he said after a pause, "was Intelligence. We sent out coast watchers and organized radio stations. It was our coast watchers who reported the Japanese fleet and made possible the American victory in the first battle of the Philippine Sea. All over the island we had watchers who sent signals with the tultugan. The tultugan is the bamboo drum. It can be heard two miles. Then another tultugan takes it up. The Japanese killed many of them, but always new men volunteered. . . ."

"What happened to Silliman University?" I asked him.

His eyes snapped. "The Japanese hate Silliman more than anything. A large proportion of our officers come from Silliman cadets. Most of the American teachers were evacuated. They were respected and trusted by the people. The Japanese burned the president's house and used Hibbard Hall for a stable and burned all the books in the library. It was the finest library south of Manila. The Japanese tried to start schools, but very few people went." He wrinkled up his nose and made a little gesture of disgust with one hand.

"Now we stand our ground, but before when the Japanese came we had to run for it. . . . Now people think we are heroes. People who come up from the lowlands have an inferiority complex." He laughed. "The girls don't want to dance with them."

Two young officers who had been working at their desks with the air of graduate students cramming for a Ph.D. came over to the table where I was sitting. The lighthaired officer had an envelope with some snapshots of lateensailed bancas and outrigger schooners and of a small white powerboat.

"These were the guerrilla navy," he said, grinning broadly. "The flagship was the *Athena*. They made a cannon for it out of a piece of iron pipe. It would fire one shot and then it had to be rebuilt. She had to be burned to keep her from falling into the hands of the enemy, but she shot down a Betty one day. . . ." He went on talking while I looked through the photographs. "This has been a strange life for us. Ever since that first weak signal from Panay was heard by an amateur in the States and relayed to the War Department and from the War Department back to General Headquarters in Australia, we have been up to our necks in it eighteen hours a day. . . ."

"But all we ever do is polish our pants on office chairs," the darkhaired officer interrupted.

"We sweated at our desk in Brisbane and we sweat at our desks in Leyte and soon we'll be sweating at our desks in Manila."

"We are the chairborne infantry," said the darkhaired officer with a bitter laugh.

"A submarine lands someplace," said the lighthaired officer. "The guerrillas come out with a brass band to take the ammo and the guns ashore. A politico makes a speech. The submarine's cooks serve coffee and doughnuts to all hands. She sails away to the tune of the 'Star Spangled Banner.' We put it all down. We classify it and tabulate it, but do we get to see it? Never."

"Somebody's got to do the paperwork," growled the darkhaired officer.

"I'm going to try to get a day off to go over with you to call on Jimmy Cushing in Cebu tomorrow, but dollars to doughnuts I shan't get to go," said the lighthaired officer cheerfully.

I never did get to make that call on Jimmy Cushing. When I met Major Telesco for breakfast long before day it turned out that the plane wasn't going to Cebu; it was going to Mindanao. The overcast was breaking up in pools of pearly light when we took off. Everybody sat around smoking cigars on the ammunition boxes that filled the center of the cabin. Out over the gulf it was clear. The clouds were white and the still water was a misty plum-blue. The rising sun lit up with amber and gold clouds piled up against the lushgreen hills back of the headlands and the empty bays and inlets of the coast of Leyte. We were in the company of a second C47. It was pleasant to see the dragonfly shapes of our fighter escorts flanking us on either side. The fighters gilded with morning light skimmed and dove and soared around us like porpoises playing round the bow of a sailing ship.

From the nose of the plane, stooping to look over the shoulders of the pilot and co-pilot, we began to make out ahead the rolling coast of Mindanao, hazy with heat. Inland, dim mountains hovered above strings of white clouds. "Where are the Japs?" I asked Major Telesco with my mouth to his ear. Grinning, he pointed directly downward. Then his face went serious as he started to study the map again. We crossed the forested lowlands of the coastal plain. Soon we were following the sheen of a snaky river inland. The map was laid out on the pilot's knee. Every face was intent on it. As we climbed, the valley deepened. Slopes dense with foliage became steeper. We were winding up a deep trench of green. The plane twisted and turned between steep hillsides where patches of morning clouds still clung to the huge trees. Ahead a great waterfall was tumbling into the canyon. The plane leapt a jagged ridge like a horse taking a jump. We were headed toward a blue pile of mountains far inland.

We buzzed low across the long meadow that still kept some of the checkerboard pattern of the original corn and camote fields. The pilot circled and buzzed again to take another look, then brought us down without a jar.

We stepped out into a broad upland valley flanked by deep gulches and spiny ridges on one side, and on the other by a great distant pile of mountains. The air was cold and sweet. It was like the high grazing country in the Rockies. For a moment the strip was clear, but immediately ragged little barefoot men with rifles began to spring up everywhere out of the grass and from under clumps of trees. They swarmed round the plane laughing and shouting. The officers managed to look quite natty in their frayed but wellwashed suntans. Before five minutes were up, they had their troops at work with much hurly-burly unloading the ammunition boxes.

"Our colonel is on his way," the officers told us proudly, as they shook hands. It was the third time planes had come to this particular field, they said.

From up the valley comes the rumble of a motor. People start to run for cover in the ditches, but it turns out not to be a hostile plane, so immediately they crowd back laughing. It is the local interurban bus, an ancient, lumbering, rattletrap yellow vehicle with open sides and benches across it like a horsecar, which advances roaring and spluttering up the dusty track along the edge of the airstrip. An American flag flies from the cracked windshield, and three pretty girls sit smiling beside the driver. "Buknidon Bus No. 2" reads in red a splattered sign across the front. Dusty clusters of threadbare guerrillas hang from the uprights that support the roof. Naked little boys run along behind.

The bus parks on the field and the troops begin to load it up with the boxes out of the plane.

Saddlehorses for us to ride are produced out of the shade of a grove of trees at the edge of the airstrip. Perhaps we might want to ride toward the village to meet Colonel Grinstead who is on his way down from his headquarters a couple of miles away in the hills. We set out at a trot along an old country road with clayey red ruts like a Virginia road that cuts straight through the fat green lands of the upland valley.

On the way we meet a bunch of people coming toward us. In the middle of them walks a tall man, head and shoulders taller than the Filipinos around him. He walks with long springy strides swinging a heavy cane. He has clear gray eyes and bushy grizzled beard. His overseas cap is set jauntily on the side of his head.

We scramble down off our ponies to shake hands. There's something easy and genial and completely selfreliant about James Grinstead's manner when you meet him that's very old-time American. You think at once of a locomotive engineer or the captain of a riverboat. He's from Oklahoma. He has that air of innate culture about him you often find in western prospectors and pioneers, the look of a man capable of sitting back and being entertained by the spectacle of his own life. His story about his beard is that he isn't going to shave it off till the Big Chief lands on Mindanao. His troops call him Santa Claus on account of it. He's an oldtimer on Mindanao, he tells us. A number of years back he retired as a sergeant from the Philippine Constabulary and set himself up near Cotogato as a coconut planter.

"A lazy man's life," he explains; "that's why I like it."

We have turned back toward the airfield and are talking as we walk along. He has a deep, resonant voice with a south-western drawl, and the amused, half deprecatory manner of a good storyteller. His eyes, under a square forehead and bushy eyebrows, twinkle as he talks.

"It's a funny war," he says; "at least I've found it so. When the Jap first came, I hid out for two months on my own place without his ever findin' me. Then I took to the hills. I haven't led such a bad life as you'd think."

While we walk along, leading our horses and talking, a formation of planes drones across the darkblue sky overhead. The Filipinos around us look up nervously from under their big hats. "They are ours," says Colonel Grinstead, laughing, "even I can tell that. . . . I'm afraid you won't find us much on the military side up here. We are so used to thinkin' any plane is a Jap that it's goin' to take us a little while to get over the habit of crawlin' in ditches."

One of the Corsairs of our fighter escort is circling to come in. We all follow the dark slender plane with our eyes as it speeds across the grass. All at once the nose digs in and the tail shoots up. The Corsair has crashed.

Major Telesco jumps into the saddle, kicks his heels into his pony, and gallops off. Somebody offers the colonel a horse. "No, thanks, I find I can get there just as fast walkin'," he drawls. We all ride after the major as fast as we can get our horses to go. When we reach the plane we see that the propeller and nose are dug into the soft dirt. Sweating and redfaced, the pilot unhurt but sore is climbing down out of his seat. "A nice target for the Japs," whispers the major. "Their Del Monte strip is only twelve miles away."

Guerrillas come running with ropes. Several of them are fetching a bamboo ladder from the staging where they fasten the sleeve to show the wind direction. Two ropes of homemade hempen fiber are fastened to the tail of the plane. Bunches of little guerrillas hang from them. The plane's tail is pulled down. Up comes its twisted propeller out of the dirt. A carabao cart is backed up to the tail, and with much pulling and hauling and sweating the Corsair is towed tailfirst off the field.

Colonel Grinstead has caught up with us and stands looking quietly at the humming swarm of his ragged troops.

"If the Jap don't pay us his regular afternoon visit . . ." he drawls with his leisurely smile. "They usually fly over just at dusk; but meanwhile," he adds in an amused and genial tone of voice, "my boys will turn that plane into a nice haystack. They are good at that. Now if you gentlemen would like to come along, I think the Rodriguezes are expectin' us for lunch."

He leads the way down a path that winds through the tall grass from the airstrip down into a leafy valley. From the edge overlooking some cornfields and a treepacked riverbank, he points out the ravine where five miles away his troops are holding back the Jap.

"When the Jap was up here, a week ago tomorrow," he says, "we held him for three days, but then the only thing we could do was get out. We went up in those hills." He turns back to point out the green ridge the other side of the airstrip. "A little way beyond that ridge is the Moro country. We stayed partway up. The Jap dug up the airstrip a little and then he pulled out and ran. Out of chow, I guess. He went back to report he'd killed a thousand guerrillas and destroyed the airstrip."

The noon sun was burning hot. We arrived sweating and thirsty at a group of pomolo trees in the corner of a field densely grown with tall shimmering corn. Behind the trees was a barn with a high porch under a galvanized iron roof. The Rodriguez family was waiting for us in a group in the shade of the porch. They looked very Spanish. There was the grayhaired man, and his wife, and the blackeyed daughters and the uncles and cousins and nephews. In the background stood friends and servants. The girls offered us fresh water to drink and pomolos, which are a primitive type of grapefruit, and brought out the few chairs the Japs had left them for us to sit on. Mr. Rodriguez explained apologetically that this barn was his home since the Japs had burned his house in the valley. He was proud to welcome us to it. He had five sons in the army. "They call it guerrillas, but we call it the Army of the Philippines."

After we had cooled off a little in the shade, they made us sit in the middle of the long table with a white tablecloth that was set the length of the porch. Americans and Filipinos sat there cooling off, talking in low voices while our host's pretty daughters passed the tuba and ran softly back and forth with dishes from the kitchen.

Only when a rumble of planes was heard overhead was there any stir. The girls and old women started to move toward the shelter down in the creekbed. The children bolted. They weren't yet used to having planes turn out friendly. Colonel Grinstead stepped out into the path and shaded his eyes to look up. "It's that same formation of ours coming back from its mission," he said. As soon as they heard his quiet confident voice, the people started coming back into the house.

While we ate we talked. Mr. Luminarias, the young deputy governor of the province, was telling about the beginning of the guerrilla movement in Mindanao. In October, 1942, he said, there had been the first rising against the Japanese-controlled police. The Filipinos had used ripe bananas, pretending they were hand grenades, and the police had surrendered and joined the guerrillas. Then in March, 1943, a government had been set up in a meeting at a school. "Since then we have complete civil government."

At first the Americans had to hide out. They were taken in by the country people, Colonel Grinstead explained. The Jap never controlled any more of Mindanao then he could see in front of his nose. Mr. Kuder, the superintendent of schools, did a great deal to influence the Moros. He stayed right on until he had to be evacuated home on account of illness.

The colonel laughed. Of course, the Americans had to keep their wits about them. Maybe the fate of those that fell into the hands of the Jap sharpened the wits of the survivors. Several Americans had been pretty badly hashed up before they were killed . . . Well, gradually with the help of young officers of the Philippine Army they built an organization. In the course of time the whole works came under the command of Colonel Fertig. Colonel Fertig was a mining engineer who had come over to Mindanao to build airstrips and gotten caught here. He'd proved a grand organizer. "Of course," added Grinstead, "we don't any of us think much of ourselves as military men."

I had met Colonel Fertig at headquarters in Tolosa a few days before. I had a vivid recollection of a quiet man with forceful gray eyes and a small goatee, who looked rather like a country doctor. He wouldn't hear of any talk of the privation and danger of his life any more than Grinstead would. Now Grinstead was explaining how Fertig never had a headquarters without electric light. Sometimes they had to use a waterwheel to turn over the generator. In Misamis Occidental they'd had street lights up to June, 1943. Lanao under Colonel Hedges had been more peaceful for the last three years than in any three years in its history. There had been remarkably little crime in guerrilla territory. Things had run surprisingly smoothly. "Of course, when the Jap came in force we had to get out the back way. We always kept the back door open."

After lunch we walked slowly through the still afternoon,

shrill with cicadas and dryflies, into the village. There was a pretty green plaza shaded by huge trees under which a few vendors squatted. Most of them were sourfaced Moros in turbans who had brought in bolts of homespun cloth for sale. There were bags of nuts and dried fruits and a few handfuls of the inevitable tiny desiccated shrimps. Quite unharmed in the middle of the grassy central square stood a stiff cement statue of Rizal. Around the plaza were hedges of flowering shrubs with vineclad bamboo arches and gates in them which opened into nicely laidout gardens. Not a house was standing. The Japs had burned every one.

While we were in the plaza we heard the distant growl of a formation of planes. We set out walking fast down the road toward the airstrip. "You never can tell what the Jap'll do, he might pay us a call," Grinstead was saying.

Soon we could make out our own olive-drab transports circling the strip. The airfield looked like a fairground. Men, women and children had trooped in from far and near. The guerrilla officers were having a hard time keeping a runway clear for the planes to land on. The colonel shook his head. "A lot of them have never seen a friendly plane in their lives," he said. "I'll be nervous as a flea on a hot griddle until those planes get out of here. . . . It's gettin' near the time when the Jap likes to come callin'."

There was a dense shouting crowd around the open side doors of the C47's. The crews were throwing out candy and cigarettes and distributing souvenirs and knickknacks with General McArthur's "I shall return" picture on them. There were Moros in the throng and the boys off the transports were carrying on a brisk trade with them for their engraved bolos and krisses. In the outskirts of the crowd all the girls in the neighborhood, in their best clothes and with flowers in their hair, were

211

strolling briskly about in twos and threes, Spanish fashion. Here and there among the people serious-looking fellows stood guard leaning on their long spears. If a guerrilla didn't have a gun he had a spear. If he didn't have a spear he had a bolo or a knife.

One of the pretty little Rodriguez girls came running across the field to where we stood under a broadspreading mango. She was carrying a plate covered with a napkin. "It is a squash pie made with cassava flour," she said, smiling. "Mother says you must taste it." She held it up under the colonel's nose.

"As if she hadn't stuffed us already," he said. "It's a funny war," he added as he pulled out his claspknife and started to divide up the pie.

While we stood in the shade munching on the pie, I asked him why in his opinion the resistance seemed to go so much better in places where a few Americans were back of it. "Well, in Mindanao the oldtime Americans have always had a pretty good reputation," he replied with his slow judicial drawl. "Not too many bastards have come in yet to ruin it. The people have confidence that we'll treat 'em square. They'd rather have an American in command than their own leaders. I'll tell you why. Whenever a Filipino gets to some position, he's assailed by a mob of relatives who want soft jobs. He'd be socially ostracized if he turned 'em down. Americans don't have such big families and they expect to support themselves by their own efforts. People respect their independence."

As we talked, we couldn't help occasionally scanning the sky with a certain apprehension. "If they come," said the colonel, "they'll make a killin'."

At last the major was beckoning to us from the door of our C47. Already the escort planes were taking off amid clouds of red dust. We shook hands all around and set off at a dogtrot toward our plane. As we were climbing the little ladder, Mr. Luminarias, the brighteyed young man in the linen suit who was deputy governor of the Province of Buknidon, came running after us and asked us please not to forget to send in books and newspapers and magazines next time.

"You do not know what it means to be out of the world," he said breathlessly. "For three years we have been cut off from the civilized world."

The boys of the crew lifted in their last souvenirs, a bundle of spears, an armful of big straw hats, and then the steps. Over the hats and bobbing heads of the crowd we had a last glimpse of Grinstead's broad forehead and gray eyes and bushy beard as he gently waved the people back from under the wings of the plane. The doors were pulled to and we settled back into the bucket seats for the takeoff.

Sydney, Australia, April, 1945

We used to make fun of the missionaries. I came away from the Philippines with respect for them. I had expected to find deep traces of Spanish culture there, but what I found was that the American Protestant missionaries and school-teachers of the early nineteen hundreds had left a much deeper mark. It was the English language and the old American system of ideas with its simple standards of right and wrong that held the heterogenous inhabitants of these hundreds of islands together as a nation. Why, I kept thinking, can't we have people like that to represent us in the world today?

After the enthusiasms of the Pacific visiting the European theater was a bitter experience. I reached the European theater too late to see it during the excitement and hazard

213

of combat. *Just as in the first war it was after the fighting stopped that the full horror of what had been going on caught up with you.*

In the Year of Our Defeat

Driving back to town in the tailend of a raw afternoon had been like driving through one of Dante's icy hells. In the freezing fog, along the road, we had passed crowds of men and women bowed under knapsacks and bundles of sticks, pulling baby carriages and carts full of wood, pushing heavily loaded bicycles. We went along honking and blinking the lights of the jeep to try to get them to move out of the way. "Damn krauts," the driver kept muttering. "They git themselves run over just on purpose. . . . I'd just as soon run 'em down as not."

We passed some trucks crowded tight with grayfaced young men in gray. "At least the military prisoners get to ride," said the lieutenant. "The lesson of this war to me is, don't ever be a civilian."

At last we made it through the crowded foggy unlit streets back to the correspondents' hotel and dragged our stiff limbs out of the open jeep. The bar wasn't functioning yet, so the lieutenant and I went up to the bedroom to thaw ourselves out over the radiator. We stood at the window a moment pulling the drenched gloves off our icy fingers and looking down the shaft of light from the window through a gap in the wall of the hotel next door into an emptiness of dangling plumbing where a piece of a stairway with red flowered carpeting on it stopped abruptly at nothing. Turning back into the warm, well-lighted, perfectly standardized hotel bedroom, we found that we had both felt the same momentary sense of surprise that it was us in here with the warm conquerors instead of out there with the dead jerries.

The lieutenant worked in Intelligence. He was a young man from Brooklyn with a thoughtful ruddy face and full lips.

Suddenly he sat down on the edge of the bed and started to talk. "My people are Jewish," he began, "so don't think I'm not bitter against the krauts. I'm for shooting the war criminals wherever we can prove they are guilty and getting it over with. But for God's sake, tell me what we are trying to do."

He got up and began to walk back and forth. "Well, they tell you it's like the fire department . . . the fire department has to do a certain amount of damage, even blow up buildings, to put the fire out. Sure, but you don't see the fire department starting new fires all over town just because one block is burning. Or do you? Hatred is like a fire. You've got to put it out. I've been interrogating German officers for the War Crimes Commission, and when I find them halfstarved to death right in our own P.W. cages and being treated like you wouldn't treat a dog, I ask myself some questions. Sometimes I have to get them fed up and hospitalized before I can get a coherent story out of them. Brutality is more contagious than typhus and a hell of a lot more difficult to stamp out. . . . Right here in Frankfurt we countenance things that would have given us cold chills back home. . . . I'm not blaming the regular army men for all of it, either. Regular Army men are a hell of a fine bunch of men and I've come to admire them very much, but the trouble is they have no training in political things. They are trained to follow directives from Washington. They do, and slavishly. . . . I do blame them for not having the courage to follow their own decent instincts. That's how General Patton got into trouble. . . . Patton is one of those men who never opens his mouth without putting his foot in it, and God knows he's a tough baby, but his instincts were all right. Throwing him overboard was cowardice. All these directives about 'don't coddle the German' have thrown open the gates for every criminal tendency we've got in us. Just because the Germans did these things is no reason for us to do them. Well, I know war isn't a pretty business, but this isn't war. This is peace. . . . Hell, let's go down and get a drink before I blow my top and start talking."

Nuremburg Diary

The day is bright and cold. A sharp sun searches out every detail of the heaped ruins of the old city of toymakers and meistersingers, points up the tall slender arches of smashed churches, rounds out the curves of broken bits of renaissance carving. In an open space in the rubbish near the nineteenth-century bronze statue of Albrecht Dürer, German women in coats and sweaters, surrounded by a pack of towheaded children, are putting potatoes to boil in a stove made out of a torn sheet of galvanized roofing. We ask them where they live. They point to the concrete entrance of an airraid shelter that opens beside the chipped pedestal of the statue. A man we talk to has just arrived from Breslau. He is a farmer dispossessed by the Poles. As we turn to leave, a little shower of stones comes our way from some bigger children who are playing on top of a mountain of bricks and ground-up stone. When we look up, they dash out of sight behind tottering walls. On a wall down the street a freshly chalked swastika stares us in the face.

Out at the great battered building in fake medieval style of the old Bavarian Palace of Justice there is a great bustle of jeeps, command cars, and converted German buses. Military police scrutinize your pass. A tank with a star on it nestles nonchalantly against the wall beside the entrance. Inside, a sound of sawing echoes through the long valuted corridors. German prisoners of war on stepladders are applying a fresh coat of water-paint to the walls. Battalions of German scrubwomen in clean dresses and heavy knitted stockings rammed into big boots are swabbing the marble floors. Thronging the corridors are Americans in uniform and out of uniform with a familiar Washington look about their faces.

The vaults resound with the cheerful clack of the heels of American girl secretaries. There are French lady reporters in highpiled Paris turbans. There are Russians and whispering Britishers. There are all the uniforms of the four nations. There's a Post Exchange and a snackbar and a Washington-style cafeteria. In the offices the furnishings have quite an American look, but out of the thick stone walls of the echoing corridors of the old German courthouse and jail, there oozes a sweat of misery, Teutonic and alien.

It's the day before the trial. People are a little edgy. They wag their heads and tell you the trial won't start on time. The French are peevish. The Russians have asked for a delay. Press conferences are inconclusive. In the freshly redecorated courtroom with its sagegreen curtains and crimson chairs, it's like the dress rehearsal of an amateur play. Interpreters sit behind their glass screen practicing with the earphones. The electricians are testing out the great clusters of floodlights that hang from the ceiling. An American sergeant, with the concerned look of a propertyman, is smoothing out the folds of the four flags that stand behind the judges' dais. Guards with white helmet linings on their heads and white batons and white pistol-holsters are being shown to their stations. The cast is jumpy. How are we ever going to be able to get the curtain up tomorrow?

Down the long hall there's a deserted office from which you can look down through a broken window into a little exercise yard planted with skinny trees and patches of grass cut into picturepuzzle shapes by crisscrossing cement paths. Several men in American fieldjackets, each an equal distance from the other, are walking briskly about. American guards stride watchfully among them. We can see the rifle of the guard on the parapet below pass and repass under the window. We look at them for a while in silence, keeping back from the window to be out of sight of the guard. "Funny to think those guys may hang in a couple of months," blurts out somebody. "They look like anybody."

"In spite of everything I could do," said Colonel Andrus at his afternoon press conference, "one of my prisoners got sick." The colonel looked heartbroken. Colonel Andrus—he hated to be called the jailer, but that was what he was—was a worried-looking man with a round face and glasses and a close-clipped mustache. He had a timid smile. His hairbrush haircut gave him an incongruously boyish look. He spoke of his prisoners as if they were a set of dangerous but valuable zoological specimens that had to be kept in good health at whatever cost. Intense preoccupation with the importance of his task seemed to have sharpened the military punctilio of originally mild and disarming manners. The prisoner he was speaking of was Kaltenbrunner. He added:

"There has occurred a spontaneous hemorrhage of a small blood vessel in the back of the cranium. I'll read you the Latin name. It is not really dangerous. . . . More severe it would have been fatal. It will be impossible for him to appear in court tomorrow. This li'l hemorrhage is being stopped, but he will have to be kept completely quiet for some time."

"Did he say anything?" asked a reporter.

The colonel picked up a paper off his desk. He read it off slowly and carefully: " 'I am very sorry I cannot be in court tomorrow' was what the prisoner remarked."

"What caused him to take sick?" asked another reporter.

"His illness was caused by stress of emotion. He has been hysterical for the last three weeks. He has had crying fits in his cell. He is the bully type, strong and hard when on top, cringing and crying when not," answered the colonel. "He's much influenced by the period of excitement and worry lately."

No, Colonel Andrus could not tell which hospital he had been taken to. He was receiving suitable care in a United States Army hospital, that was all he could say. Otherwise the behavior of the prisoners had been uniformly correct. Hess had gained slightly in health, weight, and appearance since his arrival. He complained of abdominal cramps. . . . Frank arrived with a partial paralysis of the left wrist due to selfinflicted wounds . . . improved under heat treatment. . . . Frick's condition was essentially negative, not ill but not very vigorous. . . . Funk had complained of a variety of pains and aches largely imaginary. . . . Goering now admitted that he was in better health then he had been for twenty years. His drug habit had been eliminated. His nervous heart palpitation had disappeared. He had reduced to two hundred and twenty pounds. He had no organic heart ailment of any kind. . . . Jodl's lumbago had been cured by heat treatment. . . . Keitel had a little difficulty with flat feet due to insufficient exercise, now eliminated by exercise. . . . Von Ribbentrop had suffered some neuralgia which had been relieved by heat treatment. . . .

"Where was this heat treatment given?"

"It was all given in their cells."

"Colonel, what are the prisoners going to wear?"

"That has been a problem. I have had to scrounge clothes for them. Those who have presentable uniforms will wear them, but without badges or insignia. Those who have no clothes of their own have been issued conservative irongray civilian suits and conservative pinstriped shirts."

"What is their state of mind, Colonel?"

"The prisoners show no sign of emotion. Their attitude is thoughtful. . . . At seven o'clock they get up and clean their cells with a broom and a mop. They have cereal for breakfast. . . . For dinner today they had soup, hash, spaghetti, and coffee. Tonight they will have bean stew, bread, and tea. They are fed U. S. rations. At first we tried feeding them the corresponding German rations, but they didn't thrive. . . . No, the prisoners have no knives or forks. They eat with a spoon which is taken away from them immediately after each meal."

"Thank you, Colonel Andrus."

The colonel smiled his timid smile.

Nuremburg, November 20, 1945:

Coming in from the raw air of a gray day, the courtroom seems warm, luxurious, radiant with silky white light. The prisoners are already there, sitting in two rows under a rank of young freshfaced American guards in white helmetcasings. The guards stand still with the serious faces of a highschool basketball team waiting to be photographed.

There, crumpled and worn by defeat, are the faces that glared for years from the frontpages of the world. There's Goering in a pearlgray doublebreasted uniform with brass buttons and the weazening, leaky-balloon look of a fat man who has lost a great deal of weight. Hess's putty face has fallen away till it's nothing but a pinched nose and hollow eyes. Ribbentrop, in dark glasses, has the uneasy trapped expression of a defaulting bank cashier. Streicher's a horrible cartoon of a foxy grandpa. Funk is a little round man with pendulous greyhound jowls and frightened dog's eyes. Schacht glares like an angry walrus. The military men sit up straight and quiet. Except for Hess, who slumps as if in a coma, the accused have an easy expectant look as if they had come to see the play rather than to act in it. Goering is very much the master of ceremonies. He looks around with appreciative interest at every detail of the courtroom. Sometimes his face wears the naughty-boy expression of a repentant drunkard. He is determined to be himself. He bows to an American lady he knows in the press seats. It's a spoiled, genial, outgoing, shrewdly selfsatisfied kind of a face, an actor's face. Not without charm. Nero must have had a face like that. While the courtroom waits for the judges, a plump American sailor with a shock of red hair and the manners of a window-dresser, moves cheerfully and carefully among the accused, checking on their earphones.

"Attenshun!" calls a tall man in a frock coat. The judges are filing in with a closed nutcracker look about their mouths. First come two Frenchmen, one with bushy Clemenceau mustaches. Then come the two Americans. The light gleams on Francis Biddle's tall forehead above his long sanctimonious face with its thin nose. Then come two Britishers with that indescribable Hogarthian look of the Inns of Court. And last the two Russians in uniform, looking much younger than the rest.

There's not a sound in the courtroom. The two British judges bow slightly in the direction of the motley collection of German lawyers for the defense, who sit on long benches in front of the accused, some in black robes and purple hats, some in dress civilian clothes; one man wears the purple robes of a doctor of law. Lord Justice Lawrence starts to talk in a low precise casual voice.

The earphones resound hollowly. At first the voices seem to clatter and ramble from far away down some echoing prison corridor. Then they clear. The accoustics are so good in the court-

221

room, you only need the earphones for translation.

Sidney Alderman has started to read the indictment. An Englishman takes his place, then a Frenchman, then a Russian. All day the reading goes on. Out of the voices of the prosecutors, out of the tense out-of-breath voices of the interpreters, a refrain is built up in our ears ". . . Shooting, starvation and torture . . . tortured and killed . . . shooting, beating and hanging . . . shooting, starvation and torture. . . ."

Goering shakes his head with an air of martyrdom. Streicher develops a tic in the corners of his mouth. Keitel, looking more like a buck sergeant than ever, is woodenly munching on a piece of bread. Rosenberg sits up suddenly when his name is mentioned, pulls at the neck of his blue shirt and straightens his tie. Occasionally he strips his lips off his teeth with a nervous doglike movement.

". . . and crimes against humanity and on the high seas. . . ."

Nuremburg, November 21:

Justice Lawrence has overruled a defense motion that called into question the jurisdiction of the Court and has granted a recess for the defendants to consult with their lawyers before pleading. In varying tones—defiant, outraged, deprecatory—the defendants plead *nicht schultig*.

Robert Jackson steps to the microphone to open the case for the prosecution. He has a broad forehead and an expression of good humor about his mouth. He wears round spectacles. The brown hair clipped close to his round head has a look of youth. He seems completely absorbed in the day's work. He talks slowly in an even explanatory tone without betraying a trace of selfimportance in his voice.

"The privilege of opening the first trial in history for crimes against the peace of the world imposes a grave responsibility."

The prisoners at the bar, deceived perhaps by his mild unassuming manner, listen at first quite cheerfully. Being able to hear their own voices in court when they plead seems to have bucked them up. At least they are still public characters. Goering's broad countenance has lost the peevish spoiltchild look it took on when Justice Lawrence refused to allow him to make a statement. Now he sits back listening with almost indulgent attention.

"In the prisoners' dock sit twenty broken men. Reproached by the humiliation of those they have led almost as bitterly as by the desolation of those they have attacked, their personal capacity for evil is forever past. . . ."

As the day wears on and Jackson, reasonably, dispassionately, and with magnificent clarity, unfolds the case against them, taking the evidence out of their own mouths, out of their own written orders, a change comes over the accused. They stir uneasily in their seats. They give strange starts and shudders when they hear their own words quoted out of their own secret diaries against them. When the prosecutor reaches the crimes against the Jews, they freeze into an agony of attention.

The voice of the German translator follows the prosecutor's voice, a shrill vengeful echo. Through the glass partition beside the prisoners' box you can see the taut face between gleaming earphones of the darkhaired woman who is making the translation. There's a look of horror on her face. Sometimes her throat seems to stiffen so that she can hardly speak the terrible words.

They are cringing now. Frank's dark eyes seem bulging out of his head. Rosenberg draws the stiff fingers of one hand down his face. Schacht's countenance is drawn into deep creases of nightmare. Streicher's head leans far over on his shoulder as if it were about to fall off his body.

Jackson goes on quietly and rationally to describe the actions of madmen. Sometimes there is a touch of puzzlement in his voice as if he could hardly believe the documents he is reading from. It is the voice of a reasonable man appalled by the crimes he has discovered. Echoing it the choked shrill voice of the interpreter hovers over the prisoners' box like a gadfly.

The Nazi leaders stare with twisted mouths out into the white light of the courtroom. For the first time, perhaps, they have seen themselves as the world seems them.

". . . You will say I have robbed you of your sleep. . . . These are the things that have turned the stomach of the world. . . ."

Jackson turns a page on his manuscript. As the tension relaxes, people stir a little in the courtroom. Behind the glass windows under the ceiling you can see the screwed-up faces of the photographers. From somewhere comes the gentle whirr of a movingpicture camera. A pale young soldier, who might be a pupil in a highschool class who has stepped up to help the teacher, is rolling up the white screen on the side wall to uncover a map that shows with colored bands the progressive stages of Nazi aggression. With the calm explanatory voice of a man delivering a lecture in a history course, Jackson begins his exposition of the assault on Europe. Occasionally he points to the map.

The defendants are sitting up attentively. To look at the map is a relief. Some of their faces show something like a glow of pride at the thought of how near they came to winning. They have managed to pull their features together. Ribbentrop has taken off his glasses and is stroking his heavy eyes with the tips of his fingers. When Goering stumbles out to the latrine between two guards, it is with faltering steps as if his eyesight had suddenly grown dim, but when he comes back, walking with a jaunty selfimportant stride, there is almost a smile on his great fatty face. Only Hess is still slumped in his seat with his thin blue jowl dropped on his chest, paying no attention to anything.

Austria, Czechoslovakia, Poland, the history of the early years of the war unfolds. The defendants sit up with squared shoulders during the recitation of their victories.

Gradually as the afternoon slips by, we forget to look in the ranked faces of the prisoners. Robert Jackson, his voice firmer and louder, has launched into the theory he is laying down that aggressive war is in itself a crime under the law of nations.

"To apply the sanctions of the law to those whose conduct is found criminal by the standards I have outlined is the responsibility committed to this tribunal. It is the first court ever to undertake the difficult task of overcoming the confusion of many tongues and the conflicting concepts of just procedure among diverse systems of law so as to reach a common judgment. . . . The real complaining party at your bar is civilization. . . . It points to the weariness of flesh, the exhaustion of resources, and the destruction of what was beautiful or useful in so much of the world. . . . Civilization asks whether law is so laggard as to be utterly helpless to deal with crimes of this magnitude by criminals of this order of importance. . . ."

Robert Jackson has finished speaking. The Court rises. People move slowly and thoughtfully from their seats. I doubt if there is a man or woman in the courtroom who does not feel that great and courageous words have been spoken. We Americans get a little proudly to our feet because it was a countryman of ours who spoke them.

Nuremburg, November 22:

Last night, out at the impossible schloss that the Eberhard Faber family built for themselves in Stein, out of pencil profits and vainglory, and that the occupying authorities took over to house the correspondents covering the Nuremberg trials, I was walking up the huge awkward marble staircase, looking at the red carpets, and the garish mosaics, and the chandeliers, and the statues that had an air of having been carved out of soap. I had been talking to some of the French journalists who had been so skeptical of the Anglo-American plans for the trial before it started. They were full of admiration for Robert Jackson's opening of the case for the prosecution. They had agreed with me that he had done a magnificent job. A renewed respect for Americans had crept into their manner. In their minds Jackson's speech had reestablished the American ethical viewpoint as the basis for an international law. It was a pleasure to hear intelligent Europeans speak of America in terms other than of thinly disguised ridicule and scorn. It was all very cheering. The feeling of pride in your country is one of the best feelings in the world.

I was walking up the stairs to the bar in search of a crony to have a drink of Scotch with when, on the landing in front of the library, a man I did not know addressed me in French. He was not a Frenchman, as he spoke the language with an accent. He might have been a Pole or a South Slav. He certainly came from eastern Europe. He was a mediumsized man with dark brows and a square illshaven jaw. He looked in my face, out of sharp black eyes, and asked me a question in a deferential tone of voice: "Pardon, Monsieur, is it true that you were much impressed by the proceedings?"

226

From his manner of speaking I should have imagined him to be a lawyer or a college professor. He was evidently a man who had done considerable reading and considerable talking in public.

If I had a moment, he added politely, he would like to ask me some further questions. I suggested that he have a drink with me, but he refused. We walked back down the stairway, and went out of doors and sauntered back and forth in the clammy mist out in the flagged courtyard where the jeeps were parked. He lit a cigarette as we walked up and down. It was too dark to see his face.

"I am not saying that these men should not die," he said. "If it depended on me, I should order them shot tomorrow, but I just want to ask you, as a representative of a certain type of opinion in your country, if you think there is anything to be gained by piling new hypocrisy on the monstrous hypocrisies of the world. Justice is something we crave in Europe as much as we crave food, more perhaps. Is this trial helping in the re-establishment of real justice?"

I said I thought it was. Naturally I admitted we didn't come into court with entirely clean hands. No nation could. But if it were possible to establish the legal principle that aggressive war is a crime, wouldn't it arm and implement the principles of the United Nations?

"You mean that every war should be followed by a bloody prosecution, not only of the leaders of the losing side, but of their helpless followers. If you establish the principle that the nazi organizations are criminal in themselves, will you condemn every member of them to death?"

I tried to tell him that fortunately the Anglo-Saxons were not a logical people. I admitted that it was hard to tell where our justice ended and our frameups began. I did insist that sometimes by our great state frameups we established valuable historical precedents. Charles Stuart did not get a fair trial, but his execution established the principle of royal responsibility in England.

We took a couple of turns in silence. Suddenly he asked me sharply:

"Pardon me if I inquire what crimes against humanity the nazi leaders are accused of that the Allied leaders have not committed or condoned. What did the nazis do in effect as cruel as your wholesale bombings of civilian centers?"

"They started it, didn't they?"

"Justice, monsieur, deals with the facts. The slaughter in the German cities was much greater than in England. How can you justify the massacre of the helpless refugees in Dresden? Let us turn for a moment to the betrayal of peaceful states. What have the Nazis done that compares with your handing-over of Poland, your own ally, into the hands of the darkest totalitarian tyranny in history? I need not mention Estonia, Latvia, Lithuania. Perhaps you have not visited Yugoslavia?"

He paused, but he started talking again before I could find an answer.

"Crimes against humanity," he said bitterly. "Isn't it a crime against humanity to allow fifteen million people to be driven out of their homes merely because they are accused of being Germans? In Austria you are doing it yourselves. Why do you Americans feel this desire for vengeance? I can understand it in the Russians who suffered fearful injuries, but your cities were not laid waste, your wives and children were not starved and murdered. Monsieur, do not misunderstand me; I hate the crimes of the nazis, but what I fear is that with your plausible oratory you are putting the seal of respectability on crimes more hideous than those these men committed. How would it be if it turned out that out of these dreadful men you were making martyrs instead of condemned criminals? In a civilized community, the fact that a man tried to burn your house down does not justify you in burning his. Can you be sure that if you legalize these methods of vengeance on the vanquished in Europe, they will not cross over the ocean to America? Instead of establishing the rule of the law in Europe, isn't everything you are doing helping to make certain the rule of violence?"

"That's not our intention. . . . I am sure that is not Justice Jackson's intention," I stammered.

"The nazis did not intend to bring ruin on Germany. You must pardon me, monsieur. Intentions aren't enough."

I could not answer him. I said goodnight, and went back into the schloss and went gloomily to bed.

Nuremberg, November, 1946

Retreat from Europe

The train of scaling Mitropa sleepers stood dingy among the pine trees at the suburban station, the tired old engine sending up an occasional cottony blob of steam into the cold slate sky of an afternoon of whistling east wind. The man who had the other berth in the compartment was an American college professor who had been in Germany several months on a mission. He was a large grayhaired man with a large nose set in a large tired wrinkled face. Immediately we started talking about the Russians. In Berlin there is little else to talk about. Wherever you go the Russians are the positive force. What did I think, he asked me, about the attitude of our people in Berlin toward the Russians? I said it was puzzling.

"Puzzling!" he said. "It's stark raving crazy."

"We ought to get to know a little more about the kind

of people we are dealing with," said the redhaired captain who was standing in the vestibule. We invited him in and he sat on the edge of the lower berth with his hands on his knees.

"If the Russians were a choir of angels," said the professor, "it wouldn't be safe to make the concessions we make. Of course in fairness to the men we have in charge for us, we have to admit that they inherited from the Big Three an unworkable proposition."

He added that he thought it had been pretty well proved to everybody's satisfaction that appeasement was a dangerous business. He could understand how Americans should lose interest in Europe and want to go home, but he couldn't understand how a whole nation could take on the psychology of the victim so quickly. . . . We were collectively just like Chamberlain with his umbrella: "Peace in our time."

What did he suppose the Russians thought of us? I asked him.

He said he had an idea. He spoke German, he explained, pretty fluently. Talking to Germans who were impregnated with Russian ideas he had discovered that the communists thought of us in the same terms the nazis did. That was one of the things that made it so easy for ex-nazis and communists to work together. They spoke of Americans as barbarous children. They admitted that we had been able to build up an effective industrial organization and that our industrial organization had won the war for us. But now we were done, they said. War production had been American capitalism's last great effort. Our way of life and our prattle about liberty were the reflection of an age that was past. As a nation we were already dead and didn't know it.

"Well, they seem to be a wee mite barbarous themselves, according to our way of thinking," said the redhaired captain.

"Some of our boys act pretty rough, but if it came to a contest in barbarism, the Russians would win hands down."

"They don't mean what you mean," said the professor. "They mean that we are behind the times . . . still living in the nineteenth century. That we don't understand the world of manipulated political power. . . . They think we have no notion but profits. . . . Money profits as the aim of life seem childish to men brought up in a system where direct power over the life and death of other men is the stakes. . . . Social engineering. That's much stronger meat."

The train was moving slowly through Potsdam. We crossed a canal choked with a tangle of broken bridges. Against the gray horizon moved long mansarded buildings pitted with shellholes, eighteenth-century façades torn and scaled like discarded stage scenery, smashed cupolas and belfries, pushed in pediments, snapped-off chimneypots at the gable ends of shattered slate roofs.

A railroad station slid by crowded with Russian soldiers in long greatcoats. Their massed faces passed by the window, a pale blur in the dusk. They were watching the American train go past. There was every type of face, but not a smile.

"Aw, hell," said the captain. "I can't make 'em out." He moved out into the vestibule again.

"They aren't so different from other people," said the professor in his quiet throaty voice as the station buildings gave place to wide plains sowed in wheat, fading off into the evening murk. "Of course not," he went on in a louder voice as if answering a question in his own mind. "Except for their tremendous indoctrination. . . . After all, we know what the nazis could do to the German mind in twelve years. The communists have had a quarter of a century to work on the Slavs." He paused. "We should never underestimate the Russians," he said

231

again. We sat listening to the loudening beat of the wheels over the rails. "They are one of the most talented peoples on earth, but between them and us there stands the Kremlin propaganda. . . . Hitler was right about the power of the lie."

The train had speeded up now. Bright raindrops slanted across the windows. It was quite dark. We made an effort to talk of other things.

After supper I lay in my berth trying to piece together my few days in Berlin. I lay in the berth on the Frankfurt train that was jogging steadily, thank God, away from Berlin, listening to the rumblebump of the square wheels of the decrepit Mitropa sleepingcar.

The ruin of the city was so immense it took on the grandeur of a natural phenomenon like the Garden of the Gods or the Painted Desert . . . you drove in past the shattered university and the heaps that had been Friedrichstrasse and the empty spaces where a little of the shell of the Adlon still stood. The Brandenburg Gate was oddly intact. Through it you looked out over the waste, punctuated by a few stumps of trees and a few statues, that used to be the Tiergarten. At the further end of the Tiergarten were crowds of furtive people with bundles under their arms scattered in groups over a wide area that looked like an American city dump.

That was the black market. Walking among them I couldn't help thinking of the black markets in Moscow in the old days. Here were the same harassed faces, the same satchels and briefcases stuffed with the miserable débris of a lost way of life. People kept looking over their shoulders as they went about their bargaining and bartering with the same expression of timid puzzlement I used to see in Moscow. They had been brought up to consider trade an honorable and respected way of life. Suddenly it had become illegal and underground. A year ago they were respectable German burghers. Today they were criminals.

Everywhere workmen with cables were pulling down broken brick walls. Among the ruins you passed groups of German women, old women, young women, women who looked as if they were accustomed to labor and women who had never wielded any tool heavier than a needle in their lives, carrying buckets full of bricks out of the crumbling heaps. Others stood at the brickpiles in the street rubbing the bricks together to clean them. They were frowsty and their faces were gray with dust and the skin under their eyes was blue with fatigue. The weather was raw and cold with that drizzling mixture of sleet and rain that is a specialty of Berlin. The women had bundled themselves up with all the clothes they had to keep warm. Long strings of them passing the heavy buckets from hand to hand toiled over the rubbish heaps.

"Oh, they like to do it," one young American had assured me cheerfully. "If they do heavy labor they get a heavy labor card . . . more food . . . greedy bitches."

Berlin was not just one more beaten-up city. There, that point in a ruined people's misery had been reached where the victims were degraded beneath the reach of human sympathy. After that point no amount of suffering affects the spectator who is out of it. Maybe it was such a mechanism that enabled the Germans to look with complacency on the extermination of their Jewish neighbors, and that enabled the Russian Communists to see without tears the results on the lives of other men of the Kremlin's various feats of social engineering, and that enabled perfectly decent Americans, brought up in the habits of democracy, to remain indifferent to the plight of the tortured peoples of eastern Europe. Once war has broken the fabric of human society, a chain reaction seems to set in, which keeps on after the fighting has stopped, tearing down the decencies and the inhibitions that hold civilization together.

Praying to whatever forces of good there are in the world that no fate like the Germans' would ever come to the people of my country, I finally fell asleep.

Waiting for breakfast in the morning in the corridor of the diner, I fell to talking to the redheaded captain again. He was from San Francisco. He had practiced law there. He was now in Military Government and he was fed up to the ears.

"I get a feeling," he said in a low bitter voice, "that there is a sort of competition among our politicians as to who shall sell the United States further down the river. If the American people want to commit suicide, I suppose in a democratic country it's the politician's business to tie the noose for us so that we can slip it comfortably around our necks. . . . It's all this apologizing that makes me sick. With all our faults we have invented a social system by which the majority of men for the first time in human history get a break, and instead of being cocky about it we apologize about it. . . . We built up the greatest army in the world and won the war with it, and now we're letting everything go to pieces because we don't know what to do next. . . . We apologized to the French for saving their country and we apologize to the British and we apologize to the Russians. . . . First thing you know we'll be apologizing to the Germans for licking them. . . . And they all hate our guts and it damn well serves us right."

Paris, December, 1946

VII

THE FAILURE OF MARXISM

The soldier coming home from the wars has always had a tough time. The fact of killing has carried a sort of catharsis with it. The fighting man's mind isn't distorted by hatred as the stay-at-home civilian's is. He usually comes home with a commonsense outlook on what he's been through. Though in the first war the nearest I had gotten to combat was driving an ambulance, I can remember very clearly how hard the returned doughboy found it to talk to civilians. We found people back home still all hopped up with German atrocities and brave little Belgium. Their thinking was frozen in the mold of the interallied propaganda. We knew that atrocities were universal in war. We tried to explain how the fighting man felt. It got so that to keep out of arguments we only talked frankly among ourselves. In that case a reaction set in. In two or three years the wartime psychology had melted away and the returned soldier, against loud opposition we mustn't forget, was allowed to have his say.

I found myself equally at cross purposes with the stay at homes when I got back from World War II. Those of us who protested against the abdication of the American will to victory were talked down whenever we raised our voices. The wartime obsessions, though they never reached the depth of hysteria of the wartime obsessions of the first war, lingered on in the public mind year after year.

The language of protest of the oldtime Greenwich Village radicals had become the language of an entrenched political party. Many an old radical had the amusing and somewhat alarming experience of finding himself hoist by his own petard. We had run mad for government ownership of this and that and for trade unions and for a minimum wage and unemployment relief because we thought those things would increase the happiness and dignity of the majority of men. A great many of the things we had argued for had come to pass under the New Deal in the United States and under the Labour government in England. They had become established institutions flanked by all the vested interests that fact implies. When some of us, still applying the standards we had learned in trying to defend Sacco and Vanzetti and the Harlan miners, the Spanish republicans and a hundred other less publicized victims of oppression of one sort or another, started looking with a critical but not necessarily unfriendly eye at the new institutions, we got a good shellacking from the defenders of the established order for our pains. The businessman, who used to defend himself with such fury, was now fair game, but you criticized a socialized institution at your own risk.

If some of us, who had seen the Abominable Snowmen, pointed out that the Communist Party was a greater danger to individual liberty than all the old power mad bankers and industrialists from hell to breakfast, we were promptly written down in the bad books as reactionaries.

Socialism is Not Enough

Not long ago I found myself talking to a pleasant and well-informed woman reporter in a newspaper office in a prosperous city in the Middlewestern corn belt. Although the region is usually chalked up as "black Republican" in politics, the paper she worked for wore a "liberal" complexion. I was trying to explain to her that socialism as I had seen it working last summer in Great Britain was not necessarily a force for progress. "But I thought you were a liberal," she kept saying almost tearfully, "and now you have turned reactionary." "The socialists are the conservatives now," I told her, "and the Communists are the real reactionaries." But she remained unconvinced. The reason our conversation was so fruitless was that she had decided that certain words like "liberal," "labor" and "rationing" had a virtuous connotation and there was no way of getting her to look directly at the events that lay behind the words.

It was just this sort of wall of incomprehension you used to meet years ago when you argued the right of working people to form unions and to strike for improved working conditions, or tried to explain that we ought to show a sympathetic interest in the social experiments that were going on in the Soviet Union. Then it was the capitalist slogans that were holding the fort; but during the past twenty years a new set of words has gradually become charged with a virtuous aura in the public mind. Now *public ownership, planned economy, controls* and *socialized* have become words heavy with virtue, while *profits, free enterprise, investment* and even *dividends* have taken on an evil context that needs to be explained away.

The public mind in America that twenty years ago dismissed unheard anything that smacked of a socialistic notion is now receptive to socialistic notions. Partly this comes from a reasoned change of attitude brought about by the success of some of the socialistic measures of Franklin Roosevelt's New Deal, but partly it comes from the unthinking acceptance of the vocabulary of "liberal" propaganda that spread out in ripples from New Deal Washington, becoming vaguer and more confused and more destructive of clear thinking as the ideas that engendered it lost their vitality at the source. It is in this confused region of the popular mind that the communists have been able to carry on their most successful propaganda operations. Thus it comes to pass that the "liberals" who think a man is defeated in argument when they call him a "reactionary" show very little curiosity about the actual functioning of socialistic going concerns. The "liberal" vocabulary that had some meaning in the Twenties has now become a definite hindrance to understanding events in the world of the Fifties.

Enough socialized systems and institutions have been going concerns over a long enough period of time for us at least to begin to get some idea of how they are working out. It's a most curious comment on the blindness induced by dogmatically held beliefs that in all the avalanches of print for and against socialism and free enterprise there's so little comparative examination of capitalist and socialist organizations; there's so little effort to try to discover how they work out for the men and women directly involved.

As citizens of a selfgoverning community it is our first duty continually to be asking ourselves what it is we want from our institutions.

At home in America we have seen enough of the working of socialized enterprises, successful and unsuccessful, to begin to understand that from the point of view of the wellbeing of men and women the contradiction is not between "capitalism" and "socialism" but between the sort of organization that stimulates growth and the sort that fastens on society the dead hand of bureaucratic routine or the suckers of sterile vested interests. The road must be kept open for experiment. By our habit of government we are committed to trying to keep a rough balance between the demands of different sections of the population. We haven't solved the problem of defending every man's freedom against domination by other men, but we have made a little bit of a beginning.

The rest of the world is becoming a museum of socialist failures. Our first problem now is to understand clearly the needs of our own society and its relationship to the shaky socialized regimes of Europe and to the regime of the law of the club that centers in the Soviet Union. To do this we must free our minds of the verbiage left over from the noble aspirations of socialist theory. Ideas like everything else in the world become senile and decay.

It seems likely, from what we hear faintly through the screen of lies that hems in the Soviet Union, that even there the illusions have lost their power in the face of the regime's failure to produce even the rudiments of decent living for its subjects. Even some Americans opposed to the communists talk as if it were an excess of progressiveness and idealism that caused Russian socialism to fail. We find Frenchmen and Americans and Canadians, in all other respects apparently capable of sane and normal thinking, who are willing to turn their backs on the traditions they were brought up in and to give their allegiance to the Kremlin. The success of the aggressions of the Soviet state in the last few years rests in great part on the Kremlin's command over adherents and sympathizers in the outside world. Largely because the rest of the world has not understood it the Russian socialized state has been allowed to develop into a military force for pillage and conquest. Still the faith of many of our "liberals" in the Kremlin's idealistic aims has not faltered.

Those of us who believed in socialism in the radical twenties hoped it would promote selfgovernment, expand individual liberty and make for wider distribution of the good things of life. It is obvious now that the Soviet Union is not the place to look for these things. Not even the American communists really claim any of these achievements; what they say among themselves is that present miseries will be atoned for by the regime of justice and bliss that will be established once communism has completed the conquest of the world.

The Russians are barbarians, the Western socialists will tell you; in England it will all be different.

How different *is* it? If you go around Great Britain asking questions of as many different kinds of people as possible, as I did last summer, you sense that in its ultimate implications British socialism is turning out to be not so very different from the Russian brand. Of course there's not the police terror of Stalin nor the Hitlerian pomp and parade through which the Kremlin daily expresses its power over the bodies and minds of men. There's not the proselytizing enthusiasm of a quasi-religious dogma that accompanies the agents and armies of expanding Russia. There's not the daily and visible and universal servitude; but neither has socialism brought any broadening of personal liberty. On the contrary: personal liberty in Great Britain has been contracted.

The very humane and wellintentioned people who are running the Labour government are the first to deplore the losses of liberty you bring to their attention. They reassure you with pious hopes that the "direction of labor" measure, which limits the individual's right to work where or when he likes, will be only a passing phase. Listening to these pious hopes, I couldn't help remembering similar reassurances from equally humane and wellintentioned Russian communists who used to tell me, in the early days, that military communism was a passing phase which would disappear as soon as reactionary opposition was crushed. Thirty years have gone by, and military communism marches on to fresh massacres. A man has a right to ask the British Labour Party whether thirty years from now direction of labor won't be the cornerstone of a new system of exploitation of the productive workers by a new ruling class.

If there is one thing that mankind should have learned from the agonies of the last four decades it is that it's never safe to do evil that good may come of it. The good gets lost and the evil goes on.

Of course we must admit that the present situation of the people of Great Britain would be difficult enough in any case. The island's economy was built up as the processing and financing center of an empire which has irrevocably gone. The class that had ruled that economy through control of the government, ownership of the land and domination of centralized finance and industry had become overweeningly rich and powerful. In their wealth and selfsatisfaction the owners of Britain neglected to keep their industries tooled up to date or to protect the standard of living of their working people or to conserve their natural resources. When the Labour government came in after the war it inherited a concern that had long been bankrupt.

Government control of virtually the entire economy had already been instituted during the war. About all the Labour government has done is to amplify the wartime apparatus of bureaucratic management. The living standards of the working people who were Labour's chief constituents had improved during the war, and the Labour government has continued that improvement, particularly for the lowest-paid third. Because there isn't enough to go around anyway, this has been done at the expense of the middle class, traditionally the nursery of British brains and initiative. Virtually everybody has been reduced by high taxes and high prices to the same level of subsistence. Incentive for effort and innovation has tended to disappear. A man is better off if he soldiers along in the shop and spends his Saturdays betting on the races than if he works his head off trying to rise in the world. The more his income rises the more taxation will take his earnings away from him and the more he'll feel the dead weight of the bureaucratic tangle hampering his every move.

Bernard Baruch's remark, that socialism might not succeed in distributing wealth but would certainly distribute poverty, has never been better exemplified. Up to now socialism in Great Britain has accomplished very little more than to freeze the bankrupt capitalist economy at its point of collapse. Its bureaucratic machinery, operating along the lines of the machinery of bankrupt capitalism, has not been able to stimulate the sort of revolutionary initiative and thoroughgoing reorganization of the economy that might give the British people a chance to escape from their dilemma. Socialism has acted as a brake instead of as a stimulus to enterprise.

Man does not live by bread alone, the socialists will tell you. The answer is that stronger than the urge to eat is the urge to exercise power over other men. In the past British institutions have done a moderately good job in curbing this deadliest of instincts, but in spite of political democracy British capitalism too often gave too much power to people whose only social gift was the knack of accumulating money. Now British socialism gives too much power to people whose only knack is getting themselves elected to offices in trade unions. At the same time the liberty of movement and the freedom of action that allowed people to escape from under the heel of the capitalist have been seriously weakened.

England has a new ruling class. Added to such remnants of the old ruling class as have remained in office through holding administrative jobs in government, industry and the civil service, is an infusion of new blood from the trade-union leadership, leavened by an occasional intellectual who has talked or written his way into office. Now, the main training of trade-union officials is in hamstringing production for the purpose of wringing concessions from the owners for the workers. Neither idealistic intellectuals nor civil service employees have any training in industrial production. The result is that at the very moment when the British people need to throw all their energy into discovering new ways of producing food and clothing and housing and export goods, they find themselves in the hands of a ruling class that is hampered by tradition and training from doing anything effective to stimulate production. In recent months there has developed a tendency to give technicians an increasingly bigger share in policymaking, but on the whole Britain's new ruling class tends to be so blinded by the utopian glamour of the word "socialism" that it has found it difficult to envisage the problem which confronts the nation.

Well if the government can't help them, why can't they help themselves? The British people, in my opinion, represent in themselves at this moment just about the highest development of Western civilized man. In the middle and upper classes you find a higher level of education than we have reached in America. The level of individual skill and craftsmanship in most trades is higher than ours. In the professionally trained part of the population, though there may be some flagging of creative spirit, there's still a great reservoir of first-rate brains. The British people proved themselves to be still a great people by the dignity and discipline with which they fought off the German air attacks during the war. This great highly trained, highly disciplined and civilized nation is in danger of dying of inanition because in all the elaborate structure of the state there are so few cracks left where individual initiative can take hold.

One symptom of the loss of concern for individual liberty that seems inevitably to follow the socialization of enterprise appears in the growing toleration of new forms of slavery. We are growing used to the stories of the vast slave camps in the Soviet Union and its satellite countries, but it comes somewhat as a shock to find the humane British tolerating the use of gangs of German prisoners to do agricultural labor. In all my conversations with farmers in England last summer I found only one man who disapproved of the practice. The farmers paid the prisoners' wages to the government and the government allowed the prisoners nothing more than pocket money. The farmers found that they got more work out of the prisoners if they fed them a hot meal in the middle of the day, but they didn't seem to feel that the working of prisoners of war in this way constituted a backsliding in civilization; most of them regretted that the prisoners would soon be sent home. The wages of agricultural workers in England have been much improved in recent years and the socialists take justifiable pride in this achievement. The question they didn't ask themselves, when they tolerated the enslavement of the defeated Germans was how long a highly paid plowman or tractor operator would be able to compete with slave labor.

This brings us squarely up against the dilemma of our time. Under the cover of the dazzle of socialist illusions, and just at the moment when our technology is opening up the certainty of really widespread well-being in material things, the masses of mankind, under the rule of communist dictatorships, are being plunged back into a regime of servitude such as has not existed in the West since the days of serfdom. We can't go on forever blaming on war damage a situation that results from the fact that the socialized economies in France and England have not been able to produce. So far the socialized economies, instead of opening up new aspects of selfgovernment and broader reaches of liberty for the individual, have backslid with dizzy speed into aboriginal oppressions. In the Soviet Union, failure to solve the problems of production at home has thrown Russian communism into a dangerous habit of aggression upon the rest of the world. As for Great Britain, we can hope that they will find a way to combine socialism with liberty, or at least that the failure of the socialized economy to provide its people with a decent life at home will produce a new explosion of British migration and colonization that will transmit to the future world of the West the valuable heritages of English culture. In America what we don't want to forget is that we won't have any Western world fit for a free man to live in unless we keep the avenues open for the freedom and growth of the individual man in the constantly proliferating hierarchical structure of modern industry.

Socialism is not the answer to the too great concentration of power that is the curse of capitalism. We've got to do better than that.

Palisades, N.Y., December, 1947

But has Marxism failed? It certainly has retained a sort of negative hold on the mind of the educated classes in this country that makes it hard to induce them to examine any very divergent ideas. Our college population isn't exactly socialist, but its hackles rise if you try to clear any of the socialist preconceptions out of the way in order to discuss industrial society from some different point of view.

Traveling across the continent to deliver some lectures in the fall of 1954, I had occasion to stick my nose into a number of schools and colleges. It's the first time I've had any real contact with our institutions of learning since I emerged out of the dim light of the academic halls some thirty-nine years ago.

In those days business was the great vested interest. Even the more broadminded teachers, in whose minds the humane or scholarly moods predominated, were pained when a pert youth questioned any of the preconceptions of the businessman. "Profit" was a sacred word. The professors took a dim view of criticisms of laissez faire. The educated people the colleges were turning out identified their own interests and prestige with the interests and prestige of the business class. If you stepped on a businessman's toes their corns ached.

In 1927 President Lowell of Harvard, a kindly man of unblemished private life, put his name to the report that sent Sacco and Vanzetti to their death. To his way of thinking an anarchist or communist—he never managed to get the difference between them through his head—was an agitator capable of any crime. He certainly would have been horrified if you had told him that, in performing what he considered a painful civic duty, he was merely acting in defense of capitalist vested interests. He was applauded for his courage by most of the college presidents of his day.

Today you find that the vested interest is government. Where in my day we used to wisecrack that the colleges were geared to turn out football players and bond salesmen, today you could say that they are turning out football players and bureaucrats. The college man is educated to identify himself with government. I mean with institutional authority. Government, we must remember, has many phases. There is the United States government; and then there are a host of other governments in fact if not in name, the office forces of the corporations that govern production and the office forces of the trade unions that govern the workingman. The man who values the good opinion of his fellows today is pained by any pert remark that questions the right of the men who sit in the offices to run the lives of the rest of us.

Institutions of learning eternally form the sacred ark in which the ruling dogmas of any particular era are protected from the criticisms of the profane. Remember the Sorbonne in the great days of the canon law. A historian today could make out a very good case for sampling the opinions of college presidents as a way of uncovering the mentality of whatever ruling class is emerging. Since the business of a college president is to raise money, he has to be the type of man who will appeal to those who control the available funds. Forty years ago he had to be congenial with the individual capitalists of the day. Now the money, even when it has the names of individual fortunes still attached to it, is in the hands of institutions. So the college presidents of our day have to have the institutional mentality. How can they help feeling tender toward socialized institutions, whatever form these may take?

The institutional mind drifts naturally into concepts of socialism, which, after all, only means a society run from one central office. The odd tenderness toward communism and communist causes, that seems to be felt by a good many men of the foundations and colleges, might be explained along the same lines. Communism is the most vigorous form of control from a central office that exists in the world today.

If the office workers who man these institutions were even neutral in the battle to dislodge the communists from strategic positions so many of them wouldn't discharge their ire upon the anticommunists instead of on the communists, now would they?

Isn't it possible that the same sort of new ruling class

that reached power by violent means in the Soviet Union has reached power by peaceful means in this country and England? The New Deal revolution took the management of the economy out of the hands of the capitalist. Revolutions, even though they are brought about by popular pressure, often end by installing some new group in power. Today we are more and more governed, instead of by the oldfashioned politicians, by people who are adept at institutional manipulation. We haven't quite found the terms that describe them exactly. James Burnham took a fling at a definition when he wrote of "the managerial revolution." When we like our new rulers we call them public servants. When we are mad at them we call them bureaucrats. I'm not quarreling with their right to administer. It will be the business of selfgovernment to see that they remain servants of the public, of all the public.

VIII

THE CHANGING SHAPE OF SOCIETY

Men have always found it hard to keep up with the changes in the shape of society which their own inventions bring about. In times of drastic technological change like our own, institutions evolve so rapidly that all the old frames of reference go by the board. New situations arise faster than the mental processes can keep up with them. To a certain extent we lose the power to tell good from evil.

Men who have lost the certainty of what is good and what is bad find themselves without any sextant to check their position by. When they set out to explore the society they live in they have no way of finding out whether the terrain from which they are making their observation really remains firm and stationary. The old illustration of the man driving his dogteam northward all day over a drifting icefloe only to find himself further south that night than when he started out in the morning becomes very much to the point.

The very words we need to use to describe what we see change their meanings. Slogans and phrases that yesterday pointed steadily toward the lodestar of good today spin waveringly round the compass and tomorrow may have taken on meanings opposite from the meaning they started with. A moral judgment will turn inside out on you overnight.

The mind cannot support moral chaos for long. Men are under as strong a compulsion to invent an ethical setting for their behavior as spiders are to weave themselves webs. New cosmogonies are continually being rebuilt out of the ruins of past systems. Somehow, like the degenerate last Romans, who had forgotten the art of turning columns and had to use the débris of old temples to build Christian basilicas with, we have to improvise at least enough of an edifice out of the fallen dogmas of the past to furnish a platform from which to rebuild the society we live in.

The creation of a world view is the work of a generation rather than of an individual, but we each of us, for better or for worse, must add our brick to the edifice. A generation can't go much further than the average of the achievements of the men who comprise it, but every outstanding effort affects that average. Every one of us has to go as far forward as he can. The first step is to try to form for ourselves an accurate picture of the society we live in.

Start from your street or from the apartment house where you live; you'll find that most of the men and women you know make their living by working for some sort of a corporate organization. Whether these concerns lend money or sell bread or manufacture automobiles or publish newspapers or peddle humanitarian ideas their scheme of behavior is remarkably similar. The corporation with its board of directors, its chain of command, its hierarchy of power is such a routine feature of our daily lives that it hardly ever occurs to us that its pattern has become only very recently the dominant social pattern of the life of a large part of the human race. Up to a hundred years ago the family was still the social unit.

The corporation is the top part of the pyramid. The working people in the factory or office or store do their work under its orders. Wherever you find it the pattern is uniform. In the

United States we call it capitalism. If you go over to England you'll find people behaving in much the same way but calling it socialism. In the Soviet Union and its satellite states you'll find a remarkably similar social structure going under the name of dictatorship of the proletariat, or by the oddest reversal of the meaning of terms, people's democracy. Other factors account for the greater wellbeing that results from the pattern in some countries than in others. The same plant will yield differently in different soils. You can be sure that if an eighteenth-century libertarian like Tom Paine were resurrected today he would find more similarities than differences in the three systems.

People have been pointing out for years that the government of the Soviet Union, leaving aside the police power—the power to kill is a very different thing from the power to fire—resembles more than anything else the government of a great American corporation. It makes you wonder whether the bogyman we in America see in the menace of socialism and that so many Europeans see in the menace of capitalism doesn't lie somewhere in the structure of industrial society itself.

We have proof by experience that when you change from capitalism to socialism the corporations which administer industry or banks or railroads or chain laundries retain their structure. What happens is that under socialism the men who reach places of power tend to do so through their political rather than their financial influence. Both systems suffer from bureaucratic intrigue and internal politics. Only occasionally does a man find himself in a job through plain ability. The fascinating thing to a dispassionate observer about the structure of life in the Soviet Union is that in their efforts to produce socialism the communist dictators have produced a brutal approximation of monopoly capitalism. Their system has all the disadvantages of our own, without any of the alleviations which come to us through competition and through the division between economic and political power which has so far made it possible for the humane traditions of the Western world to continue.

If you want to find out what is happening to a society the thing to study is the behavior of the people in it and not what they say about their behavior. But most of the writing and arguing about social systems is about ideologies and not about behavior. The processes of thought are constantly being confused by a basic lag in the recognition of events. Groups of words that were once fairly descriptive of a given situation will survive for generations becoming more and more charged with righteous emotion as they become less and less descriptive of the situation involved.

If, having tried to forget political slogans and ideological camouflage, you spend an afternoon talking with the men who work in one of the great stratified industrial enterprises either in this country or in England you'll notice two things. First you'll discover that the antithesis between capitalism and socialism is beside the point, that it doesn't affect the way in which the people who work the machines and sit at the directors' tables and run the teletypes and sweep out the offices actually behave. Second, you will be struck in either case, by the centralization of power and the isolation of the individual in his routine at an office desk, or in his job on the assembly line, or even at the more varied work of turret or lathe.

We mustn't forget that changing the name of an industrial system doesn't change the fact that the kind of man who has only learned to drive a tractor will go on driving a tractor and the kind of man who has only learned to sit at a desk and organize other men's work will go on doing it and the man who gets his pleasure from power to boss his fellow man will continue to find a way to boss his fellow man.

The knot which our society must untie is the problem of controlling the power over men's lives of these stratified corporations, which, whether their top management calls itself capitalist or socialist, are so admirably adapted by the pull of centralization to despotic rule. Machinery must be invented to control the power of the administrators not only in the public interest but in the interest of each private individual man. In this country some of that machinery has existed for many years. Take the Sherman Anti-trust Law for an example.

An inseparable part of this problem is the problem of communication between the isolated units which are the cogs in our society. An isolated man is an ignorant man. He has no frame of reference by which to test the selfserving propaganda which is daily pumped in his ears by the political climbers who use corporations, labor unions, stratified organizations of any kind, as ladders to positions from which they may ride to glory on the backs of their fellows.

Even a hundred years ago in this country most of the operations of agriculture and industry were within the reach of the average man's radius of information. A Connecticut farmer living outside of Stamford, say, knew how you kept store. He understood the business of buying and selling from personal experience on the marketplace. He knew how a bank worked: the banker kept a stack of goldpieces in a safe and lent them out to you at interest under proper security. A clipper ship was a complicated machine but he'd sailed a small sloop enough as a boy to understand what made it go through the water. Commerce was a matter of ships and buying and selling. The world outside was not too different from its microcosm in the farming community where he lived. Most of the events which occurred in it were comprehensible to a man of average intelligence. When the farmer went to town to listen to a politician tell him how to vote he could test the reliability of the orator's words against his own experience of practical life, against his fairly wide acquaintanceship with various types of men, farmers, mechanics, millers, merchants, the local judge and the doctor and the lawyer. For final arbiter he had his Bible, and the inner voice of traditional ethics.

Look at this man's grandson living in the same house. Like as not he works in an office and commutes into New York. He knows his family and his wife's family and a few neighbors and the men in the office of similar rank in the concern. When he was in school he used to know something about sports but now he follows them through the newspapers. He understands his car and his lawnmower but he can't mend the washing machine when it gets out of order. Ask him what the place of money is in our economy or how powerful the executive is in our government. He can't tell you and you can't tell him. All you can do is treat each other to the views of some favorite columnist.

His friends are in the same boat. He hobnobs with a few other men of similar experience and outlook in some club or lodge, and apart from that all he knows about the world is what he reads in the papers, hears over the radio or sees in the movies.

These agencies of selfserving propaganda from one group or another tease and inflame his mind with a succession of unrelated stimuli. These stimuli are rarely sustained enough to evoke the response of careful study and understanding and the resulting satisfaction which is implicit in the word understanding, so in the end they leave him frustrated. The mind of a frustrated man becomes a sink of fear, ignorance and hatred; his main response to the problems of community and national life, which demand cogitation and decision, is a stubborn apathy.

Apathy is one of the characteristic responses of any living

organism when it is subjected to stimuli too intense or too complicated to cope with. The cure for apathy is comprehension. What happens when a problem has been made comprehensible is that it has been reduced to understandable component parts so that unfamiliar elements can be measured off by analogy against familiar elements which have already become usable terms in a man's own experience. The same man who stubbornly refuses to think out the problems of a presidential election will use his brains lucidly at a meeting of a union local or a parent-teacher association. The continuance of selfgoverning institutions will depend upon the invention of methods of communication by which the operations of the great macrocosms that rule our lives can be reduced to terms which each averagely intelligent man can understand, truly understand the way a good mechanic understands the working of an internal combustion engine.

Selfgovernment demands real and not parroted information. If we are to govern ourselves we have to know how the machinery of our society works. We have to learn to measure the drift of change. As a society changes the men change who are its component parts. There has been too little exploration of industrial society in the terms of human behavior. One reason is that obsession with socialism-capitalism antithesis (with socialism equals good, capitalism equals bad or vice versa) has kept investigators from seeing clearly the prospects that were opening out under their noses.

A sectarian approach to a study of society means a search for a bogyman. You don't need to understand why people behave as they do if you've already made up your mind who is to blame. If you are going to study an ant's nest you have to start out with a mind blank of preconceptions about the behavior of social insects. Difficult as it is to be unprejudiced about ants it's a whole lot more difficult to be unprejudiced about people. The fact that it is difficult doesn't mean it is not possible.

The intellectual tools with which to examine societies in the spirit of the search for knowledge rather than for party purposes are already in the language. In the parts of the world where free inquiry is still allowed by the police the investigation of society is easier to undertake than it was twenty-five years ago. In America at least the study of behavior, in the good old empirical tradition, has not run its course nor reached its highest fruition. We've just begun to take up the problem. An entire science lies ahead. In that science we may find the tools with which to build out of our runaway institutions a society which will be tolerably stable because it will offer participation to each individual man.

The principles of representative government by checks and balances based on law and not on administrative whim are as sound as they ever were. What has happened is that the political structure no longer conforms to the economic and social structure. Paralleling the political setup we have a host of new forms of goverment set up by the needs of industrial management and labor and of all the various classes of men that make up our society. Pressure groups are organs that have appeared because they were really needed, as links and channels between the corporate organizations that make up the community and the national and state and municipal governments. Some of these new organs are socially good and some of them are bad. We must start weeding out the bad and saving the good. The nation must be like a battleship stripping for action. We can no longer keep on board any apparatus that doesn't contribute directly to our safety.

If we are to save the republic we must continually be aware of the aims of the republic. Our safety lies in the fulfillment of these aims. Lincoln said that the United States differed from other nations in that it was dedicated to a proposition. That proposition has remained basically unchanged through our history, though the means of putting it into effect change as the shape of society changes. That proposition implies that the cohesive force which holds our nation together is not a religious creed or a common ancestry but the daily effort to give to every man as much opportunity as is possible to fulfill himself in his own way, protected by law from the arbitrary measures of those in authority. The men who founded this nation tried the unheard-of experiment of founding a state which would be the servant instead of the master of its citizens, of all its citizens.

Our safety in each crisis in our history has been measured by how near we came to achieving that aim. Our crimes and failures as a nation, and there have been plenty of them, have always occurred in situations that found the electorate and its leaders forgetful of the basic reason for the existence of the United States. In the old days our isolation gave us a vast margin for error. We are now entering a period when the margin for error is narrowing with breathtaking rapidity. The time is coming when every citizen will have to ask himself at every hour of the day: is what I am doing helping save the republic or is it not?

We need to harness our technical knowledge more directly than we have in the past to the task of increasing liberty and opportunity day by day. Instead of asking is this measure or that turn of affairs tending to benefit this or that class of citizens we must ask: is it tending to increase personal liberty for all? Testing organizations by that standard we will find that some services can be performed most efficiently by the federal government, some by the states and cities, some by licensed monopolies, or cooperatives, some by private enterprise. Our nation is an immensely complicated edifice built on a series of constantly changing adjustments brought about by the stresses and strains of the struggle for survival among the multitude of organizations

257

that make up our corporate life. The only gauge we have of its worth as a method of organizing society is how it affects each separate individual citizen.

Every society has to be born again from time to time. Even in our short history as a nation we have had a series of rebirths; the various openings of the West, the inception of the railroad age, the invention of assembly line production, the renewed search for community planning and improvement and the re-newal of the sense of responsibility of one for all and all for one that accompanied the first enthusiasms of the New Deal, have all been national rebirths. Since the aims of the New Deal were forgotten and degraded in lowest-common-denominator politics political inventiveness has been stalled in the doldrums. The time has come for a fresh surge of invention. We have to remember, before it is too late, that this nation was founded not to furnish glamorous offices for politicians, or to produce good and services, or handouts of easy money, but to produce free men.

The prospect before us is one of mighty effort against great odds but it is not all black. You can't travel back and forth across the continent without seeing here and there the begin-nings of a better balanced society. Our economic problems are the problems of surplus; it's hard to get used to that when all our thinking is based on notions of scarcity. There is now no visible limit to the productivity of agriculture or of manufacturing. In spite of all the prophecies of the Marxist wiseacres our society has not yet solidified into rigid classes. Not even the struggle between the management of industry and the leadership of labor has produced a proletariat. We are still a mass of vague and rambling individuals who have barely begun to build ourselves a civilization. We lack standards, we lack ethics, we lack art, we lack that instinctive sense of direction that is the sign of an achieved civilization. But some of our faults may very well turn out to be virtues. We have not yet let ourselves be rammed into the mold of a stratified society.

There are only rare moments in history when a community of men finds itself in the position to choose alternatives. We are in that position. For a very few short years we will be able to make the choice between a stratified autocratic society more or less on the Russian model and the selfgoverning republic which is our heritage. The republic must find its origins in the shop, in the union local, in the management conference room, in the school district meeting, in the county seat and the small town and the city ward. The republic can only be attained by intelligence and courage and the selfsacrifice of the individuals who must dedicate their lives to leavening and informing the mass. They must find the brains and the will. If enough of us want a selfgoverning society in which every man can participate to the fullest of his ability we can attain it.

Nobody needs to be told that in atomic energy the rulers of the world have a destructive force in their hands which is virtually absolute. The scientists have handed them over Jove's thunderbolt. The only way to keep a rein on that power is by enforcing the scheme of ethics that has grown up out of Christianity among people of selfgoverning institutions. The ordinarily decent impulses the ordinary man learned at his mother's knee are our last line of defense against the wickedness of overweening power at home and abroad. In the end the traditional ethics will be the spearhead of the attack that will bring us victory. The Communist cult of power, plain, cannot give men the happiness that they get from conforming to the rules of live and let live, of do unto others as you would be done by which have been built up through ages of trial and error.

The defections from the communist world have proved this. Men and women risk their lives daily in search of a moral order based on independent judgment and individual responsibility. The events of the last ten years have proved that a solid scheme of ethics is the most practical thing in the world. In our dealings with foreign nations, when we have behaved according to our better instincts, as in the reversal of the vengeance policy against Germany and our liberal treatment of Japan and the Marshall plan for rebuilding Europe, our efforts have been on the whole successful. The crimes and errors which have endangered our future as a nation, and the future of everything we hold worth while in civilization, have been committed by our leaders when, blinded by the self-righteousness which is the curse of power, they have consented to acts and committed acts against helpless peoples which would have been repugnant to any ordinary moderately moral man. Freedom without morals is a negative thing. What we must fight for is the freedom to do right.

The life of a nation, like the life of a man, is a gamble against odds. It takes courage and persistence and skill to swim against the current that runs so fast toward destruction. Once we have chosen our aim we must expend ourselves recklessly upon it. With all its faults and weaknesses our society has the best chance any society ever had to mitigate the domination of man by men, but only by the expenditure of all our brains and·all our work in the service of the underlying proposition upon which the republic was founded.

Spence's Point, February, 1950

IX

THE AMERICAN CAUSE

Not long ago I received a letter from some German students asking me to explain to them in three hundred words why they should admire the United States. "Young people in Germany," they wrote "as in other places in the world are disillusioned, weary of pronouncements on the slogan level. They are not satisfied with negations, they have been told over and over again what to hate and what to fight. . . . They want to know what to be and what to do."

This is what I didn't tell them: I didn't tell them that they should admire the United States for the victories of our armed forces or because we had first developed the atomic bomb or the hydrogen bomb, or because we had shinier automobiles or more washing machines and deep freeze or more televisions or ran up more passenger miles of airplane travel a year than any other people in the world. I didn't tell them to admire us for getting more productive work done with less backbreaking than any other people in the world or for our high wages, or our social security system. I didn't tell them to admire us because our popular leaders had the sweetest smiles before the television cameras or because we lived on a magnificent continent that offered an unbelievable variety of climates, mountains, plains, rivers, estuaries, seashores. Some of these are very good things but they are not things that would help them "to know what to be and what to do."

The Theme Is Freedom

This is what I told them: I told them they should admire the United States not for what we were but for what we might become. Selfgoverning democracy was not an established creed, but a program for growth. I reminded them that industrial society was a new thing in the world and that although we Americans had gone further than any people in spreading out its material benefits we were just beginning, amid crimes, illusions, mistakes and false starts, to get to work on how to spread out what people needed much more: the sense of belonging, the faith in human dignity, the confidence of each man in the greatness of his own soul without which life is a meaningless servitude. I told them to admire our failures because they might contain the seeds of great victories to come, not of the victories that come through massacring men, women and children, but of the victories that come through overcoming the evil inherent in mankind through urgent and warmhearted use of our best brains. I told them to admire us for our foolish trust in other peoples, for our failure to create an empire when empire building was easy. I told them to admire us for our still unstratified society, where every man has the chance, if he has the will and the wit, to invent his own thoughts and to make his own way. I told them to admire us for the hope we still have that there is enough goodness in man to use the omnipotence science has given him to ennoble his life on earth instead of degrading it. Selfgovernment, through dangers and distortions and failures, is the American cause. Faith in selfgovernment, when all is said and done, is faith in the eventual goodness of man.

Spence's Point, October, 1955

The material dealing with the Sacco Vanzetti case first appeared in *Facing the Chair*, a pamphlet published in Boston by the Sacco-Vanzetti Defence Committee in 1927.

The second, third, fourth and fifth chapters are made up of extracts from *Harlan Miners Speak*, published by Harcourt, Brace & Co. in 1932; from my *In All Countries*, 1934; *Journeys Between Wars*, 1938, and *The Ground We Stand On*, 1941, first issued under the same imprint.

The sixth chapter contains selections from *State of the Nation*, 1944 and *Tour of Duty*, 1946, published by the Houghton Mifflin Co. *The Failure of Marxism* appeared in "Life" in the winter of 1948. The eighth chapter comes from *The Prospect Before Us*, Houghton Mifflin Co., 1950. *The American Cause* first appeared as an article distributed by the Spadea Syndicate in 1955.